Satire or Evasion?

Black Perspectives on *Huckleberry Finn*

Edited by

James S. Leonard,

Thomas A. Tenney,

and Thadious M. Davis

Duke University Press   Durham and London   1992

Second printing in paperback, 1992

© 1992 Duke University Press
All rights reserved
Printed in the United States of America
on acid-free paper ∞
Library of Congress Cataloging-in-Publication Data
appear on the last printed page of this book.

"Twain's 'Nigger' Jim: The Tragic Face behind the Minstrel Mask,"
by Bernard W. Bell, © Bernard W. Bell,
is reprinted by permission.

"Morality and *Adventures of Huckleberry Finn*," by Julius Lester,
© Julius Lester, is reprinted by permission.

Bibliographic material included in the For Further Reading section
has previously appeared in *Huck Finn among the Critics*, ed.
M. Thomas Inge, *Mark Twain: A Reference Guide*, by Thomas A.
Tenney, *American Literary Realism* annual supplments from
1977 to 1983, and *Mark Twain Circular*, reprinted by permission.

Contents

Acknowledgments

The editors are grateful to the Citadel Development Foundation for research funding and to The Citadel for student assistance in the preparation of this volume. Thanks especially to Vice-President George F. Meenaghan for his continued support of Mark Twain and other research at The Citadel. We appreciate, as well, access to relevant materials at The Citadel's Daniel Library, the College of Charleston's Robert Scott Small Library, Duke University's Perkins Library, the University of North Carolina's Walter Royal Davis Library, and North Carolina State University's D. H. Hill Library.

We are indebted to Louis J. Budd, Christine E. Wharton, Liz Traynor, and Mindy Conner for insightful readings of the manuscript at various stages and to Steven Mailloux for helpful suggestions. And thanks to student assistants Mark Little and James Clabby for their valuable help in typing, proofreading, and other tedious but necessary components of the process.

Introduction:

The Controversy

over *Huckleberry Finn*

James S. Leonard

and Thomas A. Tenney

Huckleberry Finn and his friend Tom Sawyer are major players in the mythology of American childhood—emblems of freedom, high-spiritedness, and solid comradeship. They fulfill the dream of youthful innocence—the main component of that mythology—with a zest and spirit of adventure that work irresistibly on the American psyche. When the National Endowment for the Humanities recently surveyed teachers and scholars, requesting their recommendations for books to be taught in high schools, *Adventures of Huckleberry Finn* finished third in the voting, behind "Shakespeare" (*Macbeth* and *Hamlet*) and "American Historical Documents, the Declaration of Independence and the Constitution," but ahead of the Bible, "Homer" (*Odyssey* and *Iliad*), "Charles Dickens" (*Great Expectations* and *A Tale of Two Cities*), and "Plato" (*Republic*).[1] Equally notable were the results of a 1989 survey in which U.S. governors were asked to name their favorite childhood books: twelve of the fifty governors named *Huckleberry Finn,* the highest total for any book; and *The Adventures of Tom Sawyer* finished second with ten.[2] Whether the governors were being candid or their responses masked secret memories of being most moved by, say, Harold Robbins, Ian Fleming, or, in the case of the more literate, D. H. Lawrence, their public homage to Huck and Tom is clear indication of the degree to which an appeal to Twain's images of childhood are the "right" responses in American public life. Most adult and child audiences experience a positive resonance in *Huckleberry Finn*'s attacks on the evils of Twain's time (both pre– and post–Civil War), including racial abuse and intolerance. For most readers, the novel represents a still-attractive ideal of unsullied integrity.

Huckleberry Finn is, in short, an American classic; and yet it has been controversial from the beginning. When the American edition appeared in 1885 (following publication of the first English edition in late 1884), it was banned from a number of public libraries. One celebrated incident was the subject of the following account in the *Boston Transcript:*

> The Concord (Mass.) Public Library committee has decided to exclude Mark Twain's latest book from the library. One member of the committee says that, while he does not wish to call it immoral, he thinks it contains but little humor, and that of a very coarse type. He regards it as the veriest trash. The library and the other members of the committee entertain similar views, characterizing it as rough, coarse, and inelegant, dealing with a series of experiences not elevating, the whole book being more suited to the slums than to intelligent, respectable people.[3]

But the book had its defenders as well, and these praised both its humorous (if inelegant) ironies and its general wholesomeness. Today the debate over *Huckleberry Finn,* while encompassing charges that the book is irreligious, obsolete, inaccurate, or simply mindless, has focused most often on its pervasive use of the word "nigger" and its arguably disparaging portrayal of the slave Jim and other black characters. The Concord Public Library's "veriest trash" has come to be seen by some as "racist trash," pitting black parents in a debate against white educators, whose response is often little more than "How dare we criticize a classic?"

It may not be sufficient to assert that *Adventures of Huckleberry Finn* is a better book than its detractors make it out to be, and to suggest that they could see this if only they would. Classic though it may be, there are undeniable obstacles to appreciating the novel. The language of the text and some elements of characterization tend to advance ethnic and racial stereotypes, particularly of the black characters, who are repeatedly termed "niggers" and are represented as superstitious, childlike, and generally insubstantial. *Adventures of Huckleberry Finn* takes place before the Civil War, in what were obviously hard times for black Americans. The book's opponents point not just to the problem of the word "nigger" but to the painful experience for black children today of reading about African American slavery.

The burden of those days weighed on Mark Twain as well. Philip Butcher, in an article titled "Mark Twain's Installment on the National Debt," describes Twain's personal penance for the wrongs done by white Americans to black Americans and concludes that "Negroes were people to Mark Twain, people who had been wronged by his forebears and were still unjustly treated by his contemporaries. Plagued by an acute sense of outrage and guilt because of man's inhumanity to man, . . . Twain wanted to make amends for his ancestors."[4] This penance included such philanthropic efforts as paying the college tuition for at least one deserving black student. It also seems to have included a conscientious effort in his writing to overcome the prejudices and injurious tendencies left over from his childhood in Missouri and his literary apprenticeship in the frontier West and Southwest. Yet at the same time, he did not hesitate to use some of the possibly offensive material from *Huckleberry Finn* (material that portrayed Jim in accordance with the "darky" stereotype) in his public readings.

Twain, born in 1835 in Florida, Missouri, tried repeatedly to reconcile dreamy boyhood memories with the cruelty of the actual world he grew up in. *Huckleberry Finn*, with its portrayal of a teenage boy and a runaway slave making brief escapes from their too-real world, can be seen as one such effort, with Huck's developing understanding of their shared humanity providing the needed resolution. Huck experiences the difficulty of reconciling his growing respect for the kindliness, wisdom, and goodness of an individual black man with the "nigger" categorization that is so deeply ingrained in his psyche as to seem beyond question. His admiration for Jim and sense of loyalty to him seem unnatural to Huck—one of Twain's most successfully ironic variations on the theme of natural virtue disrupted by environmental distortion.

But Mark Twain, like anyone else, was not without blind spots and intolerances. Most notably, he seems to have been capable of blithely overlooking the racial implications of his productions in relation to the image of the minstrel-show "darky." The black-American-as-darky is the white fiction by which an unequal relation between races is rendered harmless, natural, just, ethical. While Twain was apparently not inclined to actually use the word "darky," it is equally evident that, despite his fondness for subverting stereotype, he was drawn to this one. Several essays in this volume (especially those in the "Blackface and White Inside" section) discuss elements of the "minstrel-show darky" in *Huckleberry Finn*'s portrayal of Jim.

Ralph Ellison, in his essay "Change the Joke and Slip the Yoke," says about minstrel entertainment, "The racial identity of the performer was unimportant, the mask was the thing (the 'thing' in more ways than one) and its function was to veil the humanity of Negroes thus reduced to a sign, and to repress the white audience's awareness of its moral identification with its own acts and with the human ambiguities pushed behind the mask."[5] Such entertainment was "escapist" in the most insidious meaning of the term. But are the minstrel trappings of Jim's character finally a degradation; or do they mostly serve as a problematizing, antisentimentalizing foil for the warm, generous, and courageous qualities that define Jim as a fundamentally admirable person? Ellison establishes the terms of the debate with his often-cited judgment that "writing at a time when the blackfaced minstrel was still popular, and shortly after a war which left even the abolitionists weary of the problems associated with the Negro, Twain fitted Jim into the outlines of the minstrel tradition, and it is from behind this stereotype mask that we see Jim's dignity and human capacity—and Twain's complexity—emerge."[6] With respect to the minstrelsy question, and *Huckleberry Finn* generally, Ellison finds the positive aspects of Twain's "complex" response to race and racism significant, though far from conclusive. Others who have considered the question, including Fredrick Woodard and Donnarae MacCann in their essay in this volume, maintain that Twain's ironic reversals do not overbalance the damage done by Jim's minstrel-show speeches and reasoning.

Twain's fondness for the minstrel show is surely entwined with his early interest and participation in the particular species of story telling known as southwestern humor—a rough-and-tumble sort of humor in which racial or other stereotypes were broadly utilized, cruelty was often tolerated or even celebrated (as in the violent endings of Twain's "The Story of the Good Little Boy" and "The Story of the Bad Little Boy"), and extreme exaggeration was the rule. The leading journal in this form, W. T. Porter's *Spirit of the Times,* lasted until 1858 and would have been readily available in Hannibal. Southwestern humorist George Washington Harris's *Sut Lovingood Yarns*—many of them harshly brutal—have been compared with tamer episodes in *Huckle-*

berry Finn. Twain originally made his reputation in this genre with such stories as "The Celebrated Jumping Frog of Calaveras County," and the continuing influence of this narrative mode is palpable in the highly controversial (structurally and thematically as well as for its racial implications) "evasion" section of *Huckleberry Finn* (the last twelve chapters). This literary tradition that helped shape Twain as a writer proved resistant to his later attempts to leave it wholly behind; boisterous echoes persisted even in his pious and adoring *Joan of Arc.*

One obvious feature of southwestern humor infecting *Huckleberry Finn* with objectionable racial overtones is "eye dialect," which pretends to represent nonstandardness by variant (in some cases, merely phonetic) spellings, though the pronunciations represented may actually be at least regionally acceptable. The speech of Jim and other black characters in the novel is marked by extreme forms of eye dialect, while that of the white characters usually is not; the result exaggerates the ignorance and/or deviance of black speakers as compared to white.

David Sewell, in *Mark Twain's Languages: Discourse, Dialogue, and Linguistic Variety,* elaborates a further difficulty in Jim's manner of speech: "That Twain's slave Jim does not speak the exaggerated farcical dialect of the blackface minstrels has misled critics into describing his speech as 'realistic' black dialect. It is, in fact, romanticized folk speech, purified of any forceful hostility that might, coming from a black speaker, have seemed threatening to a white readership even in the postwar North."[7] While dismissing some aspects of the contention that Jim's characterization relies on the image of the minstrel-show darky, Sewell, like Woodard and MacCann, underscores the innocuous character of Jim's speech, raising the possibility that Twain's emphasis on "realistic" precision in his use of dialect may conceal an underlying sense that Jim's humanity is significantly compromised by too much reliance on the conventional and inoffensive.

As for the frequent use of the word "nigger" in *Huckleberry Finn,* it goes without saying that the word was at the time of Twain's writing, and remains today, a slap in the face for black Americans. It is inevitable that black children in a classroom with whites should feel uncomfortable with the word and a book in which it appears so often, and that black parents should wish to protect their children from what the word represents. In the classroom, "nigger" is embarrassing and divisive at any grade level. John H. Wallace argues that "whatever the purpose and effect of the word 'nigger' for Twain's original white

adult audiences, its appearance in a classroom today tends to reinforce racism."[8] The word has been, and continues to be, a part of
the language of oppression. Certainly there are insulting names for
whites as well, but those names have not been used in the enforced
humiliation of a race. W. E. B. Du Bois with good reason referred to
"nigger" as "the word . . . which no white man must use."[9]

Attempts to mitigate can, of course, create their own complications. Mary Mapes Dodge, editor of *St. Nicholas Magazine* and author
of *Hans Brinker; or, The Silver Skates,* published *Tom Sawyer Abroad,*
Twain's sequel to *Huckleberry Finn* (in which Tom, Huck, and Jim go
to Egypt in a balloon) as a serial in *St. Nicholas* from November 1893
through April 1894. To protect her young readers, she expunged
references to sweating, drunkenness, and, where possible, death.
Though she allowed Jim's references to *himself* as a "nigger" to
stand—a sign, despite her sensitivities, of her confidence in the broad
acceptance of the term (at least by white audiences) in the late nineteenth century[10]—out came Huck's reference to Jim as a "nigger"
in the first paragraph; Dodge substituted other terms, including
"darky," and must have felt she had made a great improvement.[11] But
Dodge's editorial substitution only disguised the racial offensiveness,
making the socially acceptable move of deleting the overt insult while
retaining the subjugating racial stereotype.

This, in part, states the obvious: the importance of the language
context notwithstanding, there is more to racism than rhetorical
constructions. Two of the most racially inflammatory books published in America are Thomas Dixon's *The Leopard's Spots* (1902) and
The Clansman (1903; these novels were the basis for D. W. Griffith's
silent film *The Birth of a Nation,* which glorified the Ku Klux Klan).
Dixon, like Twain, when speaking himself as author uses the more
neutral word "Negro." And more in line with Dodge's practice than
Twain's, he confines the use of the term "nigger" to the speeches of
blacks and poor whites. But despite the verbal restraint, Dixon has his
hero soliloquize about black physical features, which "will register
their animal marks over the proudest intellect and the rarest beauty of
any other race. The rule that had no exception was that one drop of
Negro blood makes a Negro."[12] The rarefied language here, in its
thoroughly nonsatiric context, fails to mask—and in fact may accentuate—the brutally offensive intent.

For both Dixon and Dodge (and for the Concord Public Library),
the pertinent objection to "nigger" was its vulgarity, not its racist

implication. But that more superficial vulgarity aside, the language of whites in *Huckleberry Finn,* when understood in its "literary" context, seems to serve an ironic turn against the racist mind-set, marking speakers as ignorant, malicious, or perhaps condescending, like the doctor who says of Jim, "a nigger like that is worth a thousand dollars—and kind treatment, too." Other characters less admirable than the doctor use the word "nigger" in more self-serving and threatening ways. The vilest words and deeds are those of people such as the King and the Duke, who sell Jim back into slavery, or Pap Finn, whose drunkenness, brutality, disgusting physical appearance, and general hostility toward anything wholesome or civilized eclipse the noxious behavior of even the King and the Duke. Irony pervades the scene when the besotted Pap, unthinkingly describing a better man than himself, rages against a "govment" that allows a "free nigger" to walk around publicly in fine clothes. The use of the word "nigger" six times in his harangue plays up Pap's degeneracy; by this assignment of the word, Twain's narrative accentuates the ugliness of debauched thinking.

But as the doctor's "compliment" to Jim illustrates, Twain's account does not leave racism only to stupid, vicious individuals. Few characters in *Huckleberry Finn* are immune: the pious Miss Watson is a slave owner, and so are Mary Jane Wilks, whom Huck idolizes, and Uncle Silas Phelps, whom he calls "a mighty nice old man." Phelps sees no conflict between his slave owning and his sermon on Saint Paul's message of human brotherhood (Acts 17).[13] Huck Finn himself, though disarmingly lovable in many ways, is contaminated by the racism of his time and region; to the last chapter in the book he uses "nigger," long after rejecting most of the clichéd notions the word represents. The problematic conflation of admirable characteristics with uncritical racism adds depth to the novel but at the same time raises the probability for destructive misinterpretation.

The character-bound, plot-bound purpose of *Huckleberry Finn*'s language becomes more evident against the background of the earlier novel *Tom Sawyer,* where the condemning word is used only three times: in two separate conversations between Tom and Huck, and once by Injun Joe, who after being horsewhipped, complains of being treated "like a nigger"; Twain as third-person narrator uses "negro" or "colored." Samuel Clemens's boyhood letters, and even his early western writings, contain derogatory uses of "nigger," but he reformed dramatically when he began courting, and soon married, the daughter of abolitionist Jervis Langdon (which gives an additional twist to Huck's opinion of abolitionists and his judgment that stealing Jim out of slavery is a "dirty low-down business" [chap. 33]). In both published and unpublished writings, the mature Twain increasingly finds ironic or sarcastic, or simply "language-realistic," uses for the word "nigger." On these occasions he is invariably sympathetic to the individuals so labeled. For example, he recorded a conversation between two laundresses—ex-slaves—in an April 27, 1882, notebook entry. The exchange, which later became material for *Life on the Mississippi*, reflects interestingly both on Jim's journey south and on his earlier concern about being sold "downriver":

> At one place one of them said: "That's a mighty beautiful plantation."
> The other replied, "Lordy, Lordy, many a poor nigger has been killed there, jest for nuffin, & flung into that river thar' & thats the last of-em."
> After a pause the first said, "If we could only have the old times back again, just for a minute, just to see how it would seem."
> "Oh Lordy *I* don't want 'em back again for a minute. It was mighty rough times on the niggers."
> "Thats so. I come mighty near being sold down here [Louisiana] once; & if I had been I wouldnt been here now; been the last of me."
> The other said, "I was sold down as far as Miss. I was afraid I'd go furder down. If I had I'd never been here."[14]

Huck Finn, the first-person narrator of *Adventures of Huckleberry Finn*, is a youth from the margins of society who is awkwardly learning to overcome the prejudices of his upbringing—a "realistic" justification for using the word "nigger" so often in Huck's story. As a boy uncertain of his beliefs, Huck often regresses into locally acceptable practices and uses the word even though, ironically, he is becoming increasingly aware that Jim is a person worthy of respect. As the novel progresses, Huck realizes that Jim, like the typical—or stereotypical—white man, loves his family, values freedom and friendship, and feels that he deserves an apology when insulted. Jim, like Huck, uses the word to describe himself and others in keeping with social form and thoroughly worn habit.

More troublesome to readers, though, is the fact that Huck, as "naïve" or "unreliable" narrator, is too inexperienced to understand everything he relates. Though Huck seems generally well intentioned in his moral gropings, readers are left to sort out moments of genuine insight from Huck's false starts (or stops) along the way, sounding the distances between Huck's words and Twain's intention, as well as the more problematic difference between Twain's intention and the book's unintended effects on its readers. This boy of fourteen—uneducated, growing up in a climate of intolerance gradually and perhaps incompletely overcome through his friendship with Jim—is a signal that the burden of interpretation rests, however uneasily, with the reader.

Considerable, if not entirely consistent, thematic energy works on the central characters to disrupt stereotypes both black and white. The ironic conflict between Huck's "conscience" and his heart, between what he has been taught by his racist society and what he has learned from Jim, creates what Richard K. Barksdale (in this volume) calls "an ironic appraisal of the American racial scene circa 1884." To miss this is to see in the book (as some have) nothing more than a series of childish adventures and stupid pranks. When the book is used in the classroom, the teacher has the burdensome responsibility of helping students to make critical determinations. It is difficult to teach irony, to overcome the literal, to show that a book may mean the opposite of what its words seem to say; and the degree to which the pungency of untutored impressions may linger, continuing to resound and possibly wound in spite of explanations of ironic intention, remains a crucial impediment to use of the novel at the junior high, high school, or even undergraduate college level. Certainly, teachers who admire the book must think carefully not only about the local situation and whether they feel prepared to deal with the historical background of Huck's adventures, but also about whether they can make clear the subtle distinctions that their reading of the novel requires.

Twain scholar Henry Nash Smith remarked in an interview at the time of the novel's one hundredth anniversary: "So much discussion has built up around *Huckleberry Finn* that it's almost an impossible task to get through to the novel itself."[15] But "the novel itself" poses its own obstinacies: readers can find the dialect inscrutable, the irony bewildering, and the repeated use of offensive language highly distasteful. For youthful readers, the puzzlements and shocks are unavoidably magnified.

To counterbalance Smith's somewhat exasperated comment about the oppressive overabundance of opinion on the merits of Twain's novel, we might note Henry James's more spirited contention in "The Art of Fiction" that "art lives upon discussion, . . . upon the exchange of views and the comparison of standpoints."[16] *Huckleberry Finn* seems to have thrived accordingly. As Steven Mailloux remarks, "Mark Twain remains an active presence in the ongoing conversation of American culture. His voice, especially in *Huckleberry Finn,* has been heard for over a century now and shows no signs of falling silent. Today Twain's novels participate in the cultural conversation not only as voices but as topics."[17]

The perspectives collected here continue that conversation, as black scholars voice their views on the problems, justifications, and significances of Twain's novel in relation to its nineteenth-century context and its place in the twentieth century. Eight of the essays—those by Richard K. Barksdale, Rhett S. Jones, Julius Lester, Charles H. Nichols, Charles H. Nilon, Arnold Rampersad, David L. Smith, and Kenny J. Williams—appeared in a special issue of the *Mark Twain Journal* (Fall 1984) guest edited by Thadious Davis, and one—by Bernard W. Bell—appeared in the next issue (Spring 1985). These nine essays appear here with some further editorial changes. The essays by Mary Kemp Davis, Peaches Henry, Betty H. Jones, Carmen Subryan, John H. Wallace, and Fredrick Woodard and Donnarae MacCann were written for this volume. The views given in these essays exemplify the range of possible responses—from admiration to adamant opposition—and demonstrate, not surprisingly, that there is no single "black" position on *Huckleberry Finn* any more than there is a monolithic white one. Where the same passage from *Huckleberry Finn* is discussed in more than one essay, sometimes leading to quite different conclusions, we have tried in the introductions to the various sections (and in the notes) to indicate major occurrences of the differences, providing cross-references to help define the spectrum of opinion. If the aggregate does not result in a final mapping of the controversy over *Huckleberry Finn,* it at least sheds light (at times by lightning) on the territory.

Quotations from *Adventures of Huckleberry Finn* in this volume are drawn from the Iowa/California edition, volume 8 of *The Works of Mark Twain,* ed. Walter Blair and Victor Fischer (Berkeley: U of California P, 1988), but are cited by chapter rather than page number for ease of reference to other editions.

Notes

1. Lawrence Feinberg, "Shakespeare Leads List of Recommended Reading for Schools," *Washington Post* 12 Aug. 1985: A12.

2. *Charleston* (S.C.) *News and Courier* 16 Nov. 1989: A2 6 [from an Associated Press release].

3. *Boston Transcript* 17 March 1885.

4. Philip Butcher, "Mark Twain's Installment on the National Debt," *Southern Literary Journal* 1 (Spring 1969): 55.

5. Ralph Ellison, *Shadow and Act* (New York: Random House, 1964) 48–49.

6. Ellison 50.

7. David R. Sewell, *Mark Twain's Languages: Discourse, Dialogue, and Linguistic Variety* (Berkeley: U of California P, 1987) 95.

8. John H. Wallace, "'Huck Finn' Is a Classic: A Classic Slur on Blacks," *Crain's Chicago Business* 11 Feb. 1985.

9. W. E. B. Du Bois, "The Humor of Negroes," *Mark Twain Quarterly* [later *Mark Twain Journal*] 5.3 (Fall–Winter 1942–43): 1.

10. In fact, Dodge herself wrote a story about a comic Irish maid, Miss Malony, who called a Chinese character "a haythin nager."

11. O. M. Brack, Jr., "Mark Twain in Knee Pants: The Expurgation of *Tom Sawyer Abroad*," *Proof* 2 (1972): 145–51.

12. Thomas Dixon, *The Leopard's Spots: A Romance of the White Man's Burden—1865–1900* (New York: A. Wessels, 1908) 386.

13. God "hath made of one blood all nations of men" (Acts 17:26).

14. *Mark Twain's Notebooks and Journals*, vol. 2: *1877–1883*, ed. Frederick Anderson, Lin Salamo, and Bernard L. Stein (Berkeley: U of California P, 1975) 547.

15. Quoted in Angus Paul, "Huck and Jim Begin Their Next 100 Years of Rafting through the American Psyche," *Chronicle of Higher Education* 29 (13 Feb. 1985): 6.

16. Henry James, *Theory of Fiction: Henry James*, ed. James E. Miller, Jr. (Lincoln: U of Nebraska P, 1972) 29.

17. Steven Mailloux, *Rhetorical Power* (Ithaca, N.Y.: Cornell UP, 1989) 58.

Huck Finn

and the

Authorities

In most years since *Adventures of Huckleberry Finn* appeared in America in 1885, it has been banned somewhere, for some reason.[1] At first the charge was vulgarity, as when the Concord Public Library rejected the book for being "rough, coarse, and inelegant . . . more suited to the slums than to intelligent, respectable people." Today we might see the disparaging reference to "the slums" as being itself "rough" and "coarse" in its implications; we might even suspect that one unspoken objection to Huck Finn has been a racist, or at least elitist, dislike of the company he kept. Few readers would now condemn the book as objectionably low or coarse, but the problem of racism is not so easily dismissed. Twain's novel can be treated as a period piece, its language roughly true to a time when most blacks were slaves and insulting epithets were among their lesser problems; but that language remains painfully divisive for black and white Americans. Black parents naturally want to spare their children the discrimination and gratuitous insults that are too much a part of the history of black Americans. It may also be inevitable, and not altogether inappropriate, that resentments having less to do with the book than with the experience of growing up black in America should be incorporated into protests against *Huckleberry Finn*.

John H. Wallace's essay, "The Case against *Huck Finn*," sets the tone for objections to the novel and is of historical as well as critical significance. Wallace has figured prominently in battles to get *Huckleberry Finn* out of the schools; his essay returns to the stand he has taken elsewhere, in print and in public appearances: *Huckleberry Finn* says that black people steal, that they are not as intelligent as white people, that they are not human. Wallace's analyses of various episodes differ noticeably from most critical evaluations, including those of other contributors to this volume, by emphasizing the literal content of passages without recourse to the irony usually seen as crucial to Twain's intention. Wallace's discussion of Jim's desire to steal his wife and children out of slavery ("give a nigger an inch and he'll take an ell") can be compared with Betty Jones's remarks on the same passage; his conclusion that Twain "insinuates that black people are less intelligent than whites" when Tom says that "Jim's a nigger and wouldn't understand the reasons for" sawing off his hand or foot (chap. 35) can be compared with David Smith's account of Jim's shrewdness in various encounters with Tom and Huck; and his reference to the "killed a nigger" episode (chap. 32) as an instance in which *Huckleberry Finn* suggests that blacks are not human beings" can be compared with analyses of the passage by Smith, Peaches Henry, and Charles Nichols, as well as with Harold Beaver's remark that "he [Huck] coolly evoked her [Aunt Sally's] bigotry. If that could be taught in American schools, then neither Jim (for all his limitations) nor Twain (for his) would be such a stumbling block. For *Huckleberry Finn,* at heart, is a profoundly anti-racist book."[2]

Wallace's essay ends with a promotion for his own adapted version of *Huckleberry Finn,* one of many sanitized versions which over the years have been prepared for use in schools. But critics who see Twain's novel as effectively attacking racial bigotry argue that softening the language undermines the irony that forces and reinforces that attack. Roger Sutton, commenting on Wallace's adaptation, maintains that Wallace "has taken *Huckleberry Finn,* a book containing some strong anti-racist sentiment, and turned it into a very different book, one that is 'racist by omission' (to borrow a phrase from the Council on Interracial Books for Children). . . . With Wallace's removal of 'nigger,' and his softening of white bigotry in Twain's book, readers can conclude that life wasn't so bad for blacks in the South. Indeed, they can conclude that blacks scarcely existed. By simply referring to them as 'slaves,' readers can forget why they were enslaved to begin with."[3] But Wallace's central question lingers: is the unexpurgated text too inflammatory in an ordinary classroom situation?

Peaches Henry's essay, "The Struggle for Tolerance: Race and Censorship in *Huckleberry Finn,*" adds the perspectives of professional educational research on *Huckleberry Finn* and her own class-room experience with the problem of racist language in literary texts. Her survey of studies on teaching the novel is thorough and current. She has much to say to those who would brush aside the complaints of black parents, but she also offers evidence of the potential of Huck and Jim as a much-needed model of friendship. While Wallace recommends that, in addition to *Huckleberry Finn*, the novel *To Kill a Mockingbird* be *"listed as racist* and excluded from the classroom" (Wallace's emphasis), Henry discusses how she has dealt with *Mockingbird* in mixed classes, worked through initial discomfort over such terms as "nigger-lover," and made the reading a beneficially stimulating experience for her students. She maintains that the same can be done for Twain's novel with imaginative and sensitive teaching.

Reviewing arguments for and against *Huckleberry Finn,* Richard K. Barksdale ("History, Slavery, and Thematic Irony in *Huckleberry Finn*") proposes that many of the attacks on the book stem from feelings of guilt (among both blacks and whites) over continuing racial divisions in our society and from a consequent desire to simply forget America's scandalous racial history. Barksdale emphasizes the human bonding between Jim and Huck rather than racial division, and he finds Twain's own prejudice more antisocial than antiblack (in this agreeing with Julius Lester's essay in this volume). Unlike Wallace, he calls attention to the novel's ironic content, but also concedes the difficulty of sorting through irony's "deliberate misstatements." Barksdale believes that a clear view of *Huckleberry Finn*'s racial ironies may be overly difficult because American experience, still too much enmeshed in problems of race, undercuts aesthetic distance.

James S. Leonard and Thomas A. Tenney

Notes

1. For discussions of some of these bannings, see "For Further Reading," in this volume; in particular many of the anonymous entries, and books and articles by Baker, Brauer, Dickinson, Fiedler, Gilliam, Hearn, Hentoff, Hitchens, Kaplan, Kelly (its racist tone makes this one offensive), Ruth Stein, Wallace, and Will.

2. Harold Beaver, *Huckleberry Finn* (London: Allen & Unwin, 1987) 42–43.

3. Roger Sutton, "'Sivilizing' Huck Finn," *School Library Journal* (Aug. 1984): 44.

The Case Against

Huck Finn

John H. Wallace

The Issue

The *Adventures of Huckleberry Finn,* by Mark Twain, is the most grotesque example of racist trash ever written. During the 1981–82 school year, the media carried reports that it was challenged in Davenport, Iowa; Houston, Texas; Bucks County, Pennsylvania; and, of all places, Mark Twain Intermediate School in Fairfax County, Virginia. Parents in Waukegan, Illinois, in 1983 and in Springfield, Illinois, in 1984 asked that the book be removed from the classroom—and there are many challenges to this book that go unnoticed by the press. All of these are coming from black parents and teachers after complaints from their children or students, and frequently they are supported by white teachers, as in the case of Mark Twain Intermediate School.

For the past forty years, black families have trekked to schools in numerous districts throughout the country to say, "This book is not good for our children," only to be turned away by insensitive and often unwittingly racist teachers and administrators who respond, "This book is a classic." Classic or not, it should not be allowed to continue to cause our children embarrassment about their heritage.

Louisa May Alcott, the Concord Public Library, and others condemned the book as trash when it was published in 1885. The NAACP and the National Urban League successfully collaborated to have *Huckleberry Finn* removed from the classrooms of the public schools of New York City in 1957 because it uses the term "nigger." In 1969 Miami-Dade Junior College removed the book from its classrooms because the administration believed that the book creates an emotional block for black students which inhibits learning. It was excluded from the classrooms of the New Trier High School in Winnetka, Illinois, and removed from the required reading list in the state of Illinois in 1976.

My own research indicates that the assignment and reading aloud of *Huckleberry Finn* in our classrooms is humiliating and insulting to black students. It contributes to their feelings of low self-esteem and to the white students' disrespect for black people. It constitutes mental cruelty, harassment, and outright racial intimidation to force black students to sit in the classroom with their white peers and read *Huckleberry Finn*. The attitudes developed by the reading of such literature can lead to tensions, discontent, and even fighting. If this book is removed from the required reading lists of our schools, there should be improved student-to-student, student-to-teacher, and teacher-to-teacher relationships.

"Nigger"

According to *Webster's Dictionary,* the word "nigger" means a Negro or a member of any dark-skinned race of people and is *offensive.* Black people have never accepted "nigger" as a proper term—not in George Washington's time, Mark Twain's time, or William Faulkner's time. A few white authors, thriving on making blacks objects of ridicule and scorn by having blacks use this word as they, the white authors, were writing and speaking for blacks in a dialect they perceived to be peculiar to black people, may have given the impression that blacks accepted the term. Nothing could be further from the truth.

Some black authors have used "nigger," but not in literature to be consumed by children in the classroom. Black authors know as well as whites that there is money to be made selling books that ridicule black people. As a matter of fact, the white child learns early in life that his or her black peer makes a good butt for a joke. Much of what goes on in the classroom reinforces this behavior. Often the last word uttered before a fight is "nigger." Educators must discourage the ridicule of "different" children.

In the Classroom

Russell Baker, of the *New York Times* (14 April 1982), has said (and
Jonathan Yardley, of the *Washington Post* [10 May 1982], concurred),

> Kids are often exposed to books long before they are ready for them or
> exposed to them in a manner that seems almost calculated to evaporate
> whatever enthusiasm the students may bring to them. . . . Very few
> youngsters of high school age are ready for *Huckleberry Finn*. Leaving
> aside its subtle depiction of racial attitudes and its complex view of
> American society, the book is written in a language that will seem
> baroque, obscure and antiquated to many young people today. The
> vastly sunnier *Tom Sawyer* is a book for kids, but *Huckleberry Finn most
> emphatically is not.*

The milieu of the classroom is highly charged with emotions.
There are twenty to thirty unique personalities with hundreds of
needs to be met simultaneously. Each student wants to be accepted
and to be like the white, middle-class child whom he perceives to be
favored by the teacher. Since students do not want their differences
highlighted, it is best to accentuate their similarities; but the reading
of *Huck Finn* in class accentuates the one difference that is always
apparent—color.

My research suggests that the black child is offended by the use of
the word "nigger" anywhere, no matter what rationale the teacher
may use to justify it. If the teacher permits its use, the black child tends
to reject the teacher because the student is confident that the teacher is
prejudiced. Communications are effectively severed, thwarting the
child's education. Pejorative terms should not be granted any legit-
imacy by their use in the classroom under the guise of teaching books
of great literary merit, nor for any other reason.

Equal Protection and Opportunity in the Classroom

To paraphrase Irwin Katz,[1] the use of the word "nigger" by a pres-
tigious adult like a teacher poses a strong *social* threat to the black
child. Any expression by a white or black teacher of dislike or devalua-
tion, whether through harsh, indifferent, or patronizing behavior,
would tend to have an unfavorable effect on the performance of black

children in their school work. This is so because *various psychological theories suggest that the black students' covert reactions to the social threat would constitute an important source of intellectual impairment.*

Dorothy Gilliam, writing in the *Washington Post* of 12 April 1982, said, "First Amendment rights are crucial to a healthy society. No less crucial is the Fourteenth Amendment and its guarantee of equal protection under the law." *The use of the word "nigger" in the classroom does not provide black students with equal protection and is in violation of their constitutional rights. Without equal protection, they have neither equal access nor equal opportunity for an education.*

One group of citizens deeply committed to effecting change and to retaining certain religious beliefs sacred to themselves are members of the Jewish religion. In a publication issued by the Jewish Community Council (November 1981), the following guidelines were enunciated regarding the role of religious practices in public schools: "In no event should any student, teacher, or public school staff member feel that his or her own beliefs or practices are being questioned, infringed upon, or compromised by programs taking place in or sponsored by the public school." Further, "schools should avoid practices which operate to single out and isolate 'different' pupils and thereby [cause] embarrassment."[2]

I endorse these statements without reservation, for I believe the rationale of the Jewish Community Council is consistent with my position. I find it incongruent to contend that it is fitting and proper to shelter children from isolation, embarrassment, and ridicule due to their religious beliefs and then deny the same protection to other children because of the color of their skin. The basic issue is the same. It is our purpose to spare children from scorn, to increase personal pride, and to foster the American belief of acceptance on merit, not color, sex, religion, or origin.

The Teacher

Many "authorities" say *Huckleberry Finn* can be used in our inter-mediate and high school classrooms. They consistently put stipula-tions on its use like the following: It must be used with appropriate planning. It is the responsibility of the teacher to assist students in the understanding of the historical setting of the novel, the characters being depicted, the social context, including prejudice, which existed at the time depicted in the book. Balanced judgment on the part of the classroom teacher must be used prior to making a decision to utilize this book in an intermediate or high school program. Such judgment would include taking into account the age and maturity of the students, their ability to comprehend abstract concepts, and the methodology of presentation.

Any material that requires such conditions could be dangerous racist propaganda in the hands of even our best teachers. And "some, not all, teachers are hostile, racist, vindictive, inept, or even neurotic," though "many are compassionate and skillful."[3] Teacher attitudes are important to students. Some teachers are marginal at best, yet many school administrators are willing to trust them with a book that maligns blacks. *Huckleberry Finn* would have been out of the classroom ages ago if it used "dago," "wop," or "spic."

When "authorities" mention the "historical setting" of *Huckleberry Finn,* they suggest that it is an accurate, factual portrayal of the way things were in slavery days. In fact, the book is the outgrowth of Mark Twain's memory and imagination, written twenty years after the end of slavery. Of the two main characters depicted, one is a thief, a liar, a sacrilegious corn-cob-pipe-smoking truant; the other is a self-deprecating slave. No one would want his children to emulate this pair. Yet some "authorities" speak of Huck as a boyhood hero. Twain warns us in the beginning of *Huckleberry Finn,* "Persons attempting to find a motive in this narrative will be prosecuted; persons attempting to find a moral in it will be banished; persons attempting to find a plot in it will be shot." I think we ought to listen to Twain and stop feeding this trash to our children. It does absolutely nothing to enhance racial harmony. The prejudice that existed then is still very much apparent today. Racism against blacks is deeply rooted in the American culture and is continually reinforced by the schools, by concern for socioeconomic gain, and by the vicarious ego enhancement it brings to those who manifest it.

Huckleberry Finn is racist, whether its author intended it to be or not. The book implies that black people are not honest. For example, Huck says about Jim: "It most froze me to hear such talk. He wouldn't ever dared to talk such talk in his life before. Just see what a difference it made in him the minute he judged he was about free. It was according to the old saying, 'give a nigger an inch and he'll take an ell.' Thinks I, this is what comes of my not thinking" (chap. 16). And in another section of the book, the Duke, in reply to a question from the King, says: "Mary Jane'll be in mourning from this out; and the first you know the nigger that does up the rooms will get an order to box these duds up and put 'em away; and do you reckon a nigger can run across money and not borrow some of it?" (chap. 26).

Huckleberry Finn also insinuates that black people are less intelligent than whites. In a passage where Huck and Tom are trying to get the chains off Jim, Tom says: "They couldn't get the chain off, so they just cut their hand off and shoved. And a leg would be better still. But we got to let that go. There ain't necessity enough in this case; and, besides, Jim's a nigger, and wouldn't understand the reason for it" (chap. 35). On another occasion, when Tom and Huck are making plans to get Jim out of the barn where he is held captive, Huck says: "He told him everything. Jim, he couldn't see no sense in most of it, but he allowed we was white folks and knowed better than him; so he was satisfied, and said he would do it all just as Tom said" (chap. 36).

Twain said in *Huckleberry Finn,* more than one hundred years ago, what Dr. W. B. Shockley and A. R. Jensen are trying to prove through empirical study today.[4] This tells us something about the power of the printed word when it is taught to children by a formidable institution such as the school.

Huckleberry Finn even suggests that blacks are not human beings. When Huck arrives at Aunt Sally's house, she asks him why he is late:

> "We blowed a cylinder head."
> "Good gracious! anybody hurt?"
> "No'm. Killed a nigger."
> "Well, it's lucky; because sometimes people do get hurt." (Chap. 32)

There are indications that the racist views and attitudes implicit in the preceding quotations are as prevalent in America today as they were over one hundred years ago. *Huckleberry Finn* has not been successful in fighting race hate and prejudice, as its proponents maintain, but has helped to retain the status quo.

The Black Student

In 1963 John Fisher, former president of Columbia Teachers College, stated:

> The black American youngster happens to be a member of a large and distinctive group that for a very long time has been the object of special

political, legal, and social action. . . . To act as though any child is
separable from his history is indefensible. In terms of educational planning, it is *irresponsible*.

Every black child is the victim of the history of his race in this
country. On the day he enters kindergarten, he carries a burden *no white
child* can ever know, no matter what other handicaps or disabilities he
may suffer.[5]

The primary school child learns, almost the minute he enters
school, that black is associated with dirtiness, ugliness, and wickedness. Much of what teachers and students think of the black child is
color based. As a result, the black pupil knows his pigmentation is an
impediment to his progress.

As early as the fifth grade, the black student studies American
history and must accept his ancestors in the role of slaves. This
frustrating and painful experience leaves scars that very few educators,
writers, and especially English teachers can understand. We com-
pound these problems for black children when we force them to read
aloud the message of *Huckleberry Finn*. It is so devastatingly traumatic
that the student may never recover. How much pain must a black
child endure to secure an education? No other child is asked to suffer
so much embarrassment, humiliation, and racial intimidation at the
hands of so powerful an institution as the school. The vast majority of
black students have no tolerance for either "ironic" or "satirical"
reminders of the insults and degradation heaped upon their ancestors
in slavery and postslavery times.

Dorothy Gilliam (*Washington Post*, 12 April 1982) makes a good
case for protecting the rights of students when she says, "Where
rights conflict, one must sometimes supersede the other. Freedom of
speech does not, for example, allow words to be deliberately used in a
way that would cause someone to suffer a heart attack. By the same
token, the use of words in ways that cause psychological and emotional damage is an unacceptable exercise of free speech."

Racism

If indeed, as *Huckleberry Finn*'s proponents claim, the book gives a
positive view of blacks and has an antislavery, antiracist message, then
the Nazi party, the Ku Klux Klan, and the White Citizens Council
must see something different. Most of the hate mail received when a

school in northern Virginia restricted the use of the book was from these groups.

It is difficult to believe that Samuel Clemens would write a book against the institution of slavery; he did, after all, join a Confederate army bent on preserving that peculiar institution. Also, he could not allow Huck to help Jim to his freedom. It seems he was a hodgepodge of contradictions.

Huckleberry Finn is an American classic for no other reason than that it ridicules blacks to a greater extent than any other book given our children to read. The book and racism feed on each other and have withstood the test of time because many Americans insist on preserving our racist heritage.

Marguerite Barnett (1982) points out:

> By ridiculing blacks, exaggerating their facial features, and denying their humanity, the popular art of the Post-Civil-War period represented the political culture's attempt to deny blacks the equal status and rights awarded them in the Emancipation Proclamation. By making blacks inhuman, American whites could destroy their claim to equal treatment. Blacks as slaves posed no problem because they were under complete domination, but blacks as free men created political problems. The popular culture of the day supplied the answer by dehumanizing blacks and picturing them as childlike and inferior.[6]

In this day of enlightenment, teachers should not rely on a book that teaches the subtle sickness of racism to our young and causes so much psychological damage to a large segment of our population. We are a multicultural, pluralistic nation. We must teach our young to respect all races, ethnic groups, and religious groups in the most positive terms conceivable.

Recommendations

This book should not be used with children. It is permissible to use the original *Huckleberry Finn* with students in graduate courses of history, English, and social science if one wants to study the perpetration and perpetuation of racism. The caustic, abrasive language is less likely to offend students of that age group because they tend to be mature enough to understand and discuss issues without feeling intimidated by the instructor, fellow students, or racism.

My research relating to *Huckleberry Finn* indicates that black parents and teachers, and their children and students, have complained about books that use the word "nigger" being read aloud in class. Therefore, I recommend that books such as *Huckleberry Finn, The Slave Dancer,* and *To Kill a Mockingbird* be *listed as racist* and excluded from the classroom.

If an educator feels he or she must use *Huckleberry Finn* in the classroom, I would suggest my revised version, *The Adventures of Huckleberry Finn Adapted,* by John H. Wallace. The story is the same, but the words "nigger" and "hell" are eradicated. It no longer depicts blacks as inhuman, dishonest, or unintelligent, and it contains a glossary of Twainisms. Most adolescents will enjoy laughing at Jim and Huck in this adaptation.[7]

Notes

1. Martin Deutsch, Irwin Katz, and Arthur R. Jensen, *Social Class, Race, and Psychological Development* (New York: Holt, Rinehart, and Winston, 1968) 256–57.

2. Jewish Community Council of Greater Washington, *Guidelines on Religion and the Public School* (Washington, D.C., 1981).

3. Robert D. Strom, *The Innercity Classroom* (Columbus, Ohio: Charles E. Merrill, 1966) 104.

4. [Wallace's reference here is to doctrines of biological determinism, especially to the notion that some racial groups are genetically superior, in certain ways, to other groups—ED.]

5. Harry A. Passow, *Education in Depressed Areas* (New York: Teachers College P [Columbia U], 1963) 265.

6. Documentation on this statement by Marguerite Barnett (possibly from a dissertation) is not currently available.

7. For additional reading on the subject of racial considerations in education, see James A. Banks and Jean D. Grambs, *Black Self-Concept: Implications for Education and Social Science* (New York: McGraw-Hill, 1972); Robert F. Biehler, *Psychology Applied to Teaching* (Boston: Houghton Mifflin, 1971); Gary A. Davis and Thomas F. Warren, *Psychology of Education: New Looks* (Lexington, Mass.: Heath, 1974); Marcel L. Goldschmid, *Black Americans and White Racism* (New York: Holt, Rinehart, and Winston, 1970); Donnarae MacCann and Gloria Woodard, *The Black American in Children's Books* (Metuchen, N.J.: Scarecrow, 1972).

The Struggle

for Tolerance

Race and Censorship

in *Huckleberry Finn*

Peaches Henry

In the long controversy that has been *Huckleberry Finn*'s history, the novel has been criticized, censored, and banned for an array of perceived failings, including obscenity, atheism, bad grammar, coarse manners, low moral tone, and antisouthernism. Every bit as diverse as the reasons for attacking the novel, *Huck Finn*'s detractors encompass parents, critics, authors, religious fundamentalists, right-wing politicians, and even librarians.[1]

Ironically, Lionel Trilling, by marking *Huck Finn* as "one of the world's great books and one of the central documents of American culture,"[2] and T. S. Eliot, by declaring it "a masterpiece,"[3] struck the novel certainly its most fateful and possibly its most fatal blow. Trilling's and Eliot's resounding endorsements provided Huck with the academic respectability and clout that assured his admission into America's classrooms. Huck's entrenchment in the English curricula of junior and senior high schools coincided with *Brown* vs. *Topeka Board of Education*, the Supreme Court case that ended public school segregation, legally if not actually, in 1954. Desegregation and the civil rights movement deposited Huck in the midst of American literature classes which were no longer composed of white children only, but now were dotted with black youngsters as well. In the faces of these children of the revolution, Huck met the group that was to become his most persistent and formidable foe. For while the objections of the Gilded Age, of fundamentalist religious factions, and of unreconstructed southerners had seemed laughable and transitory, the indignation of black students and their parents at the portrayal of blacks in *Huck Finn* was not at all comical and has not been short-lived.

The presence of black students in the classrooms of white America, the attendant tensions of a country attempting to come to terms with its racial tragedies, and the new empowerment of blacks to protest led to *Huck Finn*'s greatest struggle with censorship and banning. Black protesters, offended by the repetitions of "nigger" in the mouths of white and black characters, Twain's minstrel-like portrayal of the escaped slave Jim and of black characters in general, and the negative traits assigned to blacks, objected to the use of *Huck Finn* in English courses. Though blacks may have previously complained about the racially offensive tone of the novel, it was not until September 1957 that the *New York Times* reported the first case that brought about official reaction and obtained public attention for the conflict. The New York City Board of Education had removed *Huck Finn* from the approved textbook lists of elementary and junior high schools. The book was no longer available for classroom use at the elementary and junior high school levels, but could be taught in high school and purchased for school libraries. Though the Board of Education acknowledged no outside pressure to ban the use of *Huck Finn,* a representative of one publisher said that school officials had cited "some passages derogatory to Negroes" as the reason for its contract not being renewed. The NAACP, denying that it had placed any organized pressure on the board to remove *Huck Finn,* nonetheless expressed displeasure with the presence of "racial slurs" and "belittling racial designations" in many of Twain's works.[4] Whether or not the source of dissatisfaction could be identified, disapproval of *Huck Finn*'s racial implications existed and had made itself felt.

The discontent with the racial attitudes of *Huck Finn* that began in 1957 has surfaced periodically over the past thirty years. In 1963 the Philadelphia Board of Education, after removing *Huck Finn,* replaced it with an adapted version which "tone[d] down the violence, simplifie[d] the Southern dialect, and delete[d] all derogatory references to Negroes."[5] A civil rights leader in Pasco, Washington, attacked Twain's use of "nigger" in 1967;[6] two years later Miami-Dade Junior College (Miami, Florida) excised the text from its required reading list after Negro students complained that it "embarrassed them."[7] Around 1976, striking a bargain with parents of black students who demanded the removal of *Huck Finn* from the curriculum, the administration of New Trier High School in Winnetka, Illinois, agreed to withdraw the novel from required courses and confined Huck to the environs of elective courses and the school library. This compromise did not end Huck's problems in that north-shore Chicago upper-middle-class community, however, for as recently as March 1988 black parents "discovered" Huck in American Studies, an elective course team taught by an English teacher and an American history teacher, and once again approached school administrators about banning the book.[8]

The most outspoken opponent to *Huck Finn* has been John Wallace, a former administrator at the Mark Twain Intermediate School (Fairfax County, Virginia), who in 1982, while serving on the school's Human Relations Committee, spearheaded a campaign to have Huck stricken from school curricula. A decision by the school's principal to yield to the Human Relations Committee's recommendations was later overridden by the superintendent of schools. Repeatedly scoring the book as "racist trash," Wallace has raised the issue in other school districts throughout his twenty-eight-year tenure in public education. Since the Fairfax County incident, he has appeared on ABC's "Nightline" and CNN's "Freeman Reports" and has traveled the country championing the cause of black children who he says are embarrassed and humiliated by the legitimization of "nigger" in public schools. Devoted to the eradication of *Huck Finn* from the schools, he has "authored" an adapted version of Twain's story.[9] Wallace, aggressively if not eloquently, enunciates many of the deleterious effects that parents and those who support them feel the teaching of *Huck Finn* in junior high and senior high schools has on their children.[10]

The fact that people from Texas to Iowa to Illinois to Pennsylvania to Florida to Virginia to New York City concur with Wallace's assessment of *Huck Finn* demands the attention of the academic community. To condemn concerns about the novel as the misguided rantings of "know nothings and noise makers"[11] is no longer valid or profitable; nor can the invocation of Huck's immunity under the protectorate of "classic" suffice. Such academic platitudes no longer intimidate, nor can they satisfy, parents who have walked the halls of the university and have shed their awe of academe. If the academic establishment remains unmoved by black readers' dismay, the news that *Huck Finn* ranks ninth on the list of thirty books most frequently challenged[12] should serve as testimony that the book's "racial problem" is one of more consequence than the ancillary position to which scholars have relegated it.[13] Certainly, given *Huck Finn*'s high position in the canon of American literature, its failure to take on mythic proportions for, or even to be a pleasant read for, a segment of secondary school students merits academic scrutiny.

The debate surrounding the racial implications of *Huck Finn* and its appropriateness for the secondary school classroom gives rise to myriad considerations. The actual matter and intent of the text are a source of contention. The presence of the word "nigger," the treatment of Jim and blacks in general, the somewhat difficult satiric mode, and the ambiguity of theme give pause to even the most flexible reader. Moreover, as numerous critics have pointed out, neither junior high nor high school students are necessarily flexible or subtle readers. The very profundity of the text renders the process of teaching it problematic and places special emphasis on teacher ability and attitude. Student cognitive and social maturity also takes on special significance in the face of such a complicated and subtle text.

The nature of the complexities of *Huck Finn* places the dynamics of the struggle for its inclusion in or exclusion from public school curricula in two arenas. On the one hand, the conflict manifests itself as a contest between lay readers and so-called scholarly experts, particularly as it concerns the text. Public school administrators and teachers, on the other hand, field criticisms that have to do with the context into which the novel is introduced. In neither case, however, do opponents appear to *hear* each other. Too often, concerned parents are dismissed by academia as "neurotics"[14] who have fallen prey to personal racial insecurities or have failed to grasp Twain's underlying truth. In their turn, censors regard academics as inhabitants of ivory towers who pontificate on the virtue of *Huck Finn* without recognizing its potential for harm. School officials and parents clash over the school's right to intellectual freedom and the parents' right to protect their children from perceived racism.

Critics vilify Twain most often and most vehemently for his aggressive use of the pejorative term "nigger." Detractors, refusing to accept the good intentions of a text that places the insulting epithet so often in the mouths of characters, black and white, argue that no amount of intended irony or satire can erase the humiliation experienced by black children. Reading *Huck Finn* aloud adds deliberate insult to insensitive injury, complain some. In a letter to the *New York Times,* Allan B. Ballard recalls his reaction to having *Huck Finn* read aloud "in a predominantly white junior high school in Philadelphia some 30 years ago."

> I can still recall the anger I felt as my white classmates read aloud the word "nigger." In fact, as I write this letter I am getting angry all over again. I wanted to sink into my seat. Some of the whites snickered, others giggled. I can recall nothing of the literary merits of this work that you term "the greatest of all American novels." I only recall the sense of relief I felt when I would flip ahead a few pages and see that the word "nigger" would not be read that hour.[15]

Moreover, the presentation of the novel as an "American classic" serves as an official endorsement of a term uttered by the most prejudiced racial bigots to an age group eager to experiment with any language of shock value. One reporter has likened the teaching of the novel to eighth-grade kids to "pulling the pin of a hand grenade and tossing it into the all too common American classroom."[16]

Some who have followed *Huck Finn*'s racial problems express dismay that some blacks misunderstand the ironic function Twain assigned "nigger" or that other blacks, in spite of their comprehension of the irony, will allow themselves and their progeny to be defeated by a mere pejorative. Leslie Fiedler would have parents "prize Twain's dangerous and equivocal novel not in spite of its use of that wicked epithet, but for the way in which it manages to ironize it; enabling us finally—without denying our horror or our guilt—to laugh therapeutically at the 'peculiar institution' of slavery."[17] If Wallace has taken it upon himself to speak for the opponents of *Huck Finn*, Nat Hentoff, libertarian journalist for the *Village Voice,* has taken equal duty as spokesperson for the novel's champions. Hentoff believes that confronting Huck will give students "the capacity to see past words like 'nigger' . . . into what the writer is actually *saying*." He wonders, "What's going to happen to a kid when he gets into the world if he's going to let a word paralyze him so he can't think?"[18] Citing an incident in Warrington, Pennsylvania, where a black eighth-grader was allegedly verbally and physically harassed by white students after reading *Huck Finn* in class, Hentoff declares the situation ripe for the educational plucking by any "reasonably awake teacher." He enthuses:

> What a way to get Huck and Jim, on the one hand, and all those white racists they meet, on the other hand, off the pages of the book and into that very classroom. Talk about a book coming alive!
>
> Look at that Huck Finn. Reared in racism, like all the white kids in his town. And then, on the river, on the raft with Jim, shucking off that blind ignorance because this runaway slave is the most honest, percep-

tive, fair-minded man this white boy has ever known. What a book for the children, all the children, in Warrington, Pennsylvania, in 1982![19]

Hentoff laments the fact that teachers missed such a teachable moment and mockingly reports the compromise agreed upon by parents and school officials, declaring it a "victory for niceness." Justin Kaplan flatly denies that "anyone, of any color, who had actually read *Huckleberry Finn,* instead of merely reading or hearing about it, and who had allowed himself or herself even the barest minimum of intelligent response to its underlying spirit and intention, could accuse it of being 'racist' because some of its characters use offensive racial epithets."[20] Hentoff's mocking tone and reductive language, Kaplan's disdainful and condescending attitude, and Fiedler's erroneous supposition that "nigger" can be objectified so as to allow a black person "to laugh therapeutically" at slavery illustrate the incapacity of nonblacks to comprehend the enormous emotional freight attached to the hateword "nigger" for each black person. Nigger is "fightin' words and everyone in this country, black and white, knows it."[21] In his autobiography, Langston Hughes offers a cogent explanation of the signification of "nigger" to blacks:

> The word *nigger* to colored people of high and low degree is like a red rag to a bull. Used rightly or wrongly, ironically or seriously, of necessity for the sake of realism, or impishly for the sake of comedy, it doesn't matter. Negroes do not like it in any book or play whatsoever, be the book or play ever so sympathetic in its treatment of the basic problems of the race. Even though the book or play is written by a Negro, they still do not like it.
>
> The word *nigger,* you see, sums up for us who are colored all the bitter years of insult and struggle in America.[22]

Nonblacks know implicitly that to utter "nigger" in the presence of a Negro is to throw down a gauntlet that will be taken up with a vengeance.

To dismiss the word's recurrence in the work as an accurate rendition of nineteenth-century American linguistic conventions denies what every black person knows: far more than a synonym for slave, "nigger" signifies a concept. It conjures centuries of specifically black degradation and humiliation during which the family was disintegrated, education was denied, manhood was trapped within a forced perpetual puerilism, and womanhood was destroyed by concubinage. If one grants that Twain substituted "nigger" for "slave," the implications of the word do not improve; "nigger" denotes the black man as a commodity, as chattel.[23]

In addition to serving as a reminder of the "peculiar institution," "nigger" encapsulates the decades of oppression that followed emancipation. "It means not only racist terror and lynch mobs but that victims 'deserve it.'"[24] Outside Central High in Little Rock in 1954 it was emblazoned across placards; and across the South throughout the 1950s and into the 1960s it was screamed by angry mobs. Currently, it is the chief taunt of the Ku Klux Klan and other white supremacist groups. In short, "nigger" has the odious distinction of signifying all "the shame, the frustration, the rage, the fear" that has been so much a part of the history of race relations in the United States, and blacks still consider it "'dirtier' than any of the once-taboo four-syllable Anglo-Saxon monosyllabics."[25] So to impute blacks' abhorrence of "nigger" to hypersensitivity compounds injustice with callousness and signals a refusal to acknowledge that the connotations of "that word" generate a cultural discomfort that blacks share with no other racial group.

To counteract the Pavlovian response that "nigger" triggers for many black readers, some scholars have striven to reveal the positive function the word serves in the novel by exposing the discrepancy between the dehumanizing effect of the word and the real humanity of Jim.[26] Fiedler cites the passage in which Huck lies to Aunt Sally about a steamboat explosion that hurt no one but "killed a nigger," and Aunt Sally callously responds, "Well, it's lucky, because sometimes people do get hurt" (chap. 32); he notes that the passage brims with humor at the expense of Aunt Sally and the convention to which she conforms. But Fiedler is also of the opinion that Huck does not get the joke—does not recognize the humor of the fact that he and Aunt Sally by "dehumanizing the Negro diminish their own humanity."[27] It seems to Huck's foes (and to me) that if Huck does not get the joke, then there is no joke, and he becomes as culpable as Aunt Sally.

However, Fiedler's focus on this dialogue is to the point, because racial objectors isolate it as one of the most visible and detrimental slurs of the novel. The highlighting of this passage summons contrasting perspectives on it. Kaplan argues that "one has to be deliberately dense to miss the point Mark Twain is making here and to construe such passages as evidences of his 'racism.'"[28] Detractors, drawing the obvious inference from the dialogue, arrive at a conclusion different from Kaplan's, and their response cannot simply be disregarded as that of the unsophisticated reader. In order to believe in Twain's satirical intention, one has to believe in Huck's good faith toward Jim. That is to say, one has to believe that, rather than reflecting his own adherence to such conventions, Huck simply weaves a tale that marks him as a "right-thinking" youngster.

The faith in Huck that Twain's defenders display grows out of the manner in which he acquits himself at his celebrated "crisis of conscience," less than twenty-four hours prior to his encounter with Aunt Sally. There is no denying the rightness of Huck's decision to risk his soul for Jim. But there is no tangible reason to assume that the regard Huck acquires for Jim during his odyssey down the river is generalized to encompass all blacks. Further, Huck's choice to "go to hell" has little to do with any respect he has gained for Jim as a human being with an inalienable right to be owned by no one. Rather, his personal affection for the slave governs his overthrow of societal mores. It must be remembered that Huck does not adjudge slavery to be wrong; he selectively disregards a system that he ultimately believes is right. So when he discourses with Aunt Sally, he is expressing views he still holds. His emancipatory attitudes extend no further than his love for Jim. It seems valid to argue that were he given the option of freeing other slaves, Huck would not necessarily choose manumission.

Twain's apparent "perpetuation of racial stereotypes" through his portrayal of Jim and other blacks in *Huck Finn* bears relation to his use of "nigger" and has fostered vociferous criticism from anti–*Huck Finn* forces. Like the concept "nigger," Twain's depiction of blacks, particularly Jim, represents the tendency of the dominant white culture to saddle blacks with traits that deny their humanity and mark them as inferior. Critics disparage scenes that depict blacks as childish, inherently less intelligent than whites, superstitious beyond reason and common sense, and grossly ignorant of standard English. Further, they charge that in order to entertain his white audience, Twain relied upon the stock conventions of "black minstrelsy," which "drew upon European traditions of using the mask of blackness to mock individuals or social forces."[29] Given the seemingly negative stereotypical portraits of blacks, parents concerned that children, black and white, be exposed to positive models of blacks are convinced that *Huck Finn* is inappropriate for secondary classrooms.

Critics express their greatest displeasure with Twain's presentation of Jim, the runaway slave viewed by most as second only to Huck in importance to the novel's thematic structure. Although he is the catalyst that spurs Huck along his odyssey of conscience, Jim commences the novel (and to some degree remains) as the stereotypical, superstitious "darky" that Twain's white audience would have expected and in which they would have delighted.

In his essay "Change the Joke and Slip the Yoke," Ralph Ellison examines the play Twain gives the minstrel figure. Though Twain does strike Jim in the mold of the minstrel tradition, Ellison believes that we observe "Jim's dignity and human capacity" emerge from "behind this stereotype mask." Yet by virtue of his minstrel mask, Jim's role as an adult is undercut, and he often appears more childlike than Huck. Though Ellison writes that "it is not at all odd that this black-faced figure of white fun [the minstrel darky] is for Negroes a symbol of everything they rejected in the white man's thinking about race, in themselves and in their own group," his final analysis seems to be that Jim's humanity transcends the limits of the minstrel tradition.[30]

Taking a more critical stance than Ellison, Fredrick Woodard and Donnarae MacCann, in "*Huckleberry Finn* and the Traditions of Blackface Minstrelsy," examine specific incidents throughout the novel in the light of the minstrel tradition. Denying that Jim is used to poke fun at whites, as some scholars suggest, Woodard and MacCann cite the appeal that the "ridiculous or paternalistic portrayals of Black Americans" held for "the white theatre-going audience," Twain's own delight in minstrel shows, and his "willingness to shape his message to his audience."[31] Noting that the stereotypical blackface portrayals were thought to be realistic by Twain and many of his white contemporaries, the pair highlight various incidents in *Huck Finn* that they think illustrate their contention that Jim plays the minstrel role to Huck's straight man. For instance, Huck's and Jim's debate about French (chap. 14) bears a striking resemblance to the minstrel-show dialogue that Twain deemed "happy and accurate imitation[s] of the *usual and familiar negro quarrel*."[32] Though Jim's logic is superior to Huck's, argue Woodard and MacCann, the scene plays like a minstrel-show act because "Jim has the information-base of a child."[33]

Huck Finn advocates, tending to agree with Ellison's judgment that Jim's fullness of character reveals itself, offer readings of Jim that depart sharply from the Woodard and MacCann assessment. Some view Twain's depiction of Jim early in the novel as the necessary backdrop against which Huck's gradual awareness of Jim's humanity is revealed. These early renditions of Jim serve more to lay bare Huck's initial attitudes toward race and racial relations than they do to characterize Jim, positively or negatively. As the two fugitives ride down the Mississippi deeper and deeper into slave territory, the power of Jim's personality erodes the prejudices Huck's culture (educational, political, social, and legal) has instilled. Such readings of passages that appear to emphasize Jim's superstitions, gullibility, or foolishness allow Twain to escape the charge of racism and be seen as championing blacks by exposing the falseness of stereotypes. This view of Twain's motivation is evident in letters written to the *New York Times* in protest of the New York City Board of Education's decision to ban the book in 1957:

> Of all the characters in Mark Twain's works there probably wasn't any of whom he was fonder than the one that went down the river with Huck Finn. It is true that this character is introduced as "Miss Watson's big nigger, named Jim." That was the Missouri vernacular of the day. But from there on to the end of the story Miss Watson's Jim is a warm human being, lovable and admirable.[34]

> Now, *Huckleberry Finn* . . . is a great document in the progress of human tolerance and understanding. Huck begins by regarding Jim, the fugitive slave, very much as the juvenile delinquents of Little Rock regard the Negro today. Gradually, however, he discovers that Jim, despite the efforts of society to brutalize him, is a noble human being who deserves his protection, friendship, and respect. This theme of growing love is made clear throughout the book.[35]

In another vein, some defenders of Twain's racial sensitivities assign Jim's initial portrayal a more significant role than mere backdrop. The rubric of "performed ideology" frames Steven Mailloux's interpretation of Jim as he appears in the early "philosophical debates" with Huck.[36] Mailloux explains how a "literary text can take up the ideological rhetoric of its historical moment . . . and place it on a fictional stage." As "ideological drama," the literary text—*Huckleberry Finn* in this case—invites readers to become spectators and actors at a rhetorical performance. In fact, the success of the ideological drama depends upon the reader's participation: "The humor and often the ideological point of the novel's many staged arguments . . . rely upon the reader's ability to recognize patterns of false argumentation." Within the framework of rhetorical performances, then, Jim's minstrel scenes serve "as ideological critique[s] of white supremacy." In each case, however, the dominance of Jim's humanity over the racial discourse of white supremacy hinges upon the reader's recognition of the discrepancy between the two ideologies.[37]

The interpretive job that Mailloux does on the "French question" in chapter 14 exonerates the passage of any racial negativity. Huck's disdainful comment that "you can't learn a nigger to argue" renders the debate little more than a literary version of a minstrel dialogue unless readers recognize the superior rhetorician: "Of course, readers reject the racist slur as a rationalization. They know Huck gives up because he has lost the argument: it is precisely because Jim *has* learned to argue by imitating Huck that he reduces his teacher to silence. Far from demonstrating Jim's inferior knowledge, the debate dramatizes his argumentative superiority, and in doing so makes a serious ideological point through a rhetoric of humor."[38] The vigorous critical acumen with which Mailloux approaches the role played by Jim is illustrative of the interpretative tacks taken by academics. Most view Twain's depiction of Jim as an ironic attempt to transcend the very prejudices that dissidents accuse him of perpetuating.

Though there has been copious criticism of the Jim who shuffles his way across the pages of *Huckleberry Finn*'s opening chapters, the Jim who darkens the closing chapters of the novel elicits even more (and more universally agreed-upon) disapprobation. Most see the closing sequence, which begins at Huck's encounter with Aunt Sally, as a reversal of any moral intention that the preceding chapters imply. The significance that Twain's audience has attached to the journey down the river—Jim's pursuit of freedom and Huck's gradual recognition of the slave's humanness—is rendered meaningless by the entrance of Tom Sawyer and his machinations to "free" Jim.

The particular offensiveness to blacks of the closing sequence of *Huckleberry Finn* results in part from expectations that Twain has built up during the raft ride down the river. As the two runaways drift down the Mississippi, Huck (along with the reader) watches Jim emerge as a man whose sense of dignity and self-respect dwarf the minstrel mask. No one can deny the manly indignation evinced by Jim when Huck attempts to convince him that he has only dreamed their separation during the night of the heavy fog. Huck himself is so struck by Jim's passion that he humbles himself "to a nigger" and "warn't ever sorry for it afterwards" (chap. 15).

From this point, the multidimensionality of Jim's personality erodes Huck's socialized attitudes about blacks. During the night, thinking that Huck is asleep, Jim vents the adult frustrations he does not expect Huck to understand or alleviate; he laments having to abandon his wife and two children: "Po' little Lizbeth! Po' little Johnny! It's might hard; I spec' I ain't ever gwyne to see you no mo', no mo'" (chap. 23). Berating himself for having struck his four-year-old daughter, Elizabeth, in punishment for what he thought was blatant disobedience, Jim tells Huck of his remorse after discovering that the toddler had gone deaf without his knowledge. Through such poignant moments Huck learns, to his surprise, that Jim "cared just as much for his people as white folks does for their'n. It don't seem natural, but I reckon it's so" (chap. 23).

Finally, in the welcome absence of Pap, Jim becomes a surrogate father to Huck, allowing the boy to sleep when he should stand watch on the raft, giving him the affection his natural father did not, and making sure that the raft is stocked and hidden. Thus Twain allows Jim to blossom into a mature, complex human being whom Huck admires and respects. The fullness of character with which Twain imbues Jim compels Huck to "decide, forever, betwixt two things." The reader applauds Huck's acceptance of damnation for helping Jim and affixes all expectations for the rest of the novel to this climactic moment.

Having thus tantalized readers with the prospect of harmonious relations between white and black, Twain seems to turn on his characters and his audience. Leo Marx, who mounted the best-known attack on the novel's ending in his essay "Mr. Eliot, Mr. Trilling, and *Huckleberry Finn,*" describes it as a glaring lapse "of moral vision" resulting from Twain's inability to "acknowledge the truth his novel contained."[39] Readers' discomfort with the "evasion" sequence results from discrepancies between the Jim and Huck who grow in stature on the raft and the impostors who submit to Tom. Fritz Oehschlaeger's "'Gwyne to Git Hung': The Conclusion of *Huckleberry Finn*" expresses the frustrations that many experience regarding the evasion:

> The . . . shift in tone from one of high seriousness to one of low burlesque is so abrupt as to be almost chilling. Clemens has simply made the issues too serious for us to accept a return to the boyhood world of the novel's opening. We are asked to forget Huck's process of moral education, his growing awareness of Jim's value as a human being.

> Similarly, we are asked to forget Jim's nobility, revealed to us repeatedly
> in the escape down the river. Instead, Jim becomes again the stereo-
> typed, minstrel-show "nigger" of the novel's first section, a figure to be
> manipulated, tricked, and ridiculed by the boys. Perhaps even less ac-
> ceptable is Clemens's apparent decision to allow Miss Watson a partial
> redemption through her death-bed freeing of Jim. At the end Jim is free
> and considers himself rich, and Huck is left to pursue further adventures
> in the Territory. [Yet] . . . something in us longs for quite a different
> outcome, one that would allow Jim to retain his heroic stature and force
> Huck to live up to the decision that accompanies his tearing up of the
> letter to Miss Watson.[40]

By this view, Twain's apparent abandonment of Huck's reformation
and Jim's quest for freedom constitutes an absolute betrayal. Consequently, any redemptive racial attitudes that Twain has displayed
earlier are nullified; his final portrait of Jim appears sinister and
malicious.

Scholars have attempted to read the evasion sequence in ways that
would make it palatable by placing it in sync with the preceding
chapters. In just such an attempt to render the last ten chapters less
irksome, James M. Cox attacks the very thing that has led readers to
deplore that last one-fourth—that is, the moral sentiment against
which we measure Tom's actions. Our moral sentiment, explains
Cox,[41] leads us to misconstrue Twain's intent and to declare the
ending a failure. Twain does not, as most believe, lose courage and fail
to carry through with his indictment of the racial attitudes of the Old
South. On the contrary, the closing sequence returns the novel and
Huck to Twain's true central meaning.

For thirty-one chapters Twain wages an attack upon conscience—
not upon the southern conscience, as we want to believe, but upon
any conscience. According to Cox, "the deep wish which *Huckleberry
Finn* embodies" is "the wish for freedom from any conscience." Huck
flees conscience at every turn, making choices based on what is most
comfortable. It is this adherence to the pleasure principle that defines
Huck's identity and governs his actions toward Jim, not a racial
enlightenment, as we would hope. The moment at which Huck
forsakes the pleasure principle and of which we most approve marks
the point at which his identity and Twain's central focus, according to
Cox, are in the most jeopardy: "In the very act of choosing to go to
hell he has surrendered to the notion of a *principle* of right and wrong.
He has forsaken the world of pleasure to make a moral choice.

Precisely here is where Huck is about to negate himself—where, with an act of positive virtue, he actually commits himself to play the role of Tom Sawyer which he *has* to assume in the closing section of the book."[42] Insofar as the concluding sections bring Huck back into line with Twain's determination to subvert conscience, it remains consistent with the preceding chapters. Given this, to declare Twain's ending a failure is to deny his actual thematic intent and to increase our discomfort with the concluding segments.

Cox's argument demonstrates the ingenious lengths to which scholars go to feel comfortable with the final chapters of *Huck Finn*. But the inadequacy of such academic ingenuities in meeting this and other challenges to the novel becomes clear when one considers that the issue remains "hot" enough to make it available for debate on prime-time television.[43] What scholars must realize is that no amount of interpretive acrobatics can mediate the actual *matter* of the closing sequence. Regardless of Twain's motivation or intent, Jim does deflate and climb back into the minstrel costume. His self-respect and manly pursuit of freedom bow subserviently before the childish pranks of an adolescent white boy.

Considering the perplexity of the evasion brings us back full circle to *Huckleberry Finn*'s suitability for public schools. Given the powerlessness of highly discerning readers to resolve the novel in a way that unambiguously redeems Jim or Huck, how can students be expected to fare better with the novel's conclusion? Parents question the advisability of teaching to junior and senior high school students a text which requires such sophisticated interpretation in order for its moral statements to come clear. The teaching of such a text presumes a level of intellectual maturity not yet realized by secondary school students, particularly eighth- and ninth-grade students who are in the inchoate stages of literary studies. Parents fear that the more obvious negative aspects of Jim's depiction may overshadow the more subtle uses to which they are put. Critics such as Mailloux point to the reader as the component necessary to obviate the racism inherent in, for example, the interchange between Aunt Sally and Huck.[44] But if an eighth- or ninth-grader proves incapable of completing the process begun by Twain, then the ideological point is lost. This likely possibility causes parents to be hesitant about approving *Huck Finn* for the classroom.

Huck Finn apologists view the objection to the novel on the ground of students' cognitive immaturity as an underestimation of youngsters' abilities. In the third of his four-part series on the censorship of *Huck Finn*,[45] Hentoff boasts that the ability of children in 1982 to fathom Twain's subtleties is at least comparable to that of children who read the novel a century ago. "At 10, or 12, or 14, even with only the beginning ring of meaning," writes Hentoff, "any child who can read will not miss the doltishness and sheer meanness and great foolishness of most whites in the book, particularly in their attitudes toward blacks."[46] He continues, "Nor will the child miss the courage and invincible decency of the white boy and the black man on the river." While Hentoff's confidence in the American schoolchild is commendable, his enthusiasm reveals a naïvete about junior high school students' critical insight. As Cox's and Mailloux's articles show, the points of the novel are anything but "as big as barn doors." Therefore, the cognitive maturity of students and the grade-level placement of the novel are of grave importance.

That *Huckleberry Finn* brims with satire and irony is a truism of academic discourse. But a study conducted in 1983 to examine "the effects of reading *Huckleberry Finn* on the racial attitudes of ninth grade students" corroborates the contention that junior high school students lack the critical perception to successfully negotiate the satire present in the novel. According to the committee that directed the study, the collected data indicated "that the elements of satire which are crucial to an understanding of the novel go largely unobserved by students."[47] That approximately one-third of the group (those students who studied the novel as an instructional unit) regarded *Huckleberry Finn* as merely an adventure story "after several weeks of serious study" left the committee convinced "that many students are not yet ready to understand the novel on its more complex levels." Therefore, although not advising expulsion of the novel, the panel recommended its removal from the ninth-grade curriculum and placement in the eleventh- or twelfth-grade syllabus:

> This recommendation is made, not because the use of *Huckleberry Finn* promotes or furthers negative stereotyping—the preponderance of our data suggests that, if anything, it lessens such stereotyping—but because some of the literary objectives given as justification for the use of the book seem not to have been achieved. Given the degree and instances of irony and satire in the book, the difficult dialects and general reading level of the book, and the tendency of many students to read the book at the level of an adventure story, the committee believes, the novel requires more literary sophistication than can reasonably be expected from an average ninth grade student.[48]

Though the Penn State study does not support parents' calls for total removal of *Adventures of Huckleberry Finn* from the curriculum, it does validate their reservations about the presence of the work at the junior high level. Possibly a sufficiently mature audience is present in the eleventh- and twelfth-grade classes of America, but it seems not to be available in the eighth, ninth, or even tenth grades.

The volatile combination of satire, irony, and questions of race underscores an additional important facet of the controversy: teacher ability and attitude. The position of the classroom teacher in the conflict over *Huckleberry Finn* is delicate: students not only look to teachers as intellectual mentors, but turn to them for emotional and social guidance as well. So in addition to ensuring that students traverse the scholarly territory that the curriculum requires, teachers must guarantee that students complete the journey with their emotional beings intact.

The tenuous status of race relations in the United States complicates the undertaking of such an instructional unit. Cox, despite his affection for the novel and his libertarian views, admits that were he "teaching an American literature course in Bedford Stuyvesant or Watts or North Philadelphia," he might choose Twain texts other than *Adventures of Huckleberry Finn*.[49] A situation as emotionally charged as the introduction of the word "nigger" into class discussion requires a sensitivity and perspicacity that parents are unconvinced a majority of teachers possess. Those who want the "classic" expelled dread the occurrence of incidents such as the one described by Hentoff on ABC's "Nightline."[50] According to Hentoff, a teacher in Texas commenced her initial class discussion of the novel with the question "What is a nigger?" In response, the white students in the class looked around the room at the black kids. In addition to this type of ineptness, the lack of commitment to human equality on the part of some teachers looms large in the minds of would-be censors. The "inherent threat" of *Huckleberry Finn* is that in the hands of an unfit, uncommitted teacher it can become a tool of oppression and harmful indoctrination.

Assuming the inverse to be equally possible, a competent, racially accepting educator could transform the potential threat into a challenge. *Huckleberry Finn* presents the secondary teacher with a vehicle to effect powerful, positive interracial exchange among students. Though I have not taught *Huckleberry Finn* in a secondary school, I have taught Harper Lee's *To Kill a Mockingbird,* which is "tainted" with the pejorative "nigger" as well as "nigger-lover," and which is also under fire from censors. Like *Huck Finn, To Kill a Mockingbird* treats a highly emotional racial episode. Different from Twain's novel, however, is the clear-cut use of "nigger-lover" and "nigger" by characters who intend the terms to be derogatory (except where Atticus Finch, a liberal lawyer, forbids his children to use them—an important exception). Set in a small, bigoted Alabama town during the Great Depression, the Pulitzer Prize–winning novel is narrated by Atticus's daughter, Scout, a precocious tomboy. Scout, along with her older brother Jem and playmate Dill, observes the horrors of racial prejudice as they are played out in the trial of a black man, Tom Robinson, wrongfully accused of rape by a white woman.

Over a four-year period in Austin, Texas, I introduced the novel to approximately five hundred public school ninth-graders. Each time I taught the four-week unit on *To Kill a Mockingbird,* the most difficult day of instruction involved the introduction of "nigger" (actually "nigger-lover") into class discussion. My rationale for forcing the word into active class discourse proceeded from my belief that students (black and white) could only face sensitive issues of race after they had achieved a certain emotional distance from the rhetoric of race. I thought (and became convinced over the years) that open confrontation in the controlled setting of the classroom could achieve that emotional distance.

Early in the novel, when another child calls Atticus, who has agreed to defend Robinson, a "nigger-lover," Scout picks a fight with him. When Atticus learns of the fray, Scout asks if he *is* a "nigger-lover." Beautifully undercutting the malice of the phrase, Atticus responds, "Of course, I am. I try to love everybody." A discussion of this episode would constitute my first endeavor to ease my students into open dialogue about "the word" and its derivatives.

My opening query to each class—Why does Scout get into a fight at school?—was invariably answered with a paroxysm of silence. As the reality of racial discomfort and mistrust cast its shadow over the classroom, the tension would become almost palpable. Unable to utter the taboo word "nigger," students would be paralyzed, the whites by their social awareness of the moral injunction against it and the blacks by their heightened sensitivity to it. Slowly, torturously, the wall of silence would begin to crumble before students' timid attempts to approach the topic with euphemism. Finally, after some tense moments, one courageous adolescent would utter the word. As the class released an almost audible sigh of relief, the students and I would embark upon a lively and risk-taking exchange about race and its attendant complexities. The interracial understanding fostered by this careful, enlightened study of *To Kill a Mockingbird* can, I think, be achieved with a similar approach to *Huckleberry Finn*.

It must be understood, on the other hand, that the presence of incompetent, insensitive, or (sometimes unwittingly, sometimes purposefully) bigoted instructors in the public schools is no illusion. Black parents who entrust their children's well-being to such people run the risk of having their offspring traumatized and humiliated; white parents risk having their children inculcated with attitudes that run contrary to a belief in human rights and equality. The possibility of lowering black students' self-esteem and undermining their pride in their heritage is a substantial argument against sanctioning the novel's use, and the likelihood that *Huckleberry Finn* could encourage racial prejudice on the part of white students is a matter of comparable concern.

Though these qualms are legitimate and are partly supported by the Penn State study, other studies charged with the task of determining whether *Huckleberry Finn* causes, furthers, or ameliorates poor self-concept, racial shame, or negative racial stereotyping indicate that the novel's influence on a majority of students is positive. A 1972 study that measured the influence the novel had on the racial attitudes of black and white ninth-grade boys yielded only positive results.[51] Herbert Frankel, director of the study, concluded that significant changes in perceptions of blacks occurred for black *and* white students, and all shifts were of a positive nature. The data indicated that black adolescents' self-concepts were enhanced. Further, "black students tended to identify more strongly and more positively with other members of their race" as a result of having studied *Huckleberry Finn*. For white students, reading the novel "*reduce[d]* hostile or unfavorable feelings toward members of another race and *increase[d]* favorable feelings toward members of another race" (emphasis added). Students who read the novel under a teacher's guidance showed "significantly greater positive change" than those students who read the novel on their own.[52] The Penn State study upholds this last conclusion, judging the novel "suitable for serious literary study by high school students":

Our data indicate that students who read the novel as part of an instructional unit demonstrated both a deeper sensitivity to the moral and psychological issues central to the novel (a number of which deal with issues of race) and a more positive attitude on matters calling for racial understanding and acceptance. These students were also able to interpret the novel with greater literary sophistication than those students who read the novel without instruction. Additionally, these students were significantly more accepting of contacts with Blacks than were the other students involved in the study.[53]

Based on these studies completed eleven years apart (1972 and 1983), it appears that in the right circumstances *Huckleberry Finn* can be taught without perpetuating negative racial attitudes in white students or undermining racial pride in black students.

Still, in the final analysis the concerns voiced by parents and other would-be censors of *Adventures of Huckleberry Finn* are not wholly invalid. One has only to run a mental scan across the nation's news headlines to glean a portrait of the present state of American race relations. Such a glimpse betrays the ambivalence present in the status of blacks and their relations with whites. In "Breaking the Silence," a powerful statement on the plight of the "black underclass," Pete Hamill delineates the duality of the American black experience. Admitting the dismal reality of continued racist behavior, Hamill cites "the antibusing violence in liberal Boston, the Bernhard Goetz and Howard Beach cases in liberal New York, [and] a resurgent Klan in some places."[54] Then, turning to inroads forged toward equality, he mentions that "for the first time in American history, there is a substantial and expanding black middle class, . . . [a] leading contender for the Democratic nomination for President is a black man," and mayors of eight major American cities are black. Hamill's article points to a fundamental fissure in the American psyche when it comes to race. Further, these details suggest that the teaching of Twain's novel may not be the innocent pedagogical endeavor that we wish it to be.

When we move from the context into which we want to deposit *Huckleberry Finn* and consider the nature of the text and its creator, the matter becomes even more entangled. Though devotees love to praise *Huckleberry Finn* as "a savage indictment of a society that accepted slavery as a way of life"[55] or "the deadliest satire . . . ever written on . . . the inequality of [the] races,"[56] the truth is that neither the novel nor its author has escaped ambivalence about racial matters.

First, the ambiguities of the novel are multiple. The characterization of Jim is a string of inconsistencies. At one point he is the super-stitious darky; at another he is the indulgent surrogate father. On the one hand, his desire for freedom is unconquerable; on the other, he submits it to the ridiculous antics of a child. Further, while Jim flees from slavery and plots to steal his family out of bondage, most other slaves in the novel embody the romantic contentment with the "pecu-liar institution" that slaveholders tried to convince abolitionists all slaves felt.

Twain's equivocal attitude toward blacks extends beyond his fic-tion into his lifelong struggle with "the Negro question." In his autobiography Twain describes the complaisance with which he ac-cepted slavery while growing up. Leaving slaveholding Missouri seems to have had little effect on his racial outlook, because in 1853 he wrote home to his mother from New York, "I reckon I had better black my face, for in these Eastern States niggers are considerably better than white people." He served briefly as a Confederate soldier before heading west and never seemed to be morally discomfited by his defense of slavery.[57] Set over and against these unflattering details are Twain's advocacies for equality. In 1985 a letter proving that Twain had provided financial assistance to a black student at the Yale University Law School in 1885 was discovered and authenticated by Shelley Fisher Fishkin. In the letter Twain writes, "We [whites] have ground the manhood out of them, & the shame is ours, not theirs, & we should pay for it."[58] He is also known to have teamed with Booker T. Washington in championing several black causes.[59]

The factor of racial uncertainty on the part of Twain, its manifesta-tion in his best-loved piece, and its existence in American society should not be a barrier to *Huckleberry Finn*'s admittance to the class-room. Instead, this should make it the pith of the American literature curriculum. The insolubility of the race question as regards *Huckle-berry Finn* functions as a model of the fundamental racial ambiguity of the American mind-set. Active engagement with Twain's novel pro-vides one method for students to confront their own deepest racial feelings and insecurities. Though the problems of racial perspective present in *Huckleberry Finn* may never be satisfactorily explained for censors or scholars, the consideration of them may have a practical, positive bearing on the manner in which America approaches race in the coming century.

Notes

1. Justin Kaplan, *Born to Trouble: One Hundred Years of Huckleberry Finn,* Center for the Book Viewpoint Series, no. 13 (Washington, D.C.: Library of Congress, 1985) 10–11.

2. Lionel Trilling, Introduction to *Adventures of Huckleberry Finn* (New York: Rinehart, 1948) v–xviii; reprinted in Norton Critical Edition of *Adventures of Huckleberry Finn,* 2nd ed., ed. Sculley Bradley et al. (New York: Norton, 1977) 318.

3. T. S. Eliot, Introduction to *Adventures of Huckleberry Finn* (London: Cresset, 1950) vii–xvi; reprinted in Norton Critical Edition of *Adventures of Huckleberry Finn,* 2nd ed., ed. Sculley Bradley et al. (New York: Norton, 1977) 328.

4. Leonard Buder, "'Huck Finn' Barred as Textbook by City," *New York Times* 12 Sept. 1957: 1.

5. "Schools in Philadelphia Edit 'Huckleberry Finn,'" *New York Times* 17 Apr. 1963: 44.

6. "'Huckleberry Finn' Scored for References to 'Nigger,'" *New York Times* 22 Mar. 1967: 43.

7. "'Huck Finn' Not Required," *New York Times,* 15 Jan. 1969: 44.

8. Telephone interviews with Lois Fisher, New Trier High School librarian, and Eric Lair, New Trier School District assistant superintendent, 24 Mar. 1988. As of 20 April 1988, New Trier's current controversy over *Huckleberry Finn* had yet to be resolved.

9. John Wallace, *The Adventures of Huckleberry Finn Adapted* (Chicago: Wallace, 1984).

10. See Wallace's essay, "The Case against *Huck Finn,*" in this volume.

11. Christopher Hitchens, "American Notes," (London) *Times Literary Supplement* 9 Mar. 1985: 258.

12. Nicholas J. Karolides and Lee Burress, eds., *Celebrating Censored Books* (Racine, Wisc.: Wisconsin Council of Teachers of English, 1985) 6. This information is based on six national surveys of censorship pressures on the American public schools between 1965 and 1982.

13. Most scholars express opinions on whether or not to ban *Huckleberry Finn* in a paragraph or two of an article that deals mainly with another topic. Shelley Fisher Fishkin has given the issues much more attention. In addition to authenticating a letter written by Mark Twain that indicates his nonracist views (see n. 59), Fishkin has debated the issue with John Wallace on "Freeman Reports" (cnn, 14 March 1985).

14. Hitchens 258.

15. Allan B. Ballard, letter, *New York Times* 9 May 1982.

16. "Finishing the Civil War: *Huck Finn* in Racist America," *Young Spartacus* (Summer 1982): 12.

17. Leslie Fiedler, "*Huckleberry Finn:* The Book We Love to Hate," *Proteus* 1.2 (Fall 1984): 6.

18. Nat Hentoff, "Huck Finn and the Shortchanging of Black Kids," *Village Voice* 18 May 1982.

19. Hentoff.

20. Kaplan 18.

21. "Finishing the Civil War" 12.

22. Langston Hughes, *The Big Sea* (New York: Thunder's Month P, 1940) 268–69. At this point in his autobiography, Hughes discusses the furor caused by Carl Van Vechten's novel *Nigger Heaven,* published in 1926.

23. See David L. Smith's essay, "Huck, Jim, and American Racial Discourse," in this volume.

24. "Finishing the Civil War" 12.

25. Fiedler 5.

26. Again, see Smith's essay.

27. Fiedler 6; see also Smith's discussion of this passage.

28. Kaplan 19.

29. Fredrick Woodard and Donnarae MacCann, "*Huckleberry Finn* and the Traditions of Blackface Minstrelsy," *Interracial Books for Children Bulletin* 15.1–2 (1984): 4–13; reprinted in *The Black American in Books for Children: Readings in Racism,* 2nd ed., ed. Donnarae MacCann and Gloria Woodard (Metuchen, N.J.: Scarecrow, 1985) 75–103.

30. Ralph Ellison, "Change the Joke and Slip the Yoke," *Partisan Review* 25 (Spring 1958): 212–22; reprinted in Ellison's *Shadow and Act* (New York: Random House, 1964) 45–59.

31. Woodard and MacCann 76–77.

32. Mark Twain, quoted in Woodard and MacCann 76 (emphasis added).

33. Woodard and MacCann 79. See also the Woodard and MacCann essay "Minstrel Shackles and Nineteenth-Century 'Liberality' in *Huckleberry Finn,*" in this volume.

34. "Huck Finn's Friend Jim," editorial, *New York Times* 13 Sept. 1957: 22.

35. Hoxie N. Fairchild, letter, *New York Times,* 14 Sept. 1957: 18.

36. Steven Mailloux, "Reading *Huckleberry Finn:* The Rhetoric of Performed Ideology," *New Essays on "Huckleberry Finn,"* ed. Louis J. Budd (Cambridge, Eng.: Cambridge UP, 1985) 107–33. For a defense of the early Jim as an example of Twain's strategy to "elaborate [racial stereotypes] in order to undermine them," see David Smith's essay.

37. Mailloux's discussion of "rhetorical performances" in *Huckleberry Finn* bears kinship to M. M. Bakhtin's discussion of the function of heteroglossia in the comic novel. In "Discourse on the Novel," Bakhtin identifies two features that characterize "the incorporation of heteroglossia and its stylistic utilization" in the comic novel. First, the comic novel incorporates a "multiplicity of 'languages' and verbal-ideological belief systems," and for the most part these languages are not posited in particular characters, but they can be. Second, "the incorporated languages and socio-ideological belief systems . . . are unmasked and destroyed as something false, hypocritical, greedy, limited, narrowly rationalistic, inadequate to reality." *Huckleberry*

Finn seems to me to embody much of what Bakhtin says regarding hetero-glossia in the comic novel. The multiplicity of languages is clearly recognizable in the lower-class vernacular of Huck and Pap, the exaggerated slave dialect of Jim, the southern genteel tradition, the romantic diction of Scott and Dumas as it has been gleaned by Tom and filtered through Huck, and several other dialects. Twain himself acknowledges the painstaking attention he paid to language in the novel. Clearly, through his play with the "posited author" Huck, Twain's motive is to unmask and destroy various socio-ideological belief systems that are represented by language. So what Mailloux refers to as rhetorical performance Bakhtin identifies as the heteroglossia struggle. Thus Jim's successful appropriation of Huck's argumentative strategy dismantles the hegemony of white supremacy discourse present as Huck's language. M. M. Bakhtin, "Discourse in the Novel," trans. Michael Holquist and Caryl Emerson, in *The Dialogic Imagination: Four Essays,* ed. Michael Holquist (Austin: U of Texas P, 1981) 310–15.

38. Mailloux 117.

39. Leo Marx, "Mr. Eliot, Mr. Trilling, and *Huckleberry Finn,*" *American Scholar* 22.4 (1953): 423–40; reprinted in Norton Critical Edition of *Adventures of Huckleberry Finn,* 2nd ed., ed. Sculley Bradley et al. (New York: Norton, 1977) 349.

40. Frits Oelschlaeger, "'Gwyne to Git Hung': The Conclusion of *Huckleberry Finn,*" in *One Hundred Years of "Huckleberry Finn": The Boy, His Book and American Culture,* ed. Robert Sattelmeyer and J. Donald Crowley (Columbia, Mo.: U of Missouri P, 1985) 117.

41. James M. Cox, *Mark Twain: The Fate of Humor* (Princeton, N.J.: Princeton UP, 1966); reprinted as "[The Uncomfortable Ending of *Huckleberry Finn*]," in the Norton Critical Edition of *Adventures of Huckleberry Finn,* 2nd ed., ed. Sculley Bradley et al. (New York: Norton, 1977) 350–59. Though he ignores Jim and his aspiration for freedom in *Mark Twain: The Fate of Humor,* in a more recent, related article, "A Hard Book to Take," Cox returns to the evasion sequence and treats Jim's freedom in particular and the concept of freedom in general. He contends that Twain had recognized "the national lie [myth] of freedom" and that the closing movement of *Huckleberry Finn* dramatizes Twain's realization that Jim is not and never will be truly free. Further, no one, black or white, is or will be free, elaborates Cox, "despite the fictions of history and the Thirteenth Amendment." See "A Hard Book to Take," in *One Hundred Years of "Huckleberry Finn": The Boy, His Book and American Culture,* ed. Robert Sattelmeyer and J. Donald Crowley (Columbia, Mo.: U of Missouri P, 1985) 386–403.

42. Cox, *Mark Twain* 356. [See also Charles Nilon's defense of the concluding chapters of *Huckleberry Finn* in his essay, "The Ending of *Huckleberry Finn*: 'Freeing the Free Negro,'" in this volume—ED.]

43. "*Huckleberry Finn:* Literature or Racist Trash?" ABC "Nightline," 4 Feb. 1985.

44. Mailloux 117.

45. Hentoff.

46. Hentoff.

47. *The Effects of Reading "Huckleberry Finn" on the Racial Attitudes of Ninth Grade Students,* a cooperative study of the State College Area School District and the Forum on Black Affairs of Pennsylvania State University (State College, Pa., 1983) 22.

48. *The Effects of Reading "Huckleberry Finn"* 22.

49. Cox, *Mark Twain* 388.

50. *"Huckleberry Finn:* Literature or Racist Trash?"

51. Herbert Lewis Frankel, "The Effects of Reading *The Adventures of Huckleberry Finn* on the Racial Attitudes of Selected Ninth Grade Boys," diss. Temple U, May 1972, 203–4.

52. Frankel 203–4.

53. *The Effects of Reading "Huckleberry Finn"* 21.

54. Pete Hamill, "Breaking the Silence," *Esquire* 109.3 (1988): 92–93.

55. Kaplan 18.

56. "Huck Finn's Friend Jim," p. 22.

57. See Bernard Bell's essay, "Twain's 'Nigger' Jim: The Tragic Face behind the Minstrel Mask," in this volume.

58. Wil Haygood, "Twain Letter Revives Old Question: Detractors Say They Still Think 'Huck Finn' Has Racist Taint," *Boston Globe* 15 Mar. 1985: 3.

59. Jacqueline James Goodwin, "Booker T. Washington and Twain as a Team," letter, *New York Times* 24 Apr. 1985: A22.

History, Slavery, and Thematic Irony in *Huckleberry Finn*

Richard K. Barksdale

Those who argue that there is a lot of history in fiction have a more plausible argument than those who argue that there is a lot of fiction in history. When Mark Twain in the late 1870s and early 1880s wrote his *Adventures of Huckleberry Finn,* describing a series of Mississippi river-town adventures experienced by a rather ne'er-do-well young man classified by some as "po' white trash," he set his story in slavery-time Missouri. By virtue of the Missouri Compromise of 1820, that state had joined the Union as a slave state when Maine entered as a free state. Accordingly, any story having Missouri as its setting prior to 1865 had its setting in a slave state. Thus, whatever history there is in Mark Twain's novel about a rebellious teenager is slave-time history. In fact, the society, or "sivilization," that Huck was attempting to escape was a society that had slavery at its core. This was especially true along the rivers of the South, the channels of trade and commerce—the Mississippi, the Waccammaw, the Tennessee, the Tombigbee; for as Langston Hughes once wrote, the black man, whether slave or free, had long known rivers, and "his soul had grown deep like the rivers."

One gathers a deeper understanding of the meaning of living in a slave society such as the one Huck and his peers lived in when one understands that throughout the Americas, from the very beginning, there had always been slavery. This was true of Hispanic America in the sixteenth century, of all the islands of the Caribbean in the seventeenth century, of the original thirteen British colonies of the North American mainland, and of all of the states united into one nation indivisible by the Constitution of 1787. In fact, in 1787 slavery was so pervasive throughout South Carolina and Virginia that whites were in a distinct minority in those two colonies, and this fact gave the founding fathers some cause for concern. Inevitably, as the nation developed, pushing its frontier ever westward, and as slavery in the southern states became an entrenched way of life, the "peculiar institution" began to have a substantive effect on the mores, manners, and values of the new nation. Everywhere one looked in states below the Mason-Dixon line there was a substantial and growing black presence—a huge laboring and servant class—breeding, pulling, hauling, toting, hoeing, threshing, curing, refining, serving, and, above all, obeying. By the time of Huck Finn's story there were over four million, kept in forced bondage by the whip and by the immense police power of the plantation owner and his or her overseers and drivers. And, as Justice Taney stated in the 1857 *Dred Scott* decision, not one of the four million had any more legal status than an animal, and it was "fixed and universal in the civilized portion of the white race" that there was nothing about a black man ("no rights") that a white man was bound to respect.

But there was much more to slavery's story than the impact of the institution on the mores and morals of a fledgling nation. There was the slave himself, herself, or itself—the black man, the black woman, and the black child, chained in perpetual ignorance and bound for life to a master, a house, or a plantation field. The world of that slave was restricted to the land or house where he or she worked and to the dismal quarters where he or she lived. Generally, the slave had no choices about anything that affected his or her personal life, and the world beyond the master's house and land was a vast terra incognita unless the master decreed otherwise. For whatever knowledge came to the slave came only with the express permission and authorization of the master or mistress. Such a system was bound and designed to generate pain, anguish, frustration, and misery for the slave.

From such a background came Mark Twain's Jim. It is true that apologists for the southern way of life did present, for propaganda purposes, a wildly erroneous view that completely distorted slavery— a view that depicted a contented slave living in happy innocence and mutual devotion and affection with a wise and tolerant master or mistress. Such pictures of the bucolic bliss of chattel slavery were products of the romantic imagination, however, and were not in evidence in Twain's Missouri or in any of the towns, cities, or plantations that bordered the Mississippi in Huck's day. All the black men and women of those regions were, like Jim, slaves in such a grievous state of distress that they became runaways whenever an opportunity for successful flight presented itself.

So Jim, nurtured by a callous and cruel system, was naïvely ignorant of a larger world and, as a runaway, moved about fearfully and without direction or plan. That he survived in his confused freedom long enough to meet Huck was more than a minor miracle. In fact, because of the Fugitive Slave Act of 1850, all the powers of government—local, state, and federal—were ranged against Jim's survival as a free man, even in a "free" state. As a runaway slave, he was the preeminent outsider, the existential rebel—the man to be hunted down and punished by all the forces of law and order. Of course, when the hunted black fugitive and outsider meets the disaffected and poor white outsider—one long kept in childlike ignorance of a larger world by slavery's dictum and the other long victimized by his po' white trash status in a capitalist society—Twain, the storyteller, takes advantage of the situation and begins to weave incidents and events into a suspenseful narrative.

It is obvious that Twain's novel about the chance meeting of two runaways, one black and one white, is under attack today because many Americans, guilt-ridden over the racial divisions that continue to plague our society, have difficulty coping with the historical fact of slavery. Blacks, as part of their long and tortuous fight for social and legal justice, would like to blot the memory of centuries of enforced servitude off the record of history. And whites, in large measure, take no joy in remembering slave times; they would rather take patriotic pride in America's written promises of justice and equality for all, regardless of creed, race, or previous condition of servitude. Indeed, slavery times evoke bad memories for both racial groups—memories of the chaos wrought by incestuous concubinage and the birth of half-white half brothers and half-black half sisters, memories of a dehumanizing system that reduced grown black men and women to "boys" and "gals" and grown white men and women to groveling hypocrites. Blacks in particular would have their children shielded from the ignominious shame of slavery, not only because the memory of slavery exacerbates today's racial problems, but also because their children are racially traumatized by any references to their former inferior status. Thus they ask that anything that might prove to be racially divisive be banned from all educational programs. Such a ban would include Twain's *Adventures of Huckleberry Finn,* a novel in which the word "nigger," the appellation commonly used for slaves in slavery time, appears more than 200 times.

There are many arguments which can be and have been employed to counter those posed by the anti–*Huckleberry Finn* forces. One, of course, is the oft-repeated observation that any race that would ignore its history is condemned to repeat it. This admonition, if heeded, would prod black Americans to remember slavery, however painful the memory, and urge Jews to recall the Holocaust, however painful that memory. Another countering argument is that patterns of racial discrimination are so deeply interwoven in the fabric of American society that *not* reading about Huck and Jim would have no effect on lowering racial tensions or removing the sharp racial polarities that exist and will continue to exist in America. The proponents of this position argue that a novel like *Huckleberry Finn* is irrelevant. Whether the book is required reading or not, racial segregation in housing will continue to exist in all of the nation's major cities and throughout suburbia. Racial discrimination will still haunt the marketplace and employment rosters. Demoralizing statistics about the black family will continue to exist—statistics about the large number of female, single-parent families living below the poverty line, about the large number of young black men in the nation's prisons, and about the large number of teenage pregnancies. The proponents of this position argue that black America's continuing depressed status is the result of a pattern of discrimination against America's most visible minority that began with the nation's founding. In their view slavery was thus more of a symptom than a root cause of racial prejudice in America.

Some of the more radical supporters of this position argue not only that the reading or nonreading of Twain's novel is irrelevant, but that a nation consisting of an achieving majority and a nonachieving but visible minority to victimize and exploit can thereby enjoy national prosperity and good health. The argument advanced in this context is that having such a minority to victimize inflates the psychological self-esteem of the majority, and that this self-esteem is essential for the growth and development of a nation. Supporters of this point of view cite the immense success of both republican and imperial Rome, in which there was always a large lower class of plebeians, slaves, and conquered colonial subjects to be victimized and thus bolster the self-esteem of an achieving upper class. And in democratic

America, the argument continues, a powerful white majority, its motives shielded by carefully articulated verbal guarantees of democracy, freedom, and justice, proceeds to exploit, deny, and exclude America's most visible minority. In other words, the argument suggests, if there were no black minority to be victimized and exploited, white America would zealously strive to find a fit substitute in order to keep the nation on the cutting edge of progress and achievement. Obviously, in an ethical and social scenario of this kind, slavery and Twain's Jim become not root causes of current racial attitudes but providential symbols of what ought to be.

None of this supersubtle sociological and psychological theorizing, however, can successfully alleviate the trauma experienced by a young black teenager when he or she encounters racial discrimination, racial slurs, or racial epithets in a racially integrated classroom. Nor can it be expected that the average junior or senior high school English teacher will prepare the black teenager and his or her peers to read a novel like Twain's *Huckleberry Finn* with a full awareness of the far-flung historical and psychological causes and consequences. If a work of fiction demands this much preparation and student-teacher orientation, one may be fully justified in advocating that the work be removed from required reading lists and made an optional reading selection.

Unfortunately, the reasoning behind such a recommendation completely ignores, by implication at least, Twain's literary intention when he undertook to tell Huck's story. As has been suggested above, Jim's source, lineage, and status are quite clear: he was a slave who had, in protest over his condition, run away from his mistress. Similarly, Huck, saddled with an improvident, alcoholic father, was a lad without means and a self-proclaimed outcast who, because of his condition, wished to escape "sivilization." By bringing black runaway Jim into close association with white runaway Huck, Twain obviously desired to explore the ironic implications of such an association in a "sivilization" riddled by racial division and prejudice. The irony employed here is similar to that used in Pudd'nhead Wilson's story, in which Twain recounts the comitragic consequences of a situation in which a light-skinned "colored" baby is substituted for a white baby. In Huck's story, however, Twain's ironic conclusion is that two human beings, however different their backgrounds and "previous condition of servitude," will, if removed far enough from the corrupting influences of "sivilization," become friends. For Twain, like England's

Swift or Rome's Juvenal, believed that the social civilization that man labored so hard to cultivate was itself the great corrupter of man. He believed that from civilization came not only values to preserve and protect but the incentives to divide, control, and inhibit. Twain appears to be asking in his story of Huck and Jim how truly "civilized" an America is which since its beginning has cultivated and nurtured slavery. And he knew, as he observed events in the 1880s, that although slavery no longer officially existed, blacks were still a large servant and laboring class to be exploited and kept illiterate, disenfranchised, and socially and culturally oppressed.

Given the social and cultural conditions that existed in pre–Civil War America, Twain sought to explore the ironic possibilities of the development of an authentic black-white friendship. Under what circumstances could a slave and a white man develop a friendship in slave-time America? Could it occur within the system, or would it have to be a clandestine matter hidden from society at large? Twain, the ironist who doubted that social and/or moral benefits could accrue from a civilization beleaguered by greed and prejudice, concluded that, given the nature of slave-time America, a friendship of that kind could develop only outside the normal areas of civil and social discourse. In fact, Twain appears to suggest, with more than just an ironic gleam in his eye, that such a friendship could develop only on a socially isolated raft in the middle of the nation's biggest and longest river, and thus as far from the shores ruled by law and order as a person could get in middle America. But Twain the ironist did not stop there. He developed, with careful ironic forethought, an interracial friendship between two outcasts who, under civilization's auspices, were normally inveterate enemies. For, during Twain's lifetime and later, it was an observable fact that poor white trash like the Finns had nothing but hatred and disrespect for blacks. Condemned and reviled as economic and social outcasts by "respectable" society, people like the Finns looked for some inferior group on which to vent their social spleen; and in America's social hierarchy, the only class or group considered to be lower than the Finns and their kin were black slaves, who after 1865 became the openly reviled black freedmen.

Thus Twain's novel, by motive and intention, is really an ironic appraisal of the American racial scene circa 1884. Herein possibly lies the difficulty encountered in trying to teach the novel. Irony, as all students of literature know, involves a deliberate misstatement—a misstatement designed to highlight the longtime adverse effects of a grossly immoral act, a blatantly dishonest deed, or an inhumane and un-Christian practice. If the ironic statement made by an author in a work of fiction is too subtly wrought, it will not be effectively communicated to the average reader. The continuing controversy about *Adventures of Huckleberry Finn* suggests that the American reading public, in the main, has never fully understood the author's ironic message.

It is also probably true that American society—actually the same "sivilization" castigated by Huck—will never fully comprehend Mark Twain's irony, because one needs to have considerable ethical distance from the object under ironic analysis to appreciate and understand the irony. In other words, students and teachers who are immersed and involved in America's racial problems will never understand the need to develop a disciplined objectivity about those problems before they can appreciate an ironic solution to those problems. Indeed, ironic fiction, whether from the past or the present, is difficult to teach, especially to young teenagers, who usually founder on deliberately oversubtle misstatements.

So, although Jim's roots lie deep in the soil of slavery and American racism, although his is an honest and forthright portrayal of a slave runaway, and although young black teenagers are traumatized by reading about the Jims of slavery time, the great difficulty with *Adventures of Huckleberry Finn* is that it is one of America's best pieces of ironic fiction. To a nation that was and is sharply divided on matters of race, Twain's novel suggests that friendships between black and white can best be forged by the least of us, and then only under the worst of circumstances. Undoubtedly, only a reading audience of some maturity and perceptive insight—an audience that can probe for lurking truths under surface facts and figures and events—can grasp the far-reaching implications of the adventures of a white Huck and a black Jim floating down the river of American life. As Francis Bacon once wrote, "Reading maketh the full man"; but not all and sundry in our error-ridden society can sit and sup at fiction's table without occasionally feeling the pain and anguish generated by that error-ridden society.

Jim and Huck in the Nineteenth Century

Although the controversy over *Adventures of Huckleberry Finn* centers on the novel's effect on twentieth-century readers, that effect often depends on vaguely lingering impressions of the pre–Civil War era which the novel describes and the post–Civil War era in which it was written. No thoughtful analysis of the novel can safely ignore the highly charged racial contexts from which it emerged. As Steven Mailloux remarks about the contextuality of *Huckleberry Finn,* "in the reception of Twain's book, the distinction between literary and extraliterary completely breaks down."[1] The extraliterary aspects are legal as well as psychosocial. Cary Wall comments, "*Huck Finn* is full of the convulsive, thwarted attempts of the nineteenth-century South to rid itself of the twin delusions that white people are aristocrats and black people are less than human beings."[2] But the laws of the late nineteenth century also reflected a conscious attempt to suppress both the problem and its implications by institutionalizing an unequal separation, thus creating a new, if less thoroughgoing, de facto slavery in the post-slavery South. Some nineteenth-century legal events relevant to the writing and reception of *Adventures of Huckleberry Finn* are discussed below.

Fugitive Slave Acts were laws enacted by Congress in 1793 and 1850 providing for the arrest and punishment, without jury trial, of runaway slaves. Usually the punishment involved returning the slave to his or her owner. Responding to the 1850 law, some northern states mitigated the Fugitive Slave Acts insofar as possible by means of personal liberty laws to help escaped slaves.

The Missouri Compromise was an agreement negotiated in the U.S. Congress in 1820–21 by which Maine was admitted to the Union as a free state, Missouri was admitted as a slave state, and the territories north of Missouri's southern border were to be maintained as free.

The *Dred Scott case* involved a suit for his freedom filed by a Missouri slave (Dred Scott) who had lived with his master in both Illinois, a free state, and Wisconsin, a free territory. The eventual U.S. Supreme Court decision (1857) denied Scott his freedom, holding that Missouri law had still applied to him during the stay in Illinois and, more important, that since only state law could forbid slavery, no antislavery provision could legally apply in a territory (such as Wisconsin). This meant, in effect, that the Missouri Compromise had been unconstitutional and that all present and future territories would be open to slavery. Chief Justice Roger B. Taney, a former slave owner who had freed his own slaves and was personally opposed to slavery, nonetheless maintained that slavery was constitutional and that black Americans, even nonslaves, were not entitled to citizenship and had no rights under the Constitution—placing freed black Americans in a kind of constitutional limbo. Taney wrote the majority opinion for the *Dred Scott* case, including the following: "[W]hen the Constitution of the United States was framed and adopted . . . [, blacks] had for more than a century before been regarded as beings of an inferior order, and altogether unfit to associate with the white race, either in social or political relations; and so far inferior, that they had no rights which the white man was bound to respect; and that the negro might justly and lawfully be reduced to slavery for his [the white man's] benefit."[3] The furor over the Court's decision helped precipitate the Civil War.

Black Codes were laws enacted immediately after the Civil War in southern states in order to retain white control over the newly freed slaves. The Black Codes included prohibition of interracial marriage, exclusion of blacks from certain occupations, and limitations on property ownership, the right to possess weapons, and the right to testify in legal proceedings. Through a combination of vagrancy laws and apprenticeship laws, they also provided a vehicle for reemploying blacks in subservient positions strongly reminiscent of slavery. The Black Codes were quickly overridden by the Fourteenth and Fifteenth amendments and other federal legislation intended to provide basic rights of citizenship for black Americans, but later reappeared in muted form as Jim Crow laws.

Jim Crow laws were state laws which succeeded the Black Codes after Reconstruction as the legal means for controlling the freed black population. They were established in southern states beginning in the late 1870s—about the time Twain began to write *Adventures of Huckleberry Finn*—and remained in place until overthrown by the civil rights movement of the mid-twentieth century. Their principal feature was segregation of public and semipublic facilities of all sorts. Persons of mixed ancestry (in whatever proportions) were usually classified as black (see Rhett Jones's discussion of this feature of U.S. law as compared to the laws of Latin American slaveholding nations). The federal government enacted a Civil Rights Act in 1875 mandating equality in the use of most public facilities, but the law was overturned by the U.S. Supreme Court in 1883.

Focusing particularly on the "evasion" chapters at the end of the novel, Charles H. Nilon's essay, "The Ending of *Huckleberry Finn:* 'Freeing the Free Negro,'" places *Huckleberry Finn* in the context of the post-Reconstruction era of Jim Crow laws and continuing resentment against the forcible restructuring of southern society. He reads the evasion as a parable of the plight of black Americans in the late nineteenth century, demonstrating similarities between the abuse of Jim by Tom Sawyer and others and the treatment blacks received in the South from well-meaning and not-so-well-meaning whites as southern society was being readjusted to accommodate the new status of its black men and women. Henry Nash Smith says of the situation at the beginning of the evasion sequence, "As Huck approaches the Phelps plantation the writer has on his hands a hybrid— a comic story in which the protagonists have acquired something like tragic depth."[4] Nilon shows how the exaggerated, southwestern humor–style comedy of those chapters exhibits a deeply serious correspondence to the way in which white paternalism of the period dehumanized and further disenfranchised the South's black population.

Mary Kemp Davis, in her essay "The Veil Rent in Twain: Degradation and Revelation in *Adventures of Huckleberry Finn*," shifts the textual focus past the evasion to the community's treatment of Jim after his recapture. Describing Jim's role as that of sacrificial victim in a "degradation ceremony," she compares his systematic, ritualistic abuse to the mob scene in the earlier Wilks episode, in which Huck, the Duke, and the King—like Jim after his return to the Phelps farm—narrowly escape lynching. Ralph Ellison, in his book *Shadow and Act,* remarks about the plight of black Americans, "Being 'highly pigmented,' as the sociologists say, it was our Negro 'misfortune' to be caught up associatively in the negative side of [the] basic dualism of the white folk mind, and to be shackled to almost everything it would repress from conscience and consciousness."[5] Davis's analysis of ritual degradation in *Huckleberry Finn* brings to light something of the social function of racial abuse in the nineteenth-century South.

Carmen Subryan, pursuing Mark Twain's relation to the subject of racial prejudice in her essay "Mark Twain and the Black Challenge," takes Twain himself as context for *Huckleberry Finn*. She sketches the relevant biographical data—finding negative factors in his Hannibal childhood and his later allegiance to southwestern humor, but a much more positive influence in his marriage to Olivia Langdon—and surveys the corpus of his writings for their racial significance. In addition to *Huckleberry Finn,* she gives attention to *Tom Sawyer, Pudd'nhead Wilson,* and several lesser works.

David L. Smith, in "Huck, Jim, and American Racial Discourse," takes up the controversial question of language in *Huckleberry Finn,* concentrating on the ironic subversiveness of Twain's manipulation of "racial discourse"—cultural dialogue in which race is used for the purpose of regulating social relations.[6] Constructing an aggressively activist model of authorial intention for *Huckleberry Finn,* Smith launches a broad defense of the novel as a critique of late-nineteenth-century societal mores. Against the background of nineteenth-century assumptions of Afro-American inferiority, he analyzes some of the passages in which "nigger" references seem most offensive, including Pap's "govment" tirade (chap. 6), Huck's "killed a nigger" conversation with Aunt Sally (chap. 32), and the "nigger-stealing" evasion by Tom and Huck (chap. 33). His defense of the "you can't learn a nigger to argue" episode (chap. 14) provides a notable counterpoint to Subryan's condemnation of the same passage. Smith also takes up the question of Jim's superstitiousness and shows how he cleverly turns white perceptions of that superstitiousness to his own ends, first in the witch-riding incident (chap. 2), and later in the fortune-telling negotiation with Huck (chap. 4).

James S. Leonard

Notes

1. Steven Mailloux, *Rhetorical Power* (Ithaca, N.Y.: Cornell UP, 1989) 118.

2. Cary Wall, "The Boomerang of Slavery: The Child, the Aristocrat, and Hidden White Identity in *Huck Finn,*" *Southern Studies* 21 (1982): 209.

3. *Dred Scott* v. *Sanford;* quoted in Charles W. Smith, Jr., *Roger B. Taney: Jacksonian Jurist* (Chapel Hill: U of North Carolina P, 1936) 163.

4. Henry Nash Smith, *Mark Twain: The Development of a Writer* (Cambridge, Mass.: Belknap P of Harvard UP, 1962) 133.

5. Ralph Ellison, *Shadow and Act* (New York: Random House, 1964) 48.

6. See also Rhett Jones's discussion of the language and legal status of oversimplified views of racial difference in the nineteenth-century United States.

The Ending

of *Huckleberry Finn*

"Freeing the Free Negro"

Charles H. Nilon

By 1876, when Mark Twain put the unfinished *Adventures of Huckleberry Finn* aside, the restraints of military government in the South had been removed, Black Codes or laws similar in effect had been restored in most southern states, and the freedom that the black person had begun to know was now drastically limited.[1] Although Huck's Pap calls attention to educated free black people who voted and could not be sold into slavery before the Civil War, and although during the Reconstruction years black officeholders were present in the national government and in state governments in the South, increasingly from 1876 to 1895 black people were denied political recognition, forced into sharecropping, lynched (as it is proposed that Jim be), involved in convict lease systems (as George Washington Cable points out), and intimidated in many different ways. While Twain was completing *Huckleberry Finn,* black people were being "freed" much as Huck and Tom were freeing Jim, and in a style that would have pleased Tom. After the federal troops were removed, the South treated the former slaves in much the same way as Tom treats Jim, and apparently with the tacit approval of the federal government. The Phelps farm and the surrounding community are a microcosm of the way the South treated "the Negro problem."[2] The last twelve chapters of *Huckleberry Finn* show figuratively, and pass judgment on, this process of "freeing the free Negro" that Twain became increasingly aware of after 1880.[3]

Critical support for the idea that these chapters describe metaphorically what was happening in the South while Twain was writing them is found in appraisals of his work by Louis J. Budd, Philip S. Foner, Justin Kaplan, Kenneth S. Lynn, and Arthur G. Pettit.[4] These and other critics, recognizing that concerns of the sort illustrated there were present in Twain's mind as early as 1874—when his character Aunt Rachel told what it meant to be black in a particular time in history, in "A True Story"[5]—agree that Twain was aware of and disturbed by the treatment that black people received in the South during the post-Reconstruction years and that his personal response to what was happening to them increased after 1880. They suggest that he was concerned about the effects of the development of the Solid South, the dominance of the Democratic party, and the loss of black freedom in the South through the action of the Supreme Court in 1883, and that he expressed his concern about these evils.

According to some critical opinion, Twain believed the persistence of the chivalric code in the South conditioned to some extent the South's social and political behavior, including its tolerance for lynching that was exemplified in Klan activities and related acts of violence. Budd says that *Huckleberry Finn* is at its firmest in the fake rescue when it burlesques "Scott and Dumas and the phantasies of the Southern gentry," and he argues that the South's lingering chivalric ideal "encouraged the penchant for a code tolerant of violence."[6]

Most of these critics present Twain's association with George Washington Cable as evidence that what Twain expresses in the novel's last chapters may have resulted partly from Cable's influence. Guy A. Cardwell, for instance, says that Cable may have influenced Twain's thinking about southern society and treatment of black people during the period immediately prior to the completion of *Huckleberry Finn*.[7] Lynn calls attention to Twain's reference to Cable in *Life on the Mississippi* as "the masterly delineator of its [the South's] interior life and history," and he says that Cable "decided that the Negro in the Post-war South was the daily victim of persecution that made a mockery of his technical freedom."[8] When the Supreme Court upheld the emerging pattern of segregation in the South in a civil rights case of 1883, Cable responded in protest with "The Freedman's Case in Equity." When this essay appeared in print, Cable and Twain were near the midpoint of their four-month lecture tour.[9] Although there is evidence that Twain did not discuss this essay with Cable, he was nonetheless aware of it and of the sharp criticism of Cable it drew in the South. Twain also read and admired Cable's *The Grandissimes* (1880) and *Madame Delphine* (1881), and discussed the books with

Cable and with William Dean Howells. In his own way, he appears to have done in *Huckleberry Finn* something similar to what Cable says he did in *The Grandissimes*. Cable reveals in his diary that that novel "contained as plain a protest against the times in which it was written as against the earlier times in which its scenes were set."[10] This is also true of *Huckleberry Finn*. The events in it occur in the 1840s, but Twain's treatment of them, especially in his last chapters, protests against the 1880s.

Twain does figuratively in *Huckleberry Finn* what William Wells Brown does in *Clotel* (1853, 1864) and what Paul Laurence Dunbar does in *The Fanatics* (1901). Like Cable, these novelists show the dilemma of the free black person before the Civil War, and they argue, as he does in "The Freedman's Case in Equity," that black people were freer as slaves than they were after they were freed by law. Describing with considerable historical accuracy Ohio's treatment of freed slaves, Dunbar makes this point emphatically in *The Fanatics;* and Brown's heroine kills herself when there is danger that she will be sold into slavery again. William Faulkner's *The Unvanquished* (1938) and Albion Tourgée's *A Fool's Errand* (1879), *The Invisible Empire* (1880), and *Bricks without Straw* (1880) provide descriptions of the Solid South, the dominance of the Democratic party, the tolerance of violence, and the development of Jim Crow. It is Faulkner's Colonel Sartoris who as mayor decrees that no black woman should appear on the streets of Jefferson without an apron. Tourgée and Faulkner show the social and political processes used in the South to take away the black man's freedom. Tourgée, who was a contemporary and acquaintance of Twain, uses actual events that occurred in North Carolina in the two novels mentioned here. Thomas Dixon, Jr., in *The Leopard's Spots* (1902) and *The Clansman* (1905), and Thomas Nelson Page in *Red Rock* (1899), justify these practices of oppression, and Dixon recommends the use of violent means to support them. Through the metaphor of the last chapters of *Huckleberry Finn,* Twain does what Brown, Dunbar, Faulkner, and Tourgée do more directly; and through the meaning that derives from his narrative technique in these chapters he offers a judgment of the behavior and attitudes found in Dixon and Page.

Through Tom Sawyer, Twain represents the southerner who continued to accept the chivalric code and to be influenced by the mythologies of Dumas and Scott. Tom's devotion to this romanticism and to what may be called the southern mystique appears to dull his sensitivity to violence and to illustrate perhaps one source of the South's tolerance of the Klan and of lynching. Tom behaves with the same arbitrary, selfish assurance the South did when the political supports of a solid South, a single-party system, and the Supreme Court decision of 1883 made it possible to assume, as Budd suggests, "that the Bourbon Brigadiers had nullified the advances for which the Union Army had bled."[11]

The actual practices that determined the quality of the black experience in the South in the post-Reconstruction years are represented, as I have indicated, only metaphorically in the last twelve chapters of *Huckleberry Finn;* however, authors such as Tourgée provide good accounts of the practices that Twain satirizes. These practices are the subject of polemical and sociohistorical discussion in such books as Bertram Wilbur Doyle's *The Etiquette of Race Relations in the South, A Study in Social Control,* Edgar Gardner Murphy's *Problems in the Present South,* Charles S. Johnson's *Shadow of the Plantation,* and John Dollard's *Caste and Class in a Southern Town.*[12] Certain political actions and attitudes that were observable after 1876, in the opinion of authors such as these, made possible and perhaps determined the character and purpose of the practices Twain parodies in Tom's "evasion."

Rutherford B. Hayes's election in 1876 announced the Republican party's new laissez-faire policy. After 1876 the Supreme Court most often interpreted the Fourteenth and Fifteenth amendments in ways that weakened the protection of black people. It also held the state's police powers—a state's right to protect its public health, safety, and morals—to be paramount and more important than the rights given to any individual under the Fourteenth Amendment. The Court found state Jim Crow laws to be a valid exercise of a state's police powers. If a state law was not plainly discriminatory, the Court did not make an effort to ensure that it was applied alike to black and white. It appeared, however, to distinguish between race discrimination and race distinction, which was not contrary to the Constitution. National political acts and judgments in general returned black people in the South to the control of southern state governments.[13] The effect of this restored power reintroduced oppressive measures in some states that were as severe in their denial of the freedom of black people as were the Black Codes that had appeared in the southern states in the fall and winter of 1865–66 to replace the old slave codes.

It was the Tom Sawyers of the South, and of the nation, who took over the freeing of free black people after their emancipation and after the Civil War. Although the idea of freeing Jim is Huck's, Tom decides how he is to be freed, or, more precisely, that Huck and Jim will not be told that Jim is already free until Tom has used Jim for his own purposes. Some of the people in the South who spoke most seriously of preparing the former slaves for freedom were, like Tom, concerned to provide profit and pleasure for themselves. For them, as for Tom, black people were "niggers." They were inferior, and freedom for them was necessarily different from what freedom was for white people. There was no need to be especially concerned about a nigger's feelings, and Tom was not concerned about Jim's. People who behaved like Tom Sawyer defined "the Negro problem," developed the concept of gradualism, and persuaded the nation to accept the "separate but equal" principle as just. The Tom Sawyers of the South made the attempts of the Huckleberry Finns to free themselves and black people difficult and sometimes prevented or perverted those efforts.

Huck became involved in Jim's quest for freedom and in freeing himself from ignorance and prejudice when Jim and he became allies and took to the raft. Both river shores were dangerous: although Illinois was technically a free state, fugitive slave laws were in effect, and Huck too would have been subject to arrest. The extent to which he freed himself as they went down the river is seen in chapter 31 when he tries to write Miss Watson a letter telling her where Jim is. Up to this point he has been able to conduct his relationship with Jim, as he has learned and wanted to, with increasing decency. His decision not to send the letter proclaims his moral quality and his deviation from southern conventions. When he discovers that the King has turned Jim over to the Phelpses and has received forty dollars in return, Huck decides that he must find and free Jim. Like some people in the South who felt about black people and their freedom as he had learned to feel about Jim, Huck knows that if he wishes to help Jim, he will have to do it without offending those in power, to whom he cannot speak openly and honestly about his purposes. It becomes clear in chapter 31 that Huck may have to compromise and dissemble.

The reader becomes aware of Huck's necessity to pretend to be someone he is not and to accept Tom Sawyer's judgment rather than his own after Huck discovers that the King has disposed of Jim when he talks with the Duke about the predicament that Jim's loss places him in. Huck is in no position to say to the Duke what a terrible thing the King has done, or to declare his purpose to free Jim. What he says describes his reaction to Jim's absence in a way that does not offend the Duke and hides his real thoughts. Huck's disingenuousness with the Duke indicates that in the South the process of freeing the free Negro has been perverted. Huck tells the Duke, "I says to myself, ' . . . they've took my nigger, which is the only nigger I've got in the world, and now I'm in a strange country, and ain't got no property no more, nor nothing, and no way to make my living'" (chap. 31). Huck is in a strange moral terrain where he must conceal his motives from persons like the Duke, conceal his identity from Aunt Sally and others, and give Tom Sawyer's judgment priority over his own. What Huck says to the Duke is different from what the boy who was willing to go to hell rather than tell Miss Watson where her slave is would have been expected to say. With the Duke he assumes, as a protective disguise to win sympathy and prevent suspicion about his real purposes, the role of the southerner who has suffered economic loss. This behavior protects him and helps secure the information that he needs in his effort to find and free Jim. Huck's is the dilemma of the morally decent man living in the South who wants to keep his integrity and work for the freedom of former slaves.

Huck knows and understands the Duke, but he misjudges Tom Sawyer to be, in contrast to himself, a morally decent person whom he can admire. Huck knows that the Duke may take advantage of him, but he trusts Tom and expects fair dealing from him. He has no trouble telling Tom why he is at the Phelps farm and explaining the mistake Aunt Sally has made about who he is. He does not expect, however, that Tom will help him free Jim, nor does he know Tom's hidden reason: "Here was a boy that was respectable, and well brung-up; and had a character to lose; and folks at home that had characters; and he was bright and not leatherheaded, and knowing, and not ignorant; and not mean, but kind; and yet here he was, without any more pride, or rightness, or feeling, than to stoop to this business, and make himself a shame, and his family a shame, before everybody" (chap. 34). Naïvely, he assumes that Tom is actually risking his reputation by taking part in the rescue. Discovering where Jim is and finding a way to free him are Huck's responsibility, but Tom takes over and uses both Huck and Jim for purposes that have little to do with freedom.

Recounting the elaborate evasion, Twain shows clearly that Huck must follow Tom's leadership and that Jim suffers by Tom's concern for style and throwing "bulliness" into his plan. Tom's judgment of how black people should be treated is first illustrated in his behavior toward the Phelpses' slave who brings food to Jim in the cabin where he is a prisoner. When Huck and Tom enter that building with him, the slave notices that Jim knows them—that he greets them with pleasure and they greet him. When he comments on this, Tom denies that they know each other; and he forces the slave to reject the truth of what he has seen, to give up confidence in his knowledge and the accuracy of his vision. No respect is shown for him as a person. Tom persuades him to believe that witches have caused it to appear that Huck, he, and Jim greeted each other. Tom plays on the slave's superstition, using the slave's weakness to gain his own ends, as he uses Jim and other people.

Life is altered for all of the Phelps farm community by the evasion; white people as well as black are hurt by Tom's actions. The effects of "freeing the free Negro" on white people are shown as Aunt Sally and Uncle Silas respond to the evasion. As Tom's plan develops, they, like Jim, lose control of their lives. They are affected by his antics much as Nat, their slave, is; candlesticks, sheets, shirts, and spoons disappear. Aunt Sally fears that she is losing her sanity, that she has lost her ability to count. It would not be a surprise if she, like Nat, turned to witches to find an explanation for what has happened to her. Before the evasion ends, it involves many others: the neighbors are frightened; Tom is shot in the leg; people consider lynching Jim. The life of a quiet community has been disturbed by Tom's selfish game. By extension, the behavior of the South's Tom Sawyers caused decent people to live in what Huck called "a strange country."

Huck's plan for freeing Jim is honest and will work, as Tom concedes, but Tom's plan has *style* and will make Jim, Huck thinks, just as free as his plan would, and "maybe," he says, "get us all killed." Because Huck respects and trusts Tom, he expresses confidence in Tom's plan. He does not tell what the plan is because he knows that Tom will change it from time to time, "heaving in new bulliness whenever he got a chance." Huck's references to the "style" and danger in Tom's plan and to Tom's "bulliness" are significant because these aspects of the plan conceal Tom's real purposes. Although Huck's plan to free Jim would work, Tom argues, "I bet we can find a way that's twice as long." When Huck discovers a board that could be removed to provide an opening for Jim to escape, Tom says, "I should

hope we can find a way that's a little more complicated than *that*"
(chap. 34). When Huck mentions sawing Jim out, a more complicated way, Tom is pleased; that way of rescuing Jim is, he says, "real
mysterious and troublesome, and good." It has these qualities for
him, and they will contribute to his fun. He knows that Jim is already
free, but he conceals this fact from Huck and Jim with no concern for
how they will be affected.

Huck is wrong when he assumes that Tom's plan will make Jim
just as free as his own will; the plan affects both Jim and Huck
adversely. Some things that are done to Jim cause him pain and are at
least potentially dangerous. Like Huck, Jim is forced to pretend he
enjoys what he does not—though he draws the line at keeping a pet
rattlesnake. Although his personal sensitivity is offended, he endures
the presence of spiders and garter snakes and the bites of rats. He does
not do it, but Tom is willing to saw Jim's leg off to remove a chain
from it. Huck is unable to consider the full consequences of Tom's
self-serving arbitrariness (his "bulliness" or bullheadedness) on Jim.
Further, Tom's plan does more to harm Jim than simply make him
uncomfortable; it prevents him from being a man; it stimulates fear in
him just as many of the actions of white persons in the South during
the post-Reconstruction period injured black people, emotionally
and spiritually.

Huck's reference to Tom's plan getting them killed may be a reference to the fact that violence was frequently a part of the process of
coercing black behavior in the South during the post-Reconstruction
period. Tom does violence to Jim's humanity; moreover, the Tom
Sawyers of the South are often responsible for people being killed, as
Tourgée illustrates in *A Fool's Errand*. In a good number of places in
the country at that time the Klan, or persons who behaved like
Klansmen, monitored the "freeing" of black people, controlled what
jobs they could have, and determined where and how they could live.
Some people who challenged the Klan, black and white, were killed.
The lynch mob helped to limit the freedom of black persons, and
Twain was uncomfortably aware of the increase in lynching in the
South. Tom's style, or bulliness, as in the "nonnamous" letters (chap.
39) that he sends to Aunt Sally's neighbors, is responsible for his
being shot and for the talk of lynching Jim.

Huck's, Jim's, and Tom's association in the last twelve chapters of
the novel may remind the reader of the association of the rich and
poor white men in Lillian Smith's "Two Men and a Bargain,"[14] and

through that reminder suggest relationships and their import like those Twain depicts. In Smith's modern fable, a rich white man and a poor white man agree on how free black people are to be in the South. Freeing them is the subject of the discussion, as Jim and his freedom are the subject of some of Huck's and Tom's discussions; and like Jim, black people in Smith's fable have little to say in the matter. Smith makes it clear that the situation has its origin in the post-Reconstruction period when Jim Crow, as a means of social control, was accepted in the South and became legal in the "separate but equal" doctrine.

Tom in his own way presumes to accept for himself the privileges of the powerful, as the rich man does in Smith's fable; and as the rich man would, Tom assumes that Huck must accept his point of view. He takes advantage of Huck as he does of Jim, just as Smith's rich white man takes advantage of her poor white man and of black people. Huck senses that he is being taken advantage of, just as Smith's poor white man does, but does not trust his own knowledge sufficiently to act according to what he thinks is right and reasonable. As Chadwick Hansen says, Huck and Jim have no choice but to accept Tom's leadership; they are completely in his power.[15] Because the Toms of the South represent conventional authority, the Hucks must agree that they are right. Huck is, as he has said, in a strange country. The relationship among Huck, Jim, and Tom is a duplication of the relationship among white people of Tom's caste, white people of Huck's caste, and the South's black people during the post-Reconstruction years.

Twain's judgment of Tom's conduct of the evasion activities (and of the evasion activities of individuals in charge of freeing free black people in the South) is made clear when Tom provides rotten wood that will produce a dim light (phosphorescent light, foxfire) to conceal their evasion activity. Tom wants a dim light because he does not want to risk the discovery of what Huck and he are doing; nor does he want Huck to know why he is helping to free Jim. Tom's use of foxfire calls attention to the fact that certain of the actions to "free the free Negro" in the South can only be performed in a light that conceals. In other words, a logic of the quality of foxfire is sufficiently dim to make the application of Black Codes appear an appropriate means of preparing black people for freedom. The logic—the rationalizations—that some of Twain's southern contemporaries used to support the political suppression of black people was not only a logic that permitted the South to justify what it was doing in whatever ways it chose, but also a logic that would not bear close examination. Foxfire permits individuals to name things as they please. Tom says, for instance, that case knives must be used to dig the hole through which Jim is to escape, but he uses a pick and "lets on" that it is a case knife (chap. 36). He is perfectly willing, because the light of his rotten wood conceals, to call a pick a case knife. In the South that Twain satirizes, southerners speak of themselves as the black man's friends, of knowing best what he needs, and of acting to protect his interests. Frequently these affirmations of interest and goodwill, like Tom's case knives, will not bear scrutiny in good light.

The "nonnamous" letters, instances of Tom's bulliness heaved into the process of freeing Jim, move the novel toward its end and toward Twain's final comment on "freeing the free Negro." They result in two things crucially important in showing Twain's judgment of the effects of the South's treatment of black people. Through Jim's willingness to sacrifice his freedom to care for Tom, and through Tom's assumption that he can pay Jim for taking advantage of him, for playing games with Jim's life for his own amusement, Twain parodies contemporary practices and the most regrettable consequences of freeing the black man the way it was being done in the 1880s. Jim could free himself easily by slipping the chain off the leg of his bed and walking out of the cabin (and he does tell Tom that he will break out if Tom insists that he pet a rattlesnake), but Twain does not encourage the reader to speculate about Jim's responsibilities for freeing himself or for accepting the things that happen to him while he is being freed. Jim does protest some of the absurdities that Tom asks of him, but in the main he follows Tom's directions, plays the "jews-harp," and accepts all of Tom's bulliness. His trust of Tom disarms him and prevents him from working for his liberation. Perhaps black people in the 1880s contributed less to their own freedom than they could have because of paternalism and because they trusted white people whom they believed to be working in the best ways to free them.

Although by the end of the novel Jim may have become passive about his own liberation, he is clearly aware of how he regards Tom and of what he should do in Tom's own time of need: he does not hesitate to risk his freedom. When he acts to protect Tom, the reader may recognize that his failure to act more directly to free himself has come not from a fear of doing so but from a feeling, perhaps, that

Tom knew best how to free him. Jim assumes that Tom regards him as human, in the same way that he believes Tom to be human. When Huck and he talk about caring for the injured Tom, Jim says: "Well, den, dis is de way it look to me. . . . Ef it wuz *him* dat 'uz bein' sot free, en one er de boys wuz to git shot, would he say, 'Go on en save me, nemmine 'bout a doctor f'r to save dis one'? Is dat like Mars Tom Sawyer? Would he say dat? You *bet* he wouldn't! *Well,* den, is Jim gwyne to say it? No, sah—I doan' budge a step out'n dis place, 'dout a *doctor,* not if it's forty year!" (chap. 40). As his speech suggests, Jim regards Tom as his friend just as he does Huck. He believes that Tom is honest, responsible, and willing to make essential sacrifices for others when they are in need. He accepts Tom as a person of superior status much as Huck does and probably thinks Tom is wiser than Huck. He believes that Tom is interested in freeing him and that Tom knows the best way to do this. Like Huck, Jim accepts the myths of caste. It is important to notice that Jim refers to Tom as "Mars Tom Sawyer" and to Huck as "Huck." Jim's false assumptions about Tom's concern and attitudes are costly errors. Like many black people in the 1880s, Jim trusts the good intentions of whites and suffers for it. He risks his freedom to help Tom but is treated badly for acting well.

For the Phelpses' neighbors, the doctor who treats Tom's wound, and the men who recapture Jim, he remains a "nigger" in spite of his self-sacrifice and humane assistance to Tom. In the Phelpses' farm community, and in the larger South, black people who pursue their own interests and freedom, as it appears to Sister Damrell and Sister Hotchkiss that Jim is doing before Tom's emergency, are insane. For them, Jim is mad and dangerous. For the men who capture, curse, strike, and imprison him after he has helped Tom, he is crazy, a bad nigger who should be lynched as an example to show other niggers what happens to bad niggers. The doctor says that Jim is a good nigger and praises what he did for Tom, but still does not recognize his humanity. His description of Jim is reminiscent of Thomas Nelson Page's descriptions in "Marse Chan" and other stories of the faithful retainers of antebellum days: "I never see a nigger that was a better nuss or faithfuller, and yet he was resking his freedom to do it, and was all tired out, too, and I see plain enough he'd been worked main hard, lately. I liked the nigger for that; I tell you, gentlemen, a nigger like that is worth a thousand dollars—and kind treatment, too. . . . He ain't no bad nigger, gentlemen; that's what I think about him" (chap. 42). The doctor recognizes in Jim what in white people are considered admirable human qualities. Ordinarily, people who behave as Jim has in serving Tom are rewarded. To the doctor Jim's behavior means that he is not a "bad nigger"—that is, he is a good slave. The good Christians who are the Phelpses' neighbors respond to what the doctor says; his status deserves their respect. They agree with him that Jim "acted very well, and was deserving," and they promise not to "cuss him no more" (chap. 42). Twain's irony is clear. They do not curse Jim, but they also do not remove any of his chains or treat him better, as Huck hoped the doctor's speech would cause them to do.

Before being told that Miss Watson has freed him and that he is to be rewarded for giving Tom so much pleasure, Jim has risked the success of what Huck and he thought was a genuine effort to secure his freedom in order to help Tom. The freedom of black people was often risked in the post-Reconstruction South to protect the interests of white people—as Smith's fable suggests. The significance of such behavior in the novel is stated in Laurence B. Holland's comments on the events that occur after Jim's escape from the Phelpses' cabin. He says, "Saving Tom, freeing him from danger, is taking precedence over setting Jim free."[16] Tom has been hurt and he needs help, but his injury is the result of his "bulliness," the pursuit of his own pleasure, and his manipulation of other people. Holland considers the events after Tom is wounded to be the most important in the book. Jim is captured because he places Tom's care above his own freedom, a choice that affirms the quality of his humanity. However, the manner of his capture and the treatment he receives deny that humanity. Holland says that "liberation dissolves into enslavement and they come close, without actually doing so, to canceling each other out."[17] Holland continues his argument by showing that "Tom's antics confer the burden of heroism on Jim but make a cruel and diseased mockery of it," and he judges that "Tom's antics are in effect the rehearsal for the ominous enslavement that ensues when Jim is enchained 'again' in the 'same' cabin."

Another seriously disturbing effect of Jim's association with and domination by Tom, perhaps more serious than the threat that his physical freedom will be sacrificed to save Tom, is that he appears at the end of the novel to accept the value Tom places on him. Something has happened to change him from the person he was on Jackson's Island who could say, "I owns myself, en I's wuth eight hund'd dollars" (chap. 8). He does not appear to have the same goals after the evasion that he had when he and Huck took to the raft. Perhaps the humiliations inflicted on him before the evasion caused him to despair of ever being free. (It should be remembered that he anticipated being free before the evasion, and in fact was actually free although Tom withheld that information from him.) At one point Huck says to him, "*Now,* old Jim you're a free man *again*" (chap. 40; Twain's italics).

Tom's behavior (like most white behavior that he has experienced) does not encourage Jim's self-respect. In the last chapter, when Tom explains that he has exploited Jim for his own amusement, Jim shows no resentment of the way Tom took advantage of Huck's and his powerlessness. He is pleased and appears to be fully compensated by the forty dollars: "*Dah* now, Huck, what I tell you?—What I tell you dah on Jackson islan'? I *tole* you I got a hairy breas', en what's de sign un it; en I *tole* you I ben rich wunst, en gwineter to be rich *agin;* en it's come true; en heah she *is!*" ("Chapter the Last"). But although Jim may have lost respect for himself, he has kept his sensitivity to the needs of others, as is shown in his behavior when Tom is shot, and again at the end of the novel when he shows delicacy and concern for Huck's feelings in explaining to him that his father is dead.

Jim has lost a great deal. Earlier in the novel he was able to remind Huck of the mutual obligations in a friendship, and he spoke out effectively against Huck's mistreatment of a friend. He does not find a similar impropriety or exploitation in what Tom has done to him. He may have protested against spiders, rats, and snakes, and against finding metal objects in his food during the evasion, but he appears, after he is paid, to have forgotten the discomfort and lack of respect that were forced on him. It is of crucial importance that he appears also to have forgotten his interest in the condition of his wife and children (who did not belong to Miss Watson and thus could not be freed in her will as he was). His delight in being "rich" with the forty dollars Tom gave him shows how he has been injured by accepting Tom's values. Tom says he had planned to hire a brass band and march Jim back to his community in the noisy splendor of a torchlight parade so he could be admired by envious friends and former associates. The changed Jim might have enjoyed this.

Even in the end Tom shows little concern for what Jim may want to do with his life once he is free, and no regard for him as a person. His assumption that he can simply pay Jim forty dollars for his trouble underscores this. Perhaps, ultimately, he agrees with the doctor that Jim is a good nigger. His intention to provide Jim "the nigger satisfaction," as such gestures were thought to be, of a brass band and a colorful procession shows that Tom, like many southerners, assumes that black people are different—childlike, not sensitive to actions white people would find demeaning—and that they have no understanding of the meaning of freedom or the practical necessities for getting along in the world.

Figuratively, through the burlesque and parody of these last chapters, Mark Twain shows the effects of the contemporary handling of "the Negro problem." "Freeing the free Negro" strikes him as adversely as Tom's evasion affects Jim. Twain suggests that, like Jim, black people in the post-Reconstruction South were losing a sense of selfhood and often were forced to see themselves as inferior. Jim's losses suggest that the consequences of the evasion were complex and serious, as serious perhaps as the effects of chattel slavery had been.

Notes

1. A good description of Black Codes and other laws that were introduced to control the behavior of black people after the Civil War and that were, in a sense, models for laws passed after Reconstruction is found in J. W. Burgess, *Reconstruction and the Constitution, 1866–1876* (New York: Charles Scribner's Sons, 1902) 45–56; Burgess refers to Black Codes as the Mississippi Acts. Benjamin Quarles describes Black Codes briefly in *The Negro in the Making of America* (New York: Collier, 1964) 129–31. C. Van Woodward's chapter "Mudsills and Bottom Rails," in *Origins of the New South, 1877–1913* (Baton Rouge: Louisiana State UP, 1951) 205–34, is a good discussion of the black man in the South after 1876.

2. "The Negro problem" was sometimes called "the southern question," "the future of the Negro," etc. What is meant by "the Negro problem" is made clear in James Bryce's "Thoughts on the Negro Problem," *North American Review* 153 (Dec. 1891): 641–60; and in Thomas Nelson Page's "Some of Its Difficulties and Fallacies," a chapter in *The Southern Problem* (New York: Charles Scribner's Sons, 1914) 29–55. Edgar Gardner Murphy presents an excellent statement of the problem from a southerner's point of view in "The South and the Negro," in *The Present South* (New York: Longmans, Green, 1904) 153–201.

3. Roger B. Salomon devotes a good deal of attention to the way in which Twain's attitudes changed during the post-Reconstruction period in *Twain and the Image of History* (New Haven: Yale UP, 1961) 74–94. See also Kenneth S. Lynn, *Mark Twain and Southwestern Humor* (Boston: Little, Brown, 1959) 229–30.

4. Generally, Budd's *Mark Twain: Social Philosopher* (Bloomington: Indiana UP, 1962), Foner's *Mark Twain: Social Critic* (New York: International, 1958), Kaplan's *Mr. Clemens and Mark Twain* (New York: Simon and Schuster, 1966), Lynn's *Mark Twain and Southwestern Humor,* and Pettit's *Mark Twain and the South* (Lexington: U of Kentucky P, 1973) support the idea at least by implication.

5. *Atlantic Monthly* (Nov. 1874); see Budd 92; Foner 202–5; Kaplan 180–81.

6. Budd 104.

7. *Twins of Genius* (East Lansing: Michigan State UP, 1953) 68–77.

8. Lynn 231.

9. The essay was adapted from a commencement address delivered at the University of Alabama on 18 June 1884, and was published in *Century Magazine* 1 Jan. 1885, and in Cable's *The Silent South*.

10. Lynn 233.

11. Budd 92.

12. George M. Frederickson's last four chapters in *The Black Image in the White Mind* (New York: Harper & Row, 1971) 198–319, provide a good discussion of the southern ideas and practices that Twain satirizes.

13. Quarles 142–44.

14. *Killers of the Dream* (New York: Norton, 1949) 174–91.

15. "The Character of Jim and the Ending of *Huckleberry Finn,*" *Massachusetts Review* 5 (Autumn 1965): 61.

16. "'A Raft of Trouble,' Word and Deed in *Huckleberry Finn,*" *Glyph* 5 (1979): 68.

17. Holland 71.

The Veil Rent

in Twain

Degradation and

Revelation in *Adventures*

of Huckleberry Finn

Mary Kemp Davis

What at first seems to be wry humor in Huck's initial description of Jim in *Adventures of Huckleberry Finn* turns out to have sober implications in the course of the novel. Huck observes, "Miss Watson's big nigger, named Jim, was setting in the kitchen door; we could see him pretty clear, because there was a light behind him" (chap. 2). What Huck and Tom Sawyer see is not Jim at all but his silhouette; Jim is enveloped in darkness, his hulking frame thrown into relief by the light at his back. This seemingly naturalistic detail foreshadows Huck's later association with Jim when he slowly discovers that much of Jim's identity is concealed behind a mask of blackness. Even if Huck could merely shift the light from Jim's back to his face, he could not decipher Jim's identity as easily as he can the identity of Mary Jane Wilks, whom he later tells, "I don't want no better book than what your face is" (chap. 28). Jim's race is indelibly etched on his face, making it a formidable obstacle to Huck's enlightenment.

What Huck finally sees beneath this mask of blackness is "Jim's dignity and human capacity."[1] In any event, Huck's definitive assessment of Jim comes in chapter 40 on Spanish Island when he affirms, "I knowed he was white inside," shifting the angle of vision from Jim's exterior to his interior. This statement is startling, given the traditional ineradicable nature of blackness. From Jeremiah's time onward, the phrase "to wash an Ethiop white" had indicated "sheer impossibility,"[2] rather like Huck's inversion of this expression when he says, "Well, if ever I struck anything like it, I'm a nigger," referring to the King's and the Duke's masquerade in the Wilks episode (chap.

24). In the recognition scene on Spanish Island, however, Huck, who had earlier used traditional imagery in calling a stormy night on Jackson's Island "dark as sin" (chap. 9), now repudiates the curse of blackness which had shackled Jim just as securely as his chains.

Curiously, Huck's assessment of Jim's character is sandwiched between Huck's and Tom's gratuitous abuse of Jim during the three-week "evasion" episode and the equally unjustified abuse that the Pikesville community heaps upon him when he returns, reimprisoned, to the Phelps farm. Although many critics have found fault with the image of Jim during the evasion,[3] Harold Beaver's pungent remarks are worth quoting because they intimate a provocative correlation between Jim's degradation at the Phelps farm and his elevation on Spanish Island. Noting the references to "the hope of a glorious resurrection" (chap. 32), "being born again" (chap. 32), and Acts 17 (chap. 37), Beaver calls this lengthy section of the novel the "American Calvary, of Nigger Passion." He emphasizes Huck's betrayal of Jim when he submits to Tom Sawyer's tortuous schemes for freeing Jim and adds, "in making fun of the two niggers [Nat and Jim], Huck and Tom, like the Roman soldiers dolling up Jesus as King of the Jews, are restaging nothing less than a second and more prolonged passion. The Christ of this dramatic parody, this pseudo-passion or 'black' Mass, yet again, of course, being Jim."[4] Like Christ, Jim is mocked and physically assaulted; like him also Jim is patient, passive, and forgiving. Moreover, by "sacrificing his own life for Tom's," "Jim at last achieves resurrection," or his freedom.

Certainly the Phelps episode contains many allusions to Christ's Passion and Resurrection, as does the earlier Wilks episode, which contains several references to Christ's life, betrayal, and Resurrection, including references to the twelve disciples (chap. 24), Pilate (chap. 25), and Judas (chap. 28). However, we need not conclude from this that Jim *is* a black Christ. What more significantly ties the two sections together is Mark Twain's use of the "degradation ceremony" to make complex revelations about key characters, including Jim, and society. Huck, the King, and the Duke barely avoid being tarred and feathered, even lynched, in the Wilks episode, and Jim barely avoids the latter fate in the Phelps episode. One social historian has called these forms of vigilante justice "degradation ceremonies."[5] Revelation is the sine qua non of such "ceremonies,"[6] a correlation Twain exploits relentlessly. Rather than simply making the white man the black man's burden, he uses such ritualistic moments in the novel to broaden the significance of Jim's "Calvary."

It is appropriate to clarify how the terms "degradation" and "degradation ceremony" will be used in this discussion. A humorous approach to the concept of degradation occurs when the King and the Duke enter the novel. First, the Duke pretends that he is the "rightful Duke of Bridgewater." He continues, "and here am I, forlorn, torn from my high estate, hunted of men, despised by the cold world, ragged, worn, heart-broken, and *degraded* to the companionship of felons on a raft" (emphasis added). Then the King, not to be outdone, claims that he has been equally (at least) degraded: "Yes, gentlemen, you see before you, in blue jeans and misery, the wanderin', exiled, trampled-on and sufferin' rightful King of France" (chap. 19). The Duke uses and the King alludes to the term "degradation" in its denotative sense: a lowering or demotion in rank, status, or condition.

When applied to social phenomena, however, "degradation" has a more specialized meaning. For instance, Harold Garfinkel writes, "Any communicative work between persons, whereby the public identity of an actor is transformed into something looked on as lower in the local scheme of social types, [is] a 'status degradation ceremony.'" The denouncer seeks to transform the "public identity of his victim." As Garfinkel explains, "We publicly deliver the curse: 'I call upon all men to bear witness that he [the victim or object] is not as he appears but is otherwise and *in essence* of a lower species.'" The victim is not given a new identity in a status degradation ceremony; rather, his *real* identity, hidden before, is made manifest: "The former identity, at best, receives the accent of mere appearances." "What he is now is what, 'after all,' he was all along." This revelation is an essential component of the status degradation ceremony because to know the victim is not to love him. The denouncer's goal is "the ritual destruction of the person denounced."

Garfinkel emphasizes the communal nature of the degradation ceremony. The denouncer is a member of the community, shares its values, and speaks in its name—with the community's approval. The victim, by contrast, is separated from and opposed to the community. That is to say, "the denounced person must be ritually separated from a place in the legitimate order, i.e., he must be defined as standing in a place opposed to it. He must be placed 'outside,' he must be made 'strange.'" Since the victim must be seen as opposed to communal values, polarization is inherent in the ceremony. The victim must be referred to his "dialectical counterpart." If "the peaceful citizen" is the communal ideal, the victim must be seen as the "mad-dog murderer."[7]

In his book *Southern Honor: Ethics and Behavior in the Old South,* Bertram Wyatt-Brown demonstrates how Garfinkel's paradigm can be applied to slave insurrection panics, lynching, and charivari, each of which has some bearing on *Huckleberry Finn.* Of slavery he writes,

> Obedience and even the semblance of affection were the first require-
> ments of slave conduct; impudence was thought a prelude to insurgency.
> The method of testing these attributes in a public way was to create what
> one social scientist has called "degradation ceremonies," a term that has
> lately been applied to the corporeal styles of early American legal punish-
> ment. By this means the black rebel became a visible and punishable
> sacrificial victim. He was the archetypal reverse image of the self-effacing
> "uncle" that whites liked to think was the ideal servant. Whatever the
> malefactor's former character might have been, he was thereafter the
> personification of unreliability, disorder, and nameless horror.[8]

Wyatt-Brown emphasizes both the communal and the ritualistic aspects of slave trials for conspiracy. No matter how groundless the
insurrection panics or how questionable the community's methods of
isolating and prosecuting the accused, those deemed guilty "were
made sacrifices to the sacred concept of white supremacy. The rite was
a celebration of white solidarity."[9]

The ritualistic shaming and destruction of the victim were also the
salient features of lynching and charivari. Both masqueraded as communal justice and aimed to purge the community of antisocial or
subversive elements.[10] Lynching needs no definition, but it might be
useful to point out that charivari, traditionally a festive and bac-
chanalian event, encompassed the "wedding-day jest," the "public
whipping," and "tar-and-feathering." Basically, even lynching "was a
charivari with deadly as well as shaming intent."[11]

By combining the insights of Garfinkel and Wyatt-Brown, we can
make several generalizations about degradation ceremonies. First of
all, they are communal events, not personal vendettas, although one
or more persons may act as galvanizing forces. Second, the victim
becomes a one-dimensional object of censure and scorn because he
supposedly subverts communal values. Third, the victim is identified

as the reverse image of the community's idealized self. Fourth, the victim is verbally excoriated or physically punished (or both) because he is revealed to be antisocial or debased. Finally, the ceremony implicitly reinvigorates or strengthens a faltering, or at least vulnerable, community.

Many critics consider Jim "degraded" in the evasion episode of *Adventures of Huckleberry Finn*. Chadwick Hansen's and Leo Marx's viewpoints are representative. Hansen writes of Jim during the evasion: "This Jim is not the character Twain had so carefully developed, moving him from the lowest of roles to the highest. This Jim has lost all his dignity and become a subhuman creature who feels no pain and bleeds fresh ink. This Jim is a flat, cheap type, and this Jim is a measure of the failure of the ending of *Huckleberry Finn*."[12] Marx concurs with Hansen's analysis of Jim's "transformation."[13] But in a technical sense, the sociological characteristics of degradation are not present in the evasion section of Twain's novel. The true degradation ceremony, in the sense in which it has been defined in this discussion, occurs before and after Jim returns to the Phelps farm. These two scenes are actually a comic treatment of degradation ritual. The first scene is quite lighthearted, and the second veers away from a tragic denouement.

The first stage of the degradation ceremony occurs when Huck returns to the Phelps farm in chapter 41. Clearly, this is a communal event: "the place was plumb full of farmers and farmers' wives to dinner." Mrs. Hotchkiss is the chief denouncer, although she is eagerly assisted by Mrs. Damrell, Brer Penrod, Brer Hightower, Brother Marples, and the hostess, Sister Sally Phelps. Jim has not returned yet, but he and his coconspirators (reputedly slaves and Indian Territory robbers) are the chief topic of conversation. Mrs. Hotchkiss sets the tone for the discussion by stating emphatically, "I b'lieve the nigger was crazy." In fact, her first outburst, a veritable litany of denunciations, pronounces Jim crazy seven times, "crazy 's Nebokoodneezer (cf. Daniel 4). The reference to Nebuchadnezzar (and perhaps her sevenfold pronouncement) not only underscores the religiosity of this group but also serves to define Jim dialectically. In contrast to this pious assembly, Jim is not a servant of the true God. (It is irrelevant at this point that Rev. Silas Phelps has held prayers with him "every day or two" before his escape [chap. 36].) Instead, he is a mad pagan like Nebuchadnezzar, the Babylonian king whom God banished from society and forced to live with beasts. Nebuchadnezzar had ignored Daniel's warning to cease sinning and God's explicit order to show mercy to the oppressed. Ironically, no one at the table perceives that Jim has more in common with those in the latter category than with the pagan king.

That Jim was a real threat to the community is apparent from the conspiracy theory, also introduced by Mrs. Hotchkiss. She estimates that perhaps a dozen people assisted Jim. Brer Hightower, on the other hand, magnifies the danger to more than forty (another number with a fine liturgical ring to it). Because of his "secret African writ'n, done with blood" (chap. 41), his mysterious hoarding of household and other goods, and his collusion with robbers whose natural haunt is among savages in "Injun Territory," Jim is metamorphosed into a member of a secret society bent on undermining the community's sacred property rights, especially the right to hold slaves. Furthermore, he seems to have enlisted the aid of other slaves at the Phelps farm. One of these had seemed so reliable that the Phelpses had entrusted him with the key to Jim's cabin; later, they posted two more slaves at the front and back doors of their home after they received anonymous letters warning them of impending danger (chaps. 34 and 39). Not content to "fall" himself, then, Jim, it is feared, has corrupted the Phelpses' slaves and jeopardized the security of the larger community.

Perhaps Mark Twain has Aunt Sally satirize herself and the rest of these denouncers when she exclaims, "I didn't have no reasoning faculties no more." Nevertheless, the serious implications of this humorous communal dinner are apparent when Jim returns to the Phelps farm. This next sequence of events could be entitled "The 'Degradation Ceremony' That Failed."

On the morning after the dinner, "a lot of people" assemble at the Phelps farm to arraign Jim (chap. 42). Now the religious frame of reference ("the nigger's crazy—crazy 's Nebokoodneezer") is overtly abandoned in favor of a social frame of reference, the "good" versus the "bad nigger." "Good niggers" have a place, albeit a subservient one, in the community; "bad niggers" must be ferreted out and either subdued or destroyed. Having inferred that Jim is a "bad nigger," the citizens who have gathered perform their roles admirably: cursing Jim, striking the side of his head, chaining his hands and feet, and stipulating that he be restricted to a diet of bread and water until he is claimed or sold. Most important, they decide that armed white men, not trusted slaves, should be stationed outside his cabin each night.

Similarly, a bulldog, an inversion of the docile, spaniel-like slave, is supposed to guard his door every day. Economic considerations alone prevent the more impassioned among Jim's tormentors from lynching him, an outcome which would have made this degradation ceremony tragically complete.

Beaver has noticed the parallel between Jim's disguise in chapter 24 and the outfit he is wearing when he returns to the Phelps farm. In chapter 24 the Duke dresses Jim "in King Lear's outfit": "a long curtain-calico gown, and a white horse-hair wig and whiskers." He also paints "Jim's face and hands and ears and neck all over a dead dull solid blue, like a man that's been drownded nine days." Finally, as a deterrent to the curious, he places this sign in front of the wigwam on the raft: "*Sick Arab—but harmless when not out of his head.*" Noticing that Jim is wearing Aunt Sally's calico gown when he is brought back, Beaver comments, "Yet Tom had merely repeated the Duke's and the Dauphin's vindictive triumph, of degrading Jim from a black slave to an exotic, transvestite madman."[14]

The sexual ramifications of Jim's clothing might be carried a step further. Jim's feminine dress, though admittedly comic, is a visual emblem of his symbolic castration. It signifies that the community has subdued the "bad nigger" whose goals are antithetical to the community's.

Tom's doctor has a pivotal role in the proceedings. First of all, by instigating Jim's capture and accompanying him on his return, he proves to the community that he upholds the community's values and supports the institution of slavery. He tells those assembled that when he first spotted Jim, he "judged he must be a runaway nigger." Therefore, he knew spontaneously what he must do and why he should do it. Specifically, he knew not to leave Tom and Jim alone while he checked on other patients because "the nigger might get away" and then the doctor would "be to blame." He also knew that he must try to capture the fugitive. Thus, while Jim slept, he had two other men assist him in imprisoning Jim. The doctor's second role is to thwart the more serious developments of the degradation ceremony. To shield Jim from excessive abuse, he redefines him as the reverse of the "bad nigger," the enemy of the state.

What is a "bad nigger" in this context? His behavior would be diametrically opposed to the image the doctor gives of Jim. Even assuming that our "bad nigger" would have remained with Tom while Huck went for the doctor (and this is probably not too much to ask if he has already drifted eleven hundred miles downriver), he would have remained in hiding just as he and Huck had agreed (chap. 40). Also, since Tom was "out of his head" and incapable of revealing the fugitive's presence, he would have trusted the doctor to find a way to extract the bullet from Tom's leg. Far from feeling guilty about not assisting the doctor, he would have considered this a test of the white man's vaunted ingenuity and power. Then, when Tom became so crazed that he threatened to kill the doctor, he would have laughed— heartily but silently, like some demonic Natty Bumppo—at the sight of a boy holding a man at bay. And when the doctor exclaimed in exasperation, "I got to have *help,* somehow," he would have thought, like Stephen Crane's aloof Universe, that this cry created no sense of obligation in him. Finally, if he had had a momentary lapse of com-mon sense, as the world defines it, and crawled out of his hiding place to help the doctor, only to be betrayed while he slept, he would have swiftly regained it when he heard the doctor's compliment: "I never see a nigger that was a better nuss or faithfuller, and yet he was resking his freedom to do it. . . . I liked the nigger for that; . . . a nigger like that is worth a thousand dollars." Remembering bitterly that even spaniels are valued for their faithfulness but are still dogs for all that, perhaps now he would lunge for the doctor's throat, glad to forsake his "place" in the southern hierarchy.

But Jim has done none of these things, so the doctor's praise of him halts this phase of the degradation ceremony. Ironically, this phase, like the dinner scene, delineates the society without revealing Jim's essential identity. Huck has already given the normative evalua-tion of Jim in chapter 40, a chapter that resounds with religious and social ironies. On the religious level, Jim's temporary recovery of his freedom in the fortieth chapter of the novel is certainly suggestive, given the earlier allusions to Moses and the Exodus story.[15] His journey is arrested, however, when he announces that he will not leave Spanish Island ("not if it's forty year!") until Tom receives medical assistance. This impasse is potentially dangerous for a run-away slave; inertia is bound to have tragic consequences. In Jim's case, though, what could have been a curse turns out to be a boon, for Huck transforms him into an honorary white man: "I knowed he was white inside, and I reckoned he'd say what he did say—so it was all right, now, and I told Tom I was agoing for a doctor."

Beaver sees Huck's praise of Jim's character as a sign of Huck's smugness and self-delusion; Huck's appeal to white standards ("I knowed he was white inside") implies that "Jim somehow had developed a white conscience, a white sense of priorities, a white man's loyalties in so readily adopting the role of 'one of the boys.'" Beaver maintains that Huck's comment, coupled with other condescending remarks he has made previously in the novel, shows that even in his "nigger-stealing" Huck is as "racially caste-bound" as his father.[16]

But despite the racial chauvinism of Huck's remarks, Mark Twain apparently intended this affirmation to be the apogee of Huck's evolving sense of the common humanity he shares with Jim. Even the setting, Spanish Island, has social overtones. As David Brion Davis has explained, abolitionists like Theodore Parker had associated Spain with "the superstition and tyranny of medieval Europe." Parker accused Spain of reinventing "'the old sin' of Negro slavery, which was soon implanted in Virginia." Thus, "slavery was the rhetorical emblem which identified Southerners with Spanish despotism."[17] (Readers of Herman Melville might remember a masterful use of this motif in "Benito Cereno.") Conversely, with Huck's pronouncement, the raison d'être of Jim's enslavement—his race—is destroyed.

It would not be uncharitable to ask why Huck stands idly by and allows Jim to be abused when he is neither a "nigger" nor a "bad nigger." To understand Huck's behavior we should look back at the Wilks episode, where Huck actively tried to combat evil and almost wound up being a victim of a degradation ceremony himself. In the Wilks episode, the good child who seemed to be evil and the evil men who seemed to be good were drawn inexorably toward the vortex of vigilante violence. All of this illustrated to Huck the seductive power of appearances and the tenacity with which seduced men and women cling to their flawed view of reality. Far from believing that his revelation of the truth beneath appearances would have been accepted readily by the Pikesville community, then, Huck undoubtedly mused, "I been there before" (cf. "Chapter the Last").

The Wilks episode is intricately linked to the Phelps episode on the levels of plot and theme. Both episodes contain verbal denunciations of supposed miscreants and end with the dissipation of physical violence. Also, both episodes exploit the revelatory tendencies inherent in the degradation ceremony—although the revelations are more complex in the Wilks episode. In general, the Wilks episode, despite its more involved action, presages the Phelps episode. Not only does it explain why Jim's sacrificial act is so ennobling from Huck's perspective, but it also explains why Miss Watson *must* save Jim from reenslavement.

Theoretically, a degradation ceremony in whatever form is designed to unveil the "real" identity of the victim. Thus, at first glance the Wilks episode reads like a degradation ceremony gone awry. Soon after the King and the Duke arrive, one longtime friend of the Wilks family, an upstanding member of the community, accuses the King of being "a fraud" and "the thinnest kind of impostor" (chap. 25). However, it is only after the two English newcomers appear that the townspeople slowly begin to suspect that Dr. Robinson may have been right. Huck's deception is quickly apparent, but the two sets of brothers present a formidable challenge to the rather dull wits of the townspeople. First, Hines and Dr. Robinson call the King and the Duke frauds; then one frustrated person exclaims of all five people: "The whole bilin' of 'm 's frauds!" The "general investigation" becomes so tangled that the only way to unravel the mystery is for everyone to go to the graveyard to search for the tattoo marks which the real brother alleges are on Peter Wilks's chest. The crowd is extremely restive during the investigation. Even before they depart for the graveyard, one person shouts, "Le's dunk 'em! le's drown 'em! le's ride 'em on a rail!" Then a more circumspect fellow yells, "If we don't find them marks we'll lynch the whole gang." Eventually, the discovery of a bag of gold on Peter's chest diverts the crowd's attention, and the King, the Duke, and Huck escape punishment (chap. 29).

The discovery of the impostors' real identity and their flight from an outraged community are secondary to a more important theme: the romantic affirmation of the beauty, truth, and goodness of at least some human beings. In addition to projecting Huck as a hero, the Wilks episode reveals that in a world of deception and sham emotions, at least one person *is* what she seems to be (chap. 28). In this sense, Mary Jane Wilks, the nineteen-year-old redhead with whom Huck is thoroughly smitten, is a foil to the King and the Duke and an exemplar of the community ideals they oppose.

Mary Jane is an ambivalent mixture of human fallibility and human perfection. At first, like all of the townspeople except Dr. Robinson, she is taken in by the King's "tears and flapdoodle" (chap. 25). The King and the Duke understand the conventions of grief and adapt their behavior accordingly. Therefore Mary Jane, like the others who assemble, is unable to penetrate their sentimental façade. Also, she is quite a sentimentalist herself. After all, she has known Dr. Robinson for some time; he was her father's and her dead uncle's friend. Yet rather than listen to the man who has shown himself to be her "unselfish friend," she demonstrates her faith in her "uncles" by unconditionally entrusting all of her money and her two younger sisters' money to the King (chap. 25).

On the other hand, Mary Jane is compassionate toward others. When her younger sister Joanna accuses Huck of lying (which he is doing), she forces her to apologize to Huck for making him feel ashamed. Later, she is griefstricken when the King sells Peter Wilks's slaves to slave traders who disregard family ties in disposing of them. Family ties are supremely valued in this community. In fact, what is perhaps most reprehensible about the King's and the Duke's acts is that they undermine an uncle's clumsy attempts to provide for the financial security of his orphaned nieces.

Both displays of compassion motivate Huck to attempt to thwart the King's and the Duke's schemes. When Mary Jane fails to heed his counsel, Dr. Robinson, in a Pilate-like gesture, washes his hands of the matter and warns her of coming doom. His exit leaves her and her sisters exposed to the wiles of the King and the Duke. Yet Mary Jane's concern and respect for Huck in the scene with Joanna stimulate him to assume the protector's role that Dr. Robinson has temporarily abandoned. Operating in secrecy because he fears the repercussions for Jim, he first steals the money back and hides it in Peter Wilks's coffin. Later, to prevent Mary Jane from mourning over the breakup of the slave family, he drops his disguise and reveals that the King and the Duke are frauds. He also commits himself to exposing the two to the community and delivering them to legal, not vigilante, justice. Mary Jane is to be his accomplice.

Huck's gallantry and Mary Jane's eagerness to perform the role he assigns her in this counterintrigue obscure the real import of their alliance. More is involved here than the union of two good characters against two evil ones. When Huck sees Mary Jane crying, what is important to him is that she *is* what she has seemed to be. Thus, he explicitly focuses on how she confirms his prior appraisal of her. Interestingly, the scene where he asks her why she is crying parallels the scene in chapter 40 in which Huck asks Jim what they should do about Tom. As with Jim, Mary Jane's answer is what he has antici-pated: "And it was the niggers—I just expected it" (chap. 28).

Another important implication of this alliance is that since Huck is risking his life and Jim's safety with his scheme, he expects Mary Jane to intercede for him and reveal that he is her ally if he is unable to prove his innocence. Consequently, after his Tom Sawyerish plans (cf. chap. 28) fall through and he miraculously escapes the mob, his eyes are drawn irresistibly to Mary Jane's window as he speeds past her house. Huck longs for another revelation. He needs to be reassured that Mary Jane would have fulfilled the terms of their agreement had everything gone according to plan. When he sees the light in her window, his "heart swelled up sudden, like to bust" (chap. 29). Her loyalty to him is confirmed.

Mary Jane's concern for Huck's welfare and her faithfulness to him loom in Huck's memory. In a passage blending past and present perspectives, he eulogizes her unparalleled courage, beauty, and goodness and acknowledges that he has thought of her many times since:

> Pray for me! I reckoned if she knowed me she'd take a job that was more nearer her size. But I bet she done it, just the same—she was just that kind. She had the grit to pray for Judus if she took the notion—there warn't no back-down to her, I judge. . . . And when it comes to beauty—and goodness too—she lays over them all. I hain't ever seen her since that time that I see her go out of that door; no, I hain't ever seen her since; but I reckon I've thought of her a many and a many a million times, and of her saying she would pray for me; and if ever I'd a thought it would do any good for me to pray for *her*, blamed if I wouldn't a done it or bust. (Chap. 28)

Huck's extravagant praise of Mary Jane is more than an adolescent boy's flowery tribute to a lovely young woman. His praise of her is structurally linked to his response to Jim on Spanish Island. If Huck is so enchanted with this proslavery heroine who vows to save him at minimal risk to herself, it is certainly logical for him to exalt Jim for risking his own freedom to remain with Tom. Mary Jane's and Jim's actions are qualitatively different, but in a world of sordid self-interest, these two characters share a certain nobility.

Still another parallel helps to explain why the novel ends happily after Jim's "degradation." If Mary Jane Wilks, initially sentimental and gullible, is allowed to recover her inheritance, then surely Jim, even more sentimental, should eventually receive his freedom. If we accept one character's reward for human goodness, we can also accept the other's.

Leo Marx has criticized the "flimsy contrivance by which Clemens frees Jim" because it seems to vindicate the very culture he had so painstakingly criticized. He feels that the ending of the novel shows that Clemens had "only half escaped the genteel tradition, one of whose pre-eminent characteristics was an optimism undaunted by disheartening truth."[18]

We can extend this insight to Mark Twain's use of the degradation ceremony. So often, degradation ceremonies end like the tarring and feathering of the King and the Duke, in which the victims are degraded to the level of subhuman creatures (chap. 33). Rarely, as Wyatt-Brown observes, do they end like the one involving Colonel Sherburn, where the would-be victim excoriates the mob rather than the mob "degrading" the victim.[19] In the Wilks and Phelps episodes, the depressing aspects of the degradation ceremonies are relieved by the complex revelations Mark Twain makes through them. He scoops honey from the carcass of a lion and taunts us, like Samson, with a riddle (cf. Judges 14:5–12). If we fail to solve his riddle, we miss the deeper meaning of Jim's "Calvary."

Notes

1. Ralph Ellison, *Shadow and Act* (New York: New American Library, 1966) 65.

2. Winthrop D. Jordan, *White over Black: American Attitudes toward the Negro, 1550–1812* (Chapel Hill: U of North Carolina P, 1968) 15.

3. Leo Marx, "Mr. Eliot, Mr. Trilling, and *Huckleberry Finn*," *American Scholar* 22 (Autumn 1953): 424–28; Kenneth S. Lynn, *Mark Twain and Southwestern Humor* (Boston: Little, Brown, 1959) 245; Walter Blair, *Mark Twain and Huck Finn* (Berkeley: U of California P, 1960) 350; Henry Nash Smith, *Mark Twain: The Development of a Writer* (1962; New York: Atheneum, 1974) 133; Chadwick Hansen, "The Character of Jim and the Ending of *Huckleberry Finn*," *Massachusetts Review* 5 (Autumn 1963): 58–62; Louis D. Rubin, Jr., "Mark Twain's South: Tom and Huck," in *The American South: Portrait of a Culture,* ed. Louis D. Rubin, Jr. (Baton Rouge: Louisiana State UP, 1980) 204.

4. Harold Beaver, "Run, Nigger, Run: *Adventures of Huckleberry Finn* as a Fugitive Slave Narrative," *Journal of American Studies* 8 (Dec. 1974): 351.

5. Bertram Wyatt-Brown, *Southern Honor: Ethics and Behavior in the Old South* (New York: Oxford UP, 1982) 402, 406, 435–42, passim.

6. Harold Garfinkel, "Conditions of Successful Degradation Ceremonies," *American Journal of Sociology* 51 (Mar. 1956): 421–22.

7. Garfinkel 420–24.

8. Wyatt-Brown 406.

9. Wyatt-Brown 402–3.

10. Wyatt-Brown 436–37.

11. Wyatt-Brown 440, 453.

12. Hansen 59–60.

13. Marx 429–30. Although Hansen's article was published later than Marx's, Marx acknowledged his debt to Hansen's then-unpublished essay. See his fn. 5, p. 430.

14. Beaver 353.

15. See Lynn 208, 243; Joseph B. McCullough, "Uses of the Bible in *Huckleberry Finn*," *Mark Twain Journal* 19 (Winter 1978–79): 2–3; and Earl F. Briden, "Huck's Great Escape: Magic and Ritual," *Mark Twain Journal* 21 (Spring 1983): 17–18.

16. Beaver 349–52, 359.

17. David Brion Davis, *The Slave Power Conspiracy and the Paranoid Style* (Baton Rouge: Louisiana State UP, 1969) 68.

18. Marx 427, 432, 439.

19. Wyatt-Brown 435–36, 459–60.

Mark Twain and

the Black Challenge

Carmen Subryan

Mark Twain has often met with resentment for his seemingly negative portrayal of black characters and the use of the word "nigger" in some of his works. Partly because of an emotional reaction to this word, many people dismiss Twain as a racist and protest the use of his major novel, *Adventures of Huckleberry Finn,* as a required text in schools. But if it is at all possible to look beyond the pejorative term "nigger" and examine other works by Twain, along with his personal attempts to atone for the harm suffered by black people, one must conclude that as a mature adult Twain viewed the black situation as a moral challenge, and that he met that challenge successfully.

As a young southerner Mark Twain clearly did not feel positively toward blacks. Evidence of his negative view appears in his letters, notebooks, and early published writings. As Twain matured as a writer, however, he began to display a marked ambivalence about black people—an ambivalence that surfaced in such major works as *Tom Sawyer* (1876), *Huckleberry Finn* (1885), and *Pudd'nhead Wilson* (1894), and also in some of his shorter pieces. Mark Twain had a long way to go in outgrowing the racial attitudes of his time and place. He was born in the village of Florida, Missouri, on 30 November 1835, and was reared in the river town of Hannibal. Across the Mississippi lay Illinois, a free state but not a safe haven for blacks: there were slave hunters there, backed by the Fugitive Slave Acts passed by Congress. Everybody knew there could be freedom somewhere for blacks, but in Hannibal slavery was the way of life. Twain later recalled:

> In my schoolboy days I had no aversion to slavery. I was not aware that
> there was anything wrong about it. No one arraigned it in my hearing;
> the local papers said nothing against it; the local pulpit taught us that
> God approved it, that it was a holy thing, and that the doubter need only
> look in the Bible if he wished to settle his mind—and then the texts were
> read aloud to us to make the matter sure; if the slaves themselves had an
> aversion to slavery, they were wise and said nothing.[1]

Slavery was familiar and occasionally brutal. His family could sometimes afford household servants, and he remembered his father whipping one of them. In his late years he struggled with the surroundings of his boyhood and tried, somewhat incongruously at times, to see them as relatively benign. He wrote in his autobiography: "I vividly remember seeing a dozen black men and women chained to one another, once, and lying in a group on the pavement, awaiting shipment to the Southern slave market. Those were the saddest faces I have ever seen. Chained slaves could not have been a common sight, or this picture would not have made so strong and lasting an impression on me."[2] In *Following the Equator* (1897), the sight of a hotel servant in Bombay slapped for some minor mistake reminded Twain of Hannibal, where "this was the *usual* way of explaining one's desires to a slave. . . . [T]hose unresented cuffings made me sorry for the victim and ashamed for the punisher." And then he recalled a shocking incident:

> When I was ten years old I saw a man fling a lump of iron-ore at a slave-
> man in anger, for merely doing something awkwardly—as if that were a
> crime. It bounded from the man's skull, and the man fell and never spoke
> again. He was dead in an hour. I knew the man had the right to kill his
> slave if he wanted to, and yet it seemed a pitiful thing and somehow
> wrong, though why wrong I was not deep enough to explain if I had
> been asked to do it. Nobody in the village approved of that murder, but
> of course no one said much about it. (Vol. 2, chap. 2)

When Twain left Hannibal in 1853 (at the age of seventeen) to work as a journeyman printer in St. Louis, New York, and Philadelphia, he took his hometown prejudices with him. He wrote his family from New York on August 24, 1853: "I reckon I had better black my face, for in these Eastern States niggers are [judged] considerably better than white people."[3] But as with every human being who matures, a variety of influences forced Mark Twain to face the shadows lurking in his past and dispel them. The issue of slavery was an increasingly important shadow that he had to struggle with.

From 1857 to 1861 he worked first as a cub pilot, then as a full-fledged pilot on river steamboats; he left the river in early May 1861 when the Civil War ended the river trade and his career. Then twenty-five years old, he joined the Marion Rangers, an irregular Confederate unit that was disbanded a few weeks later. He afterward recalled his service, in "The Private History of a Campaign That Failed," as a time of fear and discomfort, when he and his friends shot a stranger from ambush. At best, his service was brief and unheroic, and the depth of his Confederate sentiment seems doubtful.

In July 1861 he accompanied his brother, Orion, to Nevada. Orion had received a commission signed by President Lincoln to serve as the first secretary of the new territory of Nevada. After attempts at mining and prospecting, Mark Twain began a newspaper career. He joined the *Territorial Enterprise* and later worked on the *San Francisco Morning Call*. In 1866 he was able to get a commission from the *Sacramento Union* to go to the Sandwich Islands (now Hawaii) to write a series of letters for its columns. The series was a success; he returned to San Francisco after a few months and began what would be a second triumphant career, as a popular lecturer. The *Union* letters led to a similar commission from the *San Francisco Alta California* to write a series on travels that took him back to the East Coast (by two steamships, with a trip overland across the isthmus at Nicaragua). After some weeks in New York he won the support of the *Alta* and other papers to continue his travel correspondence by joining a tour of Europe and the Near East originally arranged by Henry Ward Beecher's Plymouth Church. On 8 June 1867 he sailed from New York aboard the steamship *Quaker City* on an excursion that would become the basis for his first best-seller, *The Innocents Abroad*, published in 1869. The sight of new cultures and customs must have broadened Twain's outlook. He commented in his notebooks about the enlightened practices of the Moroccans in their treatment of slaves; and in *The Innocents Abroad* (chap. 23) he described a black man who had grown up free, far from a racist society:

> The guide I have spoken of is the only one we have had yet who knew anything. He was born in South Carolina, of slave parents. They came to Venice while he was an infant. He has grown up here. He is well

educated. He reads, writes, and speaks English, Italian, Spanish, and French, with perfect facility; is a worshipper of art and thoroughly conversant with it; knows the history of Venice by heart and never tires of talking of her illustrious career. He dressed better than any of us, I think, and is daintily polite. Negroes are deemed as good as white people, in Venice, and so this man feels no desire to go back to his native land. His judgment is correct.[4]

A far more important influence came after the cruise, when he met, courted, and married Olivia Langdon, sister of eighteen-year-old Charles Langdon, a companion on the tour. Olivia's family were prominent citizens in the town of Elmira, New York, and staunch abolitionists; their home had been a station on the Underground Railroad. Olivia's father, Jervis Langdon, was a wealthy mine owner and coal dealer who maintained his family in style in a mansion downtown. He was a charter member of the Independent Congregational Church of Elmira, composed largely of persons who had withdrawn from the First Presbyterian Church over the issue of slavery. Twain's marriage to Olivia in 1870 signaled a change for the better in his perception of black people. Her influence was pervasive in every facet of his life, including his writing, which she sometimes edited, and was supplemented by the wholesome influences of Twain's friend William Dean Howells, editor of the *Atlantic Monthly,* and liberal writers such as Harriet Beecher Stowe and Charles Dudley Warner, Twain's neighbors when he moved to Hartford, Connecticut, in 1871.

Apart from the influence of family and friends, one senses a further change in Mark Twain as he entered middle age. The ribaldry of his youth, including a love of the southwestern humor so detrimental to the black image, was now tempered. After 1869 Twain no longer, when speaking for himself, referred in print to black people as "niggers"; and although characters use the word in some of his major works, the effect is to show the limitations of those who used it. Still, Twain's changed perception of black people was neither instant nor total. It involved a series of progressions and regressions which resulted in the ambivalent portrayals of blacks that have fueled the continuing controversy over *Huckleberry Finn* and, to a lesser extent, other works by Twain.

Before 1876, when Twain published *Tom Sawyer,* he had made passing references to blacks in works such as *The Innocents Abroad* (1869), *Roughing It* (1872), and *The Gilded Age* (1873; written in collaboration with Charles Dudley Warner). These few references are a mixed bag, sometimes sympathetic and sometimes minstrel-type humor at blacks' expense. In 1874, however, he published "A True Story, Repeated Word for Word as I Heard It," based on the recollections of Mary Ann Cord, then seventy-six years old and a cook in the household of Susan Langdon Crane (Olivia's adopted sister) and her husband, Theodore.[5] Although this short story has often been quoted to demonstrate Mark Twain's sympathy for slaves, one should note what he said shortly after writing the story, when he forwarded it to William Dean Howells for the *Atlantic:* "I enclose also a 'True Story' which has no humor in it. You can pay as lightly as you choose for that, if you want it, for it is rather out of my line. I have not altered the old colored woman's story except to begin it at the beginning, instead of the middle, as she did and traveled both ways."[6] From this letter it appears that Twain thought little of the story, or perhaps of his retelling of it; he had little experience in this line of pathos. He claims to have added little or nothing of his own in his treatment of this black character, Aunt Rachel. Twain relates that, when asked how it was that she had lived so long without encountering trouble in her life, she told how her family had been sold one by one—even Henry, her youngest son, from whom she was separated only by brutal force. Years later she was reunited with Henry, who, then a Union soldier, was guarding the house at which she was a cook. Aunt Rachel's heart-rending words at the end are richly ironic: "Oh, no Misto C——, *I* hain't had no trouble. An' no *joy!*" This conclusion not only demonstrates the tragedy hidden deep within Aunt Rachel's soul, but also celebrates her triumphant resilience of spirit.

Mainly because it was considered a boys' book, *Tom Sawyer* made only a small stir in the serious literary world; but it represented an important stage in the author's development. This stage was important because Mark Twain was still functioning partly as a product of his environment; he was a southerner in whom the twin evils of racial prejudice and regional chauvinism were interwoven. Careful examination of the novel reveals that Twain's few references to blacks are wholly incidental, with no real attempt to portray character. For instance, when Tom is forced to whitewash the fence as punishment, he tries vainly at first to cajole the other children passing by into doing his job. As they saunter down the street to the well, Twain observes: "White, mulatto, negro boys and girls were always there waiting their turns, resting, trading playthings, quarreling, fighting, skylarking" (chap. 2). Tom almost prevails upon Jim, a young black boy, to whitewash the fence, but Aunt Polly, who has secretly witnessed the conversation, descends on the unsuspecting Jim, slipper in hand. In this first reference to blacks in *Tom Sawyer*, Twain portrays an easy-going, natural, and unprejudiced relationship between youths of both races.

This first description, however, differs significantly from the second reference to blacks, this time by Tom. When Huck is skeptical about Tom's assertion that "spunk-water" will cure warts, Tom asks if he has ever tried it. Huck concedes that he has not, but has heard indirectly about Bob Tanner's doing so:

> "Why, he told Jeff Thatcher, and Jeff told Johnny Baker, and Johnny told Jim Hollis, and Jim told Ben Rodgers, and Ben told a nigger, and the nigger told me. There now!"
>
> "Well, what of it? They'll all lie. Leastways all but the nigger. I don't know *him*. But I never knowed a nigger that *wouldn't* lie." (Chap. 6)

This is just a conversation between two young boys in slave times, and Tom's sweeping generalization merely groups blacks as a class with the white companions he names. Nonetheless, Tom is mindlessly reinforcing a racial stereotype, and the irony on Twain's part is at best ambiguous.

In *Huckleberry Finn,* Twain's most controversial novel (and the one with which we are principally concerned here), one can see clearly how Jim, the Negro slave, emerges not only as a comic figure but also as a sensitive, caring human being. At the beginning he acts the part of the buffoon. He appears as a big, lazy, good-for-nothing, lounging sleepily in the doorway of Miss Watson's house. Upon hearing a sound caused by Huck and Tom, Jim investigates but, finding nothing, decides to wait for the noise to recur. Soon he is again fast asleep, and Tom cannot resist the temptation to slip Jim's hat off his head and hang it on a branch. A faithful stereotype of the superstitious slave, Jim later elaborates considerably on the incident, telling everyone that witches removed his hat after riding him all over the state. According to Huck, Jim's superiority over the other slaves is so established that they travel from miles around to hear him relate his story; Jim has become "most ruined, for a servant, because he got so stuck up on account of having seen the devil and been rode by witches" (chap. 2).

As Twain's portrayal evolves, we find Jim on Jackson's Island fighting for his dignity as a human being, yet Twain still portrays him as a buffoon who is the butt of Huck's jokes. When Huck kills a rattlesnake, he places the carcass near Jim's blanket, causing the snake's mate to bite Jim. Later, as the two outcasts journey downstream, they talk of various subjects and Huck tries to get Jim to understand abstract reasoning. However, Jim cannot comprehend the wisdom in King Solomon's decision to settle an argument over the ownership of a baby by proposing that the child be chopped in two. Neither can Jim understand the idea of human beings speaking different languages. He reasons that a cat and a cow cannot "talk" the same language because they are different animals, but since human beings are all the same, they should all speak alike. Unable to answer Jim's logic, Huck dismisses it: "I see it warn't no use wasting words— you can't learn a nigger to argue. So I quit" (chap. 14). Huck's statement, despite the irony of Jim's actually having bested him in the argument, is damaging because it portrays Jim as a fool and, at least superficially, supports a broader misconception of black people as incapable of reason (and thus not fully human).

In the series of separations and reunions that occur as the two companions move downstream, their camaraderie deepens; yet Huck continues to treat Jim as if he were a fool. The crucial reunion is in chapter 15, after Jim has given Huck up for lost in a storm: "Goodness gracious, is dat you, Huck? En you ain' dead—you ain' drownded—you's back agin? It's too good for true, honey, it's too good for true. Lemme look at you, chile, lemme feel o' you. No, you ain' dead! you's back agin, 'live en soun', jis de same ole Huck—de same ole Huck, thanks to goodness!" (chap. 15). Huck responds by pretending the separation was only a dream, and Jim at first is confused, until he sees trash from the storm on the raft and rebukes Huck by reminding him of their bond of caring and concern, which Huck has turned into a joke. Describing the event from a later and more mature perspective, Huck says: "It was fifteen minutes before I could work myself up to go and humble myself to a nigger—but I done it, and I warn't ever sorry for it afterwards, neither. I didn't do him no more mean tricks, and I wouldn't done that one if I'd a knowed it would make him feel that way." In fairness to Mark Twain, this incident is a turning point in his portrayal of Jim, who at last has evolved from a stereotypical buffoon into a sensitive human being. Yet Twain displays tremendous ambivalence as to the final resolution of Jim's character, for at the end of the novel Twain reduces him again to the character of buffoon, with Tom Sawyer playing the cruelest trick on him: postponing his freedom and making a joke of it. Far worse, Twain himself played the final episodes for laughs on his lecture tours, and thought he had done well.

As late as 1894, when *Pudd'nhead Wilson* was published, the same (or a worse) stereotypical and ambivalent portrayal of a black character resurfaced. In this later novel the reader encounters the slave Roxy:

> Only one-sixteenth of her was black, and that sixteenth did not show. . . . Her complexion was very fair, with the rosy glow of vigorous health in the cheeks, her face was full of character and expression, her eyes were brown and liquid, and she had a heavy suit of fine soft hair which was also brown, but the fact was not apparent because her head was bound about with a checkered handkerchief and the hair was concealed under it. (Chap. 2)

Roxy fits exactly the nineteenth-century description of the tragic mulatto rejected by blacks and whites alike. Because of her white appearance she cannot come to terms with her blackness. At the beginning of the novel she spars verbally with Jasper, whom Twain describes as "young, coal-black, and of magnificent build." When Jasper makes known his desire to court Roxy, she responds: "*You* is, you black mud-cat! Yah-yah-yah! I got somep'n' better to do den 'sociat'n wid niggers as black as you is." And she declares jokingly that if she owned Jasper, she would sell him down the river (chap. 2).

Roxy's baby, Chambers, is one thirty-second black, and only she can tell him from her master's child, Tom Driscoll. As chapter 3 opens, she has seen a terrifying reminder that slaves can be disposed of at their masters' whims, even sold into the hell of the plantations down the river that she taunted Jasper with. Someday this could happen to her own child: "The thought crazed her with horror." To protect him from such a fate, she switches the two babies in their cradles, so Chambers becomes Tom, a slave master, and white Tom becomes the new Chambers, a slave. The consequences are disastrous; her son is spoiled, corrupted, and made brutal by the position she has given him. Caught between two races, Roxy is mistreated, disowned, and ultimately sold down the river herself by the very son for whom she has fought the white world. At the end of the novel she is a broken, lifeless individual whose only solace is religion.

Ironically, Chambers, the real Driscoll heir, becomes another tragic mulatto, who during slavery is often mistreated by both whites and blacks. Chambers becomes Tom's bodyguard and the whipping boy on whom Tom cruelly vents his frustration and anger. Even when Chambers saves Tom from drowning, Tom attacks him with a knife. Then, after Chambers is reinstated as the rightful heir to the Driscoll fortune, he cannot adapt to life in a white environment. He prefers the company of the slaves with whom he has associated for over twenty years, but now their company is forbidden.

Twain's portrayal of Roxy is ambivalent. The reader cannot decide whether Twain agrees with the laws under which a drop of "black" blood makes a person black, or is ridiculing those laws. Sterling Brown, poet and author, says the novel "falls a great way" because it leaves many readers believing that Twain agreed with Roxy's assessment of her son: "one drop of 'black' blood tainted a person's character for life."[7] The duality of possible interpretation again leaves Twain open to some critics' charges that he was a racist.

In his public life Mark Twain spoke favorably of significant black figures of the day and lectured on "black" platforms on behalf of black causes. He also paid the tuition of at least one black man through Yale Law School; his friend William Dean Howells reported on the episode: "He held himself responsible for the wrong which the white race had done the black race in slavery, and, he explained . . . he was doing it as part of the reparation due from every white to every black man."[8] In 1881, Twain, stating that he was proud to number Frederick Douglass among his personal friends, communicated to President-elect James Garfield, for whom he had once campaigned, his desire to see Douglass retain his position as marshal of the District of Columbia. No doubt Twain's intervention on behalf of Douglass facilitated Douglass's reappointment, though not to the position he had held for four years; instead he became recorder of deeds for the District of Columbia. Also, Twain, who had met Booker T. Washington in London, spoke at Carnegie Hall on behalf of Washington's Tuskegee Educational Institute.

Along with these personal attempts at reparation, Twain wrote several pieces in his later years revealing his concern over relations between the races. One of these pieces is *Which Was It?*, a little-known novel Twain began in 1899 and left uncompleted in 1902.[9] In this novel, Jasper, a defiant mulatto who has been badly used by his white master, by chance sees his master commit a murder. He conceals the information until he learns that his master has come into a large inheritance, then uses the information to make his master his slave.

Arthur G. Pettit, one of the few critics to examine *Which Was It?* in detail, devotes to the novel a chapter titled "From Stage Nigger to Mulatto Superman: The End of Nigger Jim and the Rise of Jasper."[10] To Pettit, Jasper is "the logical extension" of comments Twain wrote down privately about where he thought racial animosities might lead. Pettit asserts that Jasper "lacks compassion, and he is capable of forceful action" and that his "plot to 's'rivel' up as many members of the white race as he can through a step-by-step process of intrigue, intimidation, and brute force has a jarring note of reality to it."[11] He sums up Jasper as symbolic of the beginning of black power in the twentieth century and sounds this ominous warning: "If we put this man of mixed blood together with Clemens' dire notebook predictions about the future overthrow of the white race, we come up with a South turned on its ear. To take Jasper seriously as a symbol is to hear Mark Twain saying there will be no reconciliation of black and white. There will be nothing but bigotry, hatred, and violence."[12]

Alongside *Which Was It?* and its bold, defiant picture of a vengeful black man stand Mark Twain's editorials on lynching, which he attacked both early and late in his career as a prominent writer. As a matter of fact, Twain intended to write a book about lynching in America; he had even collected some material toward the study, but was dissuaded from his endeavor by his publisher, Frank Bliss, who described the project as foolhardy. In an early editorial, published in 1869, Twain is bitterly ironic as he denounces the "cold-blooded Yankee civilization" for hanging an innocent black man who had supposedly raped a young white woman a few years earlier. The guilty person confessed after the man had been hanged. With scathing irony Twain describes the mob concept which made the hanging possible as "a little blunder in the administration of justice by Southern mob law; but nothing to speak of. Only 'a nigger' killed by mistake"[13]—a notable forerunner of Huck Finn's remark to Aunt Sally that while no one was hurt in the steamboat accident, "a nigger" was killed. Another short essay, "The United States of Lyncherdom," published posthumously in 1923, twenty-two years after it was written, demonstrates clearly Twain's disgust with lynching, which he called a vile, cowardly act.[14] He also depicts a lynch mob with contempt in chapter 22 of *Huckleberry Finn,* though in this case the intended victim, a white man, drives off the mob with bitter sarcasm and a shotgun.

Conspicuous among Twain's writings on behalf of black people is his forceful essay titled "King Leopold's Soliloquy."[15] This work, which Twain wrote at the suggestion of E. D. Morel, director of the Congo Reform Organization in England, denounces in graphic detail the atrocities in the Congo; it was so contrary to popular opinion that at first no American publisher would touch it. In the booklet, Twain imagines King Leopold of Belgium hypocritically bemoaning the fact that other countries have exposed the slavery, looting, rape, mutilation, and death he has brought to the Congo, but they refuse to give him credit for the blessings of religion he piously claims to have given the backward masses. King Leopold reads aloud from reports documenting atrocities which outsiders have witnessed, and he tries in vain to refute them.

Placing these lesser-known works beside popular earlier pieces such as *Tom Sawyer* and *Huckleberry Finn* leads to a more balanced view of Mark Twain, who was in reality a more complex figure than many believe. Examination of Twain's portrayal of blacks in his works reveals a tremendous inconsistency. One has to admit, however, that late in his life the black cause became prominent in the consciousness of Mark Twain, this man who had traveled so far from his southern roots. In facing its challenge he came to the difficult realization not only that slavery was inhumane but also that black people were human beings. William Dean Howells recognized how much Twain had overcome in his background: "He was the most desouthernized Southerner I ever knew. No man more perfectly sensed and more entirely abhorred slavery."[16] If Twain failed to escape completely from his own times, he was well in advance of them; he still has much to say to those in our time who have not learned.

The lessons are in his works, sometimes stated boldly and forthrightly—as in his attacks on the physical abuse, enslavement, and murder of blacks—and sometimes implied quite as strongly, though indirectly. Time after time, Huck Finn is surprised to find that blacks have feelings like those of whites: love for their families, concern for younger persons, anger and pain when this concern is made the matter of a joke. After Huck learned this lesson, Twain apparently forgot it, demeaning the importance of Jim's freedom when he let Tom Sawyer take over the ending of the book. We may feel uncomfortable when Twain forgets himself this way, and wince at the language in *Huckleberry Finn,* but it is clear that Twain was doing his best, as a man of his time, to respect and support the humanity of black Americans.

Notes

1. *Mark Twain's Autobiography,* 2 vols., ed. Albert Bigelow Paine (New York: Harper & Brothers, 1924) 2:101.

2. *Autobiography* 2: 124.

3. *Mark Twain's Letters,* vol. 1: *1853–1866,* ed. Edgar Marquess Branch, Michael B. Frank, and Kenneth M. Sanderson (Berkeley: U of California P, 1988) 4.

4. A notebook entry from June 1867, when Twain was in Tangier, shows some of the openness to new ideas evidenced in the passage from *The Innocents Abroad,* but also shows that he still had something to learn: "Many of the blacks are slaves to the Moors:—when they can read first chapter of Koran, can no longer be slaves;—would have been well to adopt educational test for nigger vote in America." "Relation of master with female slave frees her." See *Mark Twain's Notebook,* Authorized Edition, ed. Albert Bigelow Paine (New York: Harper & Brothers, 1935) 65.

5. Reprinted in Mark Twain, *Sketches New and Old* (1875), available in various editions.

6. *Mark Twain–Howells Letters,* 2 vols., ed. Henry Nash Smith and William H. Gibson (Cambridge, Mass.: Belknap P of Harvard UP, 1960) 1: 22–23.

7. Sterling Brown, "Negro Characters as Seen by White Authors," *Journal of Negro Education* (Jan. 1933): 180–201.

8. William Dean Howells, *My Mark Twain: Reminiscences and Criticisms* (New York: Harper & Brothers, 1910) 35.

9. Published in *Mark Twain's "Which Was the Dream?" and Other Symbolic Writings of the Later Years,* ed. with an introduction by John S. Tuckey (Berkeley: U of California P, 1967) 177–429.

10. Arthur G. Pettit, *Mark Twain and the South* (Lexington: U of Kentucky P, 1974). [Contrary to the impression given by Pettit's chapter title, "Nigger Jim" is a name used by some critics but nowhere to be found in *Huckleberry Finn.* Possibly Theodore Dreiser's short story "Nigger Jeff" played some role in the confusion among critics on this point; see also David Smith's brief commentary on the misapplied appellation—ED.]

11. Pettit 172.

12. Pettit 173.

13. Facsimile reprint in Milton Meltzer, *Mark Twain Himself* (New York: Bonanza, 1960) 127.

14. Reprinted in Janet Smith, ed., *Mark Twain and the Damned Human Race* (New York: Hill & Wang, 1960) 96–104.

15. Reprinted in Janet Smith 181–93.

16. Howells 35.

Huck, Jim, and American Racial Discourse

David L. Smith

> They [blacks] are at least as brave, and more adventuresome [compared with whites]. But this may perhaps proceed from a want of forethought, which prevents their seeing a danger till it be present. . . . They are more ardent after their female: but love seems with them to be more an eager desire, than a tender delicate mixture of sentiment and sensation. Their griefs are transient. Those numberless afflictions, which render it doubtful whether heaven has given life to us in mercy or in wrath, are less felt, and sooner forgotten with them. In general, their existence appears to participate more of sensation than reflection. To this must be ascribed their disposition to sleep when abstracted from their diversions, and unemployed in labor.
>
> —Thomas Jefferson, *Notes on the State of Virginia*[1]

Almost any Euro-American intellectual of the nineteenth century could have written the preceding words. The notion of Negro inferiority was so deeply pervasive among those heirs of "The Enlightenment" that the categories and even the vocabulary of Negro inferiority were formalized into a tedious, unmodulated litany. This uniformity increased rather than diminished during the course of the century. As Leon Litwack and others have shown, even the abolitionists, who actively opposed slavery, frequently regarded blacks as inherently inferior. This helps to explain the widespread popularity of colonization schemes among abolitionists and other liberals.[2] As for Jefferson, it is not surprising that he held such ideas, but it is impressive that he formulated so clearly at the end of the eighteenth century what would become the dominant view of the Negro in the nine-

teenth century. In many ways this father of American democracy—
and quite possibly of five mulatto children—was a man of his time
and ahead of his time.[3]

In July 1876, exactly one century after the American Declaration
of Independence, Mark Twain began writing *Adventures of Huckleberry Finn,* a novel that illustrates trenchantly the social limitations
that American "civilization" imposes on individual freedom.[4] The
book takes special note of ways in which racism impinges upon the
lives of Afro-Americans, even when they are legally "free." It is therefore ironic that *Huckleberry Finn* has often been attacked and even
censored as a racist work. I would argue, on the contrary, that except
for Melville's work, *Huckleberry Finn* is without peer among major
Euro-American novels for its explicitly antiracist stance.[5] Those who
brand the book racist generally do so without having considered the
specific form of racial discourse to which the novel responds. Furthermore, *Huckleberry Finn* offers much more than the typical liberal
defenses of "human dignity" and protests against cruelty. Though it
contains some such elements, it is more fundamentally a critique of
those socially constituted fictions—most notably romanticism, religion, and the concept of "the Negro"—which serve to justify and
disguise selfish, cruel, and exploitative behavior.

When I speak of "racial discourse," I mean more than simply
attitudes about race or conventions of talking about race. Most importantly, I mean that race itself is a discursive formation which
delimits social relations on the basis of alleged physical differences.[6]
"Race" is a strategy for relegating a segment of the population to a
permanent inferior status. It functions by insisting that each "race"
has specific, definitive, inherent behavioral tendencies and capacities
which distinguish it from other races. Though scientifically specious,
race has been powerfully effective as an ideology and as a form of
social definition that serves the interests of Euro-American hegemony. In America, race has been deployed against numerous groups,
including Native Americans, Jews, Asians, and even—for brief periods—an assortment of European immigrants.

For obvious reasons, however, the primary emphasis historically
has been on defining "the Negro" as a deviant from Euro-American
norms. "Race" in America means white supremacy and black inferiority,[7] and "the Negro," a socially constituted fiction, is a generalized,
one-dimensional surrogate for the historical reality of Afro-American
people. It is this reified fiction that Twain attacks in *Huckleberry Finn.*

Twain adopts a strategy of subversion in his attack on race. That is, he focuses on a number of commonplaces associated with "the Negro" and then systematically dramatizes their inadequacy. He uses the term "nigger," and he shows Jim engaging in superstitious behavior. Yet he portrays Jim as a compassionate, shrewd, thoughtful, self-sacrificing, and even wise man. Indeed, his portrayal of Jim contradicts every claim presented in Jefferson's description of "the Negro." Jim is cautious, he gives excellent advice, he suffers persistent anguish over separation from his wife and children, and he even sacrifices his own sleep so that Huck may rest. Jim, in short, exhibits all the qualities that "the Negro" supposedly lacks. Twain's conclusions do more than merely subvert the justifications of slavery, which was already long since abolished. Twain began his book during the final disintegration of Reconstruction, and his satire on antebellum southern bigotry is also an implicit response to the Negrophobic climate of the post-Reconstruction era.[8] It is troubling, therefore, that so many readers have completely misunderstood Twain's subtle attack on racism.

Twain's use of the term "nigger" has provoked some readers to reject the novel.[9] As one of the most offensive words in our vocabulary, "nigger" remains heavily shrouded in taboo. A careful assessment of this term within the context of American racial discourse, however, will allow us to understand the particular way in which the author uses it. If we attend closely to Twain's use of the word, we may find in it not just a trigger to outrage but, more important, a means of understanding the precise nature of American racism and Mark Twain's attack on it.

Most obviously, Twain uses "nigger" throughout the book as a synonym for "slave." There is ample evidence from other sources that this corresponds to one usage common during the antebellum period. We first encounter it in reference to "Miss Watson's big nigger, named Jim" (chap. 2). This usage, like the term "nigger stealer," clearly designates the "nigger" as an item of property: a commodity, a slave. This passage also provides the only apparent textual justification for the common critical practice of labeling Jim "Nigger Jim," as if "nigger" were a part of his proper name. This loathsome habit goes back at least as far as Albert Bigelow Paine's biography of Twain (1912).[10] In any case, "nigger" in this sense connotes an inferior, even subhuman, creature who is properly owned by and subservient to Euro-Americans.

Both Huck and Jim use the word in this sense. For example, when Huck fabricates his tale about the riverboat accident, the following exchange occurs between him and Aunt Sally:

> "Good gracious! anybody hurt?"
> "No'm. Killed a nigger."
> "Well, it's lucky; because sometimes people do get hurt." (Chap. 32)

Huck has never met Aunt Sally prior to this scene, and in spinning a lie which this stranger will find unobjectionable, he correctly assumes that the common notion of Negro subhumanity will be appropriate. Huck's offhand remark is intended to exploit Aunt Sally's attitudes, not to express Huck's own. A nigger, Aunt Sally confirms, is not a person. Yet this exchange is hilarious precisely because we know that Huck is playing on her glib and conventional bigotry. We know that Huck's relationship to Jim has already invalidated for him such obtuse racial notions. The conception of the "nigger" is a socially constituted and sanctioned fiction, and it is just as false and absurd as Huck's explicit fabrication, which Aunt Sally also swallows whole.

In fact, the exchange between Huck and Aunt Sally reveals a great deal about how racial discourse operates. Its function is to promulgate a conception of "the Negro" as a subhuman and expendable creature who is by definition feeble-minded, immoral, lazy, and superstitious. One crucial purpose of this social fiction is to justify the abuse and exploitation of Afro-American people by substituting the essentialist fiction of "Negroism" for the actual character of individual Afro-Americans. Hence, in racial discourse every Afro-American becomes just another instance of "the Negro"—just another "nigger." Twain recognizes this invidious tendency of race thinking, however, and he takes every opportunity to expose the mismatch between racial abstractions and real human beings.

For example, when Pap drunkenly inveighs against the free mulatto from Ohio, he is outraged by what appears to him to be a crime against natural laws (chap. 6). In the first place, a "free nigger" is, for Pap, a contradiction in terms. Indeed, the man's clothes, his demeanor, his education, his profession, and even his silver-headed cane bespeak a social status normally achieved by only a small elite of white men. He is, in other words, a "nigger" who refuses to behave like one. Pap's ludicrous protestations discredit both himself and other believers in "the Negro," as many critics have noted. But it has not been sufficiently stressed that Pap's racial views correspond very closely to those of most of his white southern contemporaries, in substance if not in manner of expression. Such views were held not only by poor whites but by all "right-thinking" southerners, regardless of their social class. Indeed, not even the traumas of the Civil War could cure southerners of this folly. Furthermore, Pap's indignation at the Negro's right to vote is precisely analogous to the southern backlash against the enfranchisement of Afro-Americans during Reconstruction. Finally, Pap's comments are rather mild compared with the anti-Negro diatribes that were beginning to emerge among politicians even as Twain was writing *Huckleberry Finn*. He began writing this novel during the final days of Reconstruction, and it seems more than reasonable to assume that the shameful white supremacist bluster of that epoch—exemplified by Pap's tirade—informed Twain's critique of racism in *Huckleberry Finn*.[11]

Pap's final description of this Ohio gentleman as "a prowling, thieving, infernal, white-shirted free nigger" (chap. 6) almost totally contradicts his previous description of the man as a proud, elegant, dignified figure. Yet this contradiction is perfectly consistent with Pap's need to reassert "the Negro" in lieu of social reality. Despite the vulgarity of Pap's personal character, his thinking about race is highly conventional, and therefore respectable. But most of us cannot respect Pap's views, and when we reject them, we reject the standard racial discourse of both 1840 and 1880.

A reader who objects to the word "nigger" might still insist that Twain could have avoided using it. But it is difficult to imagine how Twain could have debunked a discourse without using the specific terms of that discourse. Even when Twain was writing his book, "nigger" was universally recognized as an insulting, demeaning word. According to Stuart Berg Flexner, "Negro" was generally pronounced "nigger" until about 1825, at which time abolitionists began objecting to that term.[12] They preferred "colored person" or "person of color." Hence, W. E. B. Du Bois reports that some black abolitionists of the early 1830s declared themselves united "as men, . . . not as slaves; as 'people of color,' not as 'Negroes.'"[13] Writing a generation later in *Army Life in a Black Regiment* (1869), Thomas Wentworth Higginson deplored the common use of "nigger" among freedmen, which he regarded as evidence of low self-esteem.[14] The objections to "nigger," then, are not a consequence of the modern sensibility but had been common for a half century before *Huckleberry Finn* was published. The specific function of this term in the book, however, is neither to offend nor merely to provide linguistic authenticity. Much more importantly, it establishes a context against which Jim's specific virtues may emerge as explicit refutations of racist presuppositions.

Of course, the concept of "nigger" entails far more than just the deployment of certain vocabulary. Most of the attacks on the book focus on its alleged perpetuation of racial stereotypes. Twain does indeed use racial stereotypes here. That practice could be excused as characteristic of the genre of humor within which Twain works. Frontier humor relies upon the use of stock types, and consequently racial stereotypes are just one of many types present in *Huckleberry Finn*. Yet while valid, such an appeal to generic convention would be unsatisfactory because it would deny Twain the credit he deserves for the sophistication of his perceptions.[15]

As a serious critic of American society, Twain recognized that racial discourse depends upon the deployment of a system of stereotypes which constitute "the Negro" as fundamentally different from and inferior to Euro-Americans. As with his handling of "nigger," Twain's strategy with racial stereotypes is to elaborate them in order to undermine them. To be sure, those critics are correct who have argued that Twain uses this narrative to reveal Jim's humanity. Jim, however, is just one individual. Twain uses the narrative to expose the cruelty and hollowness of that racial discourse which exists only to obscure the humanity of *all* Afro-American people.

One aspect of *Huckleberry Finn* that has elicited copious critical commentary is Twain's use of superstition.[16] In nineteenth-century racial discourse, "the Negro" was always defined as inherently superstitious.[17] Many critics, therefore, have cited Jim's superstitious behavior as an instance of negative stereotyping. One cannot deny that in this respect Jim closely resembles the entire tradition of comic darkies,[18] but in some instances apparent similarities conceal fundamental differences. The issue is: does Twain merely reiterate clichés, or does he use these conventional patterns to make an unconventional point? A close examination will show that, in virtually every instance, Twain uses Jim's superstition to make points that undermine rather than revalidate the dominant racial discourse.

The first incident of this superstitious behavior occurs in chapter 2, as a result of one of Tom Sawyer's pranks. When Jim falls asleep under a tree, Tom hangs Jim's hat on a branch. Subsequently Jim concocts an elaborate tale about having been hexed and ridden by witches. The tale grows more grandiose with each repetition, and eventually Jim becomes a local celebrity, sporting a five-cent piece on a string around his neck as a talisman. "Niggers would come miles to hear Jim tell about it, and he was more looked up to than any nigger in that country," the narrator reports. Jim's celebrity finally reaches the point that "Jim was most ruined, for a servant, because he got so stuck up on account of having seen the devil and been rode by witches." That is, no doubt, amusing. Yet whether Jim believes his own tale or not—and the "superstitious Negro" thesis requires us to assume that he does—the fact remains that Jim clearly benefits from becoming more a celebrity and less a "servant." It is his owner, not Jim, who suffers when Jim reduces the amount of his uncompensated labor.[19]

This incident has often been interpreted as an example of risible Negro gullibility and ignorance as exemplified by blackface minstrelsy. Such a reading has more than a little validity, but it can only partially account for the implications of this scene. If not for the final sentence, such an account might seem wholly satisfactory, but the information that Jim becomes, through his own story telling, unsuited for life as a slave introduces unexpected complications. Is it likely that Jim has been deceived by his own creative prevarications—especially given what we learn about his character subsequently? Or has he cleverly exploited the conventions of "Negro superstition" in order to turn a silly boy's prank to his own advantage?

Regardless of whether we credit Jim with forethought in this matter, it is undeniable that he turns Tom's attempt to humiliate him into a major personal triumph. In other words, Tom gives him an inch, and he takes an ell. It is also obvious that he does so by exercising remarkable skills as a rhetorician. By constructing a fictitious narrative of his own experience, Jim elevates himself above his prescribed station in life. By becoming, in effect, an author, Jim writes himself a new destiny. Jim's triumph may appear to be dependent upon the gullibility of other "superstitious" Negroes, but since we have no direct encounter with them, we cannot know whether they are unwitting victims of Jim's ruse or not. A willing audience need not be a totally credulous one. In any case, it is intelligence, not stupidity, that facilitates Jim's triumph. Tom may have had his chuckle, but the last laugh clearly belongs to Jim.

In assessing Jim's character, we should keep in mind that forethought, creativity, and shrewdness are qualities that racial dis-

course—as in the passage from Thomas Jefferson—denies to "the
Negro." In that sense, Jim's darky performance here subverts the
fundamental definition of "darky." For "the Negro" is defined to be an
object, not a subject. But does an object construct its own narrative?
Viewed in this way, the fact of superstition, which traditionally connotes ignorance and unsophistication, becomes far less important
than the ends to which superstition is put. This inference exposes,
once again, the inadequacy of a positivist epistemology, which holds,
for example, that "a rose is a rose is a rose." No one will deny the self-
evidence of a tautology; but a rose derives whatever meaning it has
from the context within which it is placed (including the context
of traditional symbolism). It is the contextualizing activity, not *das
Ding-an-sich,* which generates meaning. Again and again Twain attacks racial essentialism by directing our attention instead to the
particularity of individual action. We find that Jim is not "the Negro."
Jim is Jim, and we, like Huck, come to understand what Jim is by
attending to what he does in specific situations.

In another instance of explicitly superstitious behavior, Jim uses a
hair ball to tell Huck's fortune. One may regard this scene as a comical
example of Negro ignorance and credulity, acting in concert with the
ignorance and credulity of a fourteen-year-old white boy. That reading would allow one an unambiguous laugh at Jim's expense. If one
examines the scene carefully, however, the inadequacy of such a
reductive reading becomes apparent. Even if Jim does believe in the
supernatural powers of this hair ball, the fact remains that most of the
transaction depends upon Jim's quick wits. The soothsaying aside,
much of the exchange between Huck and Jim is an exercise in wily
and understated economic bartering. In essence, Jim wants to be paid
for his services, while Huck wants free advice. Jim insists that the hair
ball will not speak without being paid. Huck, who has a dollar, will
only admit to having a counterfeit quarter. Jim responds by pretending to be in collusion with Huck. He explains how to doctor the
quarter so that "anybody in town would take it in a minute, let alone a
hair-ball" (chap. 4). But obviously it is not the hair ball that will
benefit from acquiring and spending this counterfeit coin.[20]

In this transaction, Jim serves his own interest while appearing to
serve Huck's interest. He takes a slug which is worthless to Huck, and
through the alchemy of his own cleverness contrives to make it worth
twenty-five cents to himself. That, in antebellum America, is not a bad
price for telling a fortune. But more important, Twain shows Jim self-

consciously subverting the prescribed definition of "the Negro," even as he performs within the limitations of that role. He remains the conventional "Negro" by giving the white boy what he wants, at no real cost, and by consistently appearing to be passive and subservient to the desires of Huck and the hair ball. But in fact, he serves his own interests all along. Such resourcefulness is hardly consistent with the familiar one-dimensional concept of "the superstitious Negro."

And while Jim's reading is formulaic, it is hardly simpleminded. He sees the world as a kind of Manichean universe, in which forces of light and darkness—white and black—vie for dominance. Pap, he says, is uncertain what to do, torn between his white and black angels. Jim's advice, "to res' easy en let de ole man take his own way" (chap. 4), turns out to be good advice, because Huck enjoys life in the cabin, despite Pap's fits of drunken excess. This mixture of pleasure and pain is precisely what Jim predicts. Admittedly, Jim's conceptual framework is not original. Nonetheless, his reading carries considerable force because it corresponds so neatly to the dominant thematic patterns in this book, and, more broadly, to the sort of dualistic thinking that informs much of Twain's work. (To take an obvious example, consider the role reversals and character contrasts in *Pudd'nhead Wilson* or *The Prince and the Pauper*.) And most immediately, Jim's comments here reflect tellingly upon his situation as a black slave in racist America. The slave's fate is always torn between his master's will and his own.

In this reading and other incidents, Jim emerges as an astute and sensitive observer of human behavior, both in his comments regarding Pap and in his subtle remarks to Huck. Jim clearly possesses a subtlety and intelligence which "the Negro" allegedly lacks. Twain makes this point more clearly in the debate scene in chapter 14. True enough, most of this debate is, as several critics have noted, conventional minstrel-show banter. Nevertheless, Jim demonstrates impressive reasoning abilities, despite his factual ignorance. For instance, in their argument over "Poly-voo-franzy," Huck makes a category error by implying that the difference between languages is analogous to the difference between human language and cat language. While Jim's response—that a man should talk like a man—betrays his ignorance of cultural diversity, his argument is otherwise perceptive and structurally sound. The humor in Huck's conclusion, "you can't learn a nigger to argue," arises precisely from our recognition that Jim's argument is better than Huck's.

Throughout the novel Twain presents Jim in ways which render ludicrous the conventional wisdom about "Negro character." As an intelligent, sensitive, wily, and considerate individual, Jim demonstrates that race provides no useful index of character. While that point may seem obvious to contemporary readers, it is a point rarely made by nineteenth-century Euro-American novelists. Indeed, except for Melville, J. W. DeForest, Albion Tourgée, and George Washington Cable, white novelists virtually always portrayed Afro-American characters as exemplifications of "Negroness." In this regard the twentieth century has been little better. By presenting us with a series of glimpses which penetrate the "Negro" exterior and reveal the person beneath it, Twain debunks American racial discourse. For racial discourse maintains that the "Negro" exterior is all that a Negro really has.

This insight in itself is a notable accomplishment. Twain, however, did not view racism as an isolated phenomenon, and his effort to place racism within the context of other cultural traditions produced the most problematic aspect of his novel. For it is in the final chapters— the Tom Sawyer section—which most critics consider the weakest part of the book, that Twain links his criticisms of slavery and southern romanticism, condemning the cruelties that both of these traditions entail.[21] Critics have objected to these chapters on various grounds. Some of the most common are that Jim becomes reduced to a comic darky,[22] that Tom's antics undermine the seriousness of the novel, and that these burlesque narrative developments destroy the structural integrity of the novel. Most critics see this conclusion as an evasion of the difficult issues the novel has raised. There is no space here for a discussion of the structural issues, but it seems to me that as a critique of American racial discourse, these concluding chapters offer a harsh, coherent, and uncompromising indictment.

Tom Sawyer's absurd scheme to "rescue" Jim offends because the section has begun with Huck's justly celebrated crisis of conscience culminating in his resolve to free Jim, even if doing so condemns him to hell. The passage that leads to Huck's decision, familiar as it is, merits reexamination:

> I'd see him standing my watch on top of his'n—stead of calling me, so I could go on sleeping; and see him how glad he was when I come back out of the fog; and when I come to him again in the swamp, up there where the feud was; and such-like times; and would always call me

> honey, and pet me, and do everything he could think of for me, and how good he always was; and at last I struck the time I saved him by telling the men we had small-pox aboard, and he was so grateful, and said I was the best friend old Jim ever had in the world, and the *only* one he's got now; and then I happened to look around, and see that paper. . . . I studied a minute, sort of holding my breath, and then says to myself: "All right, then, I'll *go* to hell"—and tore it up. (Chap. 31)

The issue here is not just whether or not Huck should return a fugitive slave to its lawful owner. More fundamentally, Huck must decide whether to accept the conventional wisdom, which defines "Negroes" as subhuman commodities, or the evidence of his own experience, which has shown Jim to be a good and kind man and a true friend.

Huck makes what is obviously the morally correct decision, but his doing so represents more than simply a liberal choice of conscience over social convention. Twain explicitly makes Huck's choice a sharp attack on the southern church. Huck scolds himself: "There was the Sunday school, you could a gone to it; and if you'd a done it they'd a learnt you, there, that people that acts as I'd been acting about that nigger goes to everlasting fire" (chap. 31). Yet despite Huck's anxiety, he transcends the moral limitations of his time and place. By the time Twain wrote these words, more than twenty years of national strife, including the Civil War and Reconstruction, had established Huck's conclusion regarding slavery as a dominant national consensus; not even reactionary southerners advocated a reinstitution of slavery. But since the pre–Civil War southern church taught that slavery was God's will, Huck's decision flatly repudiates the church's teachings regarding slavery. And implicitly, it also repudiates the church as an institution by suggesting that the church functions to undermine, not to encourage, a reliance on one's conscience. To define "Negroes" as subhuman removes them from moral consideration and therefore justifies their callous exploitation. This view of religion is consistent with the cynical iconoclasm that Twain expressed in *Letters from the Earth* and other "dark" works.[23]

In this context, Tom Sawyer appears to us as a superficially charming but fundamentally distasteful interloper. His actions are governed not by conscience but rather by romantic conventions and literary "authorities." Indeed, while Tom may appear to be a kind of renegade, he is in essence thoroughly conventional in his values and proclivities. Despite all his boyish pranks, Tom represents a kind of solid respectability—a younger version of the southern gentleman as exemplified by the Grangerfords and Shepherdsons.[24] Hence, when Tom proposes to help Huck steal Jim, Huck laments that "Tom Sawyer fell, considerable, in my estimation. Only I couldn't believe it. Tom Sawyer a *nigger stealer*!" (chap. 33). Such liberating activity is proper for Huck, who is not respectable, but not for Tom, who is. As with the previous example, however, this one implies a deep criticism of the status quo. Huck's act of conscience, which most of us now (and in Twain's own time) would endorse, is possible only for an outsider. This hardly speaks well for the moral integrity of southern (or American) "civilization."

To examine Tom's role in the novel, let us begin at the end. Upon learning of the failed escape attempt and Jim's recapture, Tom cries out, self-righteously: "Turn him loose! he ain't no slave; he's as free as any cretur that walks this earth!" (chap. 42). Tom has known all along that his cruel and ludicrous scheme to rescue the captured "prisoner" was being enacted upon a free man; and indeed, only his silence regarding Jim's status allowed the scheme to proceed with Jim's cooperation. Certainly, neither Huck nor Jim would otherwise have indulged Tom's foolishness. Tom's gratuitous cruelty here in the pursuit of his own amusement corresponds to his less vicious prank against Jim in chapter 2. And just as before, Twain converts Tom's callous mischief into a personal triumph for Jim.

Not only has Jim suffered patiently, which would, in truth, represent a doubtful virtue (Jim is not Uncle Tom); he demonstrates his moral superiority by surrendering himself in order to assist the doctor in treating his wounded tormentor. This is hardly the behavior one would expect from a commodity, and it is *precisely* Jim's status—man or chattel—that has been fundamentally at issue throughout the novel. It may be true that the lengthy account of Tom's juvenile antics subverts the tone of the novel, but they also provide the necessary backdrop for Jim's noble act. Up to this point we have been able to admire Jim's good sense and to respond sentimentally to his good character. This, however, is the first time that we see him making a significant (and wholly admirable) moral decision. His act sets him apart from everyone else in the novel except Huck. And modestly (if not disingenuously), he claims to be behaving just as Tom Sawyer would. Always conscious of his role as a "Negro," Jim knows better than to claim personal credit for his good deed. Yet the contrast between Jim's behavior and Tom's is unmistakable. Huck declares that Jim is "white inside" (chap. 40). He apparently intends this as a compliment, but Tom is fortunate that Jim does not behave like most of the whites in the novel.

Twain also contrasts Jim's self-sacrificing compassion with the cruel and mean-spirited behavior of his captors, emphasizing that white skin does not justify claims of superior virtue. They abuse Jim, verbally and physically, and some want to lynch him as an example to other slaves. The moderates among them resist, however, pointing out that they could be made to pay for the destruction of private property. As Huck observes, "the people that's always the most anxious for to hang a nigger that hain't done just right, is always the very ones that ain't the most anxious to pay for him when they've got their satisfaction out of him" (chap. 42). As if these enforcers of white supremacy did not appear contemptible enough already, Twain then has the doctor describe Jim as the best and most faithful nurse he has ever seen, despite Jim's "resking his freedom" and his obvious fatigue. These vigilantes do admit that Jim deserves to be rewarded, but their idea of a reward is to cease punching and cursing him. They are not even generous enough to remove Jim's heavy shackles.

Ultimately, *Huckleberry Finn* renders a harsh judgment on American society. Freedom from slavery, the novel implies, is not freedom from gratuitous cruelty; and racism, like romanticism, is finally just an elaborate justification which the adult counterparts of Tom Sawyer use to facilitate their exploitation and abuse of other human beings. Tom feels guilty, with good reason, for having exploited Jim, but his final gesture of paying Jim off is less an insult to Jim than it is Twain's commentary on Tom himself. Just as slaveholders believe that economic relations (ownership) can justify their privilege of mistreating other human beings, Tom apparently believes that an economic exchange can suffice as atonement for his misdeeds. Perhaps he finds a forty-dollar token more affordable than an apology. But then, just as Tom could only "set a free nigger free," considering, as Huck says, "his bringing-up" (chap. 42), he similarly could hardly be expected to apologize for his pranks. Huck, by contrast, is equally rich, but he *has* apologized to Jim earlier in the novel. And this is the point of Huck's final remark rejecting the prospect of civilization. To become civilized is not just to become like Aunt Sally. More immediately, it is to become like Tom Sawyer.

Jim is indeed "as free as any cretur that walks this earth." In other words, he is a man, like all men, at the mercy of other men's arbitrary cruelties. In a sense, given Twain's view of freedom, to allow Jim to escape to the North or to have Tom announce Jim's manumission earlier would have been an evasion of the novel's ethical insights. While one may escape from legal bondage, there is no escape from the cruelties of this "civilization." There is no promised land where one may enjoy absolute personal freedom. An individual's freedom is always constrained by social relations to other people. Being legally free does not spare Jim from gratuitous humiliation and physical suffering in the final chapters, precisely because Jim is still regarded as a "nigger." Even if he were as accomplished as the mulatto from Ohio, he would not be exempt from mistreatment. Furthermore, since Tom represents the hegemonic values of his society, Jim's "freedom" amounts to little more than an obligation to live by his wits and make the best of a bad situation, just as he has always done.

Slavery and racism, then, are social evils that take their places alongside various others which the novel documents, such as the insane romanticism that inspires the Grangerfords and Shepherdsons blithely to murder each other, generation after generation. Twain rejects entirely the mystification of race and demonstrates that Jim is in most ways a better man than the men who regard him as their inferior. But he also shows how little correlation there may be between the treatment one deserves and the treatment one receives.

If this conclusion sounds uncontroversial from the perspective of the 1980s, we would do well to remember that it contradicts entirely the overwhelming and optimistic consensus of the 1880s. No other nineteenth-century novel so effectively locates racial discourse within the context of a general critique of American institutions and traditions. Indeed, the novel suggests that real individual freedom, in this land of the free, cannot be found. "American civilization" enslaves and exploits rather than liberating. It is hardly an appealing message.

Given the subtlety of Mark Twain's approach, it is not surprising that most of his contemporaries misunderstood or simply ignored the novel's demystification of race. Despite their patriotic rhetoric, they, like Pap, were unprepared to take seriously the implications of "freedom, justice, and equality." They, after all, espoused an ideology and an explicit language of race that was virtually identical to Thomas Jefferson's. Yet racial discourse flatly contradicts and ultimately renders hypocritical the egalitarian claims of liberal democracy. The heart of Twain's message to us is that an honest person must reject one or the other. But hypocrisy, not honesty, is our norm. Many of us continue to assert both racial distinction and liberal values simultaneously. If we, a century later, continue to be confused about *Adventures of Huckleberry Finn,* perhaps it is because we remain more deeply committed to both racial discourse and a self-deluding optimism than we care to admit.[25]

Notes

1. *The Portable Thomas Jefferson,* ed. Merrill D. Peterson (New York: Viking, 1975) 187–88.

2. The literature on the abolition movement and on antebellum debates regarding the Negro is, of course, voluminous. George M. Fredrickson's excellent *The Black Image in the White Mind* (New York: Harper Torchbooks, 1971) is perhaps the best general work of its kind. Fredrickson's *The Inner Civil War* (New York: Harper Torchbooks, 1971) is also valuable, especially pp. 53–64. Leon Litwack, in *North of Slavery* (Chicago: U of Chicago P, 1961) 214–46, closely examines the ambivalence of abolitionists regarding racial intermingling. Benjamin Quarles presents the most detailed examination of black abolitionists in *Black Abolitionists* (New York: Oxford UP, 1969), although Vincent Harding offers a more vivid (and overtly polemical) account of their relationships to white abolitionists; see *There Is a River* (New York: Harcourt, Brace, Jovanovich, 1981).

3. The debate over Jefferson's relationship to Sally Hemings has raged for two centuries. The most thorough scholarly accounts are by Fawn Brodie, who suggests that Jefferson did have a prolonged involvement with Hemings (*Thomas Jefferson, an Intimate History* [New York: Norton, 1974]), and by Virginius Dabney, who endeavors to exonerate Jefferson of such charges (*The Jefferson Scandals* [New York: Dodd, Mead, 1981]). Barbara Chase-Riboud presents a fictionalized version of this relationship in *Sally Hemings* (New York: Viking, 1979). The first Afro-American novel, *Clotel; or, The President's Daughter* (1853; New York: Arno, 1969), by William Wells Brown, was also based on this alleged affair.

4. For dates of composition, see Walter Blair, "When Was *Huckleberry Finn* Written?" *American Literature* 30 (Mar. 1958): 1–25.

5. For a discussion of Melville's treatment of race, Carolyn Karcher's *Shadow over the Promised Land* (Baton Rouge: Louisiana State UP, 1980) is especially valuable. Also noteworthy are two articles on "Benito Cereno": Joyce Adler, "Melville's *Benito Cereno:* Slavery and Violence in the Americas," *Science and Society* 38 (1974): 19–48; and Jean Fagan Yellin, "Black Masks: Melville's *Benito Cereno,*" *American Quarterly* 22 (Fall 1970): 678–89. Rayford Logan, *The Negro in American Life and Thought: The Nadir, 1877–1901*

(New York: Dial, 1954), and Lawrence J. Friedman, *The White Savage: Racial Fantasies in the Postbellum South* (Englewood Cliffs, N.J.: Prentice-Hall, 1970), provide detailed accounts of the racist climate in post-Reconstruction America, emphasizing the literary manifestations of such attitudes. Friedman's discussion of George Washington Cable, the outspoken southern liberal (99–118), is very informative. For a general historical overview of the period, C. Vann Woodward's *Origins of the New South* (Baton Rouge: Louisiana State UP, 1971) and *The Strange Career of Jim Crow,* 3rd ed. (New York: Oxford UP, 1974) remain unsurpassed. John W. Cell, in *The Highest Stage of White Supremacy* (New York: Cambridge UP, 1982), offers a provocative reconsideration of Woodward's arguments. Finally, Joel Williamson's *The Crucible of Race* (New York: Oxford UP, 1984) documents the excessively violent tendencies of southern racism at the end of the century.

6. My use of "racial discourse" has some affinities to Foucault's conception of "discourse." This is not, however, a strictly Foucaultian reading. While Foucault's definition of discursive practices provides one of the most sophisticated tools presently available for cultural analysis, his conception of power seems to me problematic. I prefer an account of power which allows for a consideration of interest and hegemony. Theorists such as Marshall Berman, *All That Is Solid Melts into Air* (New York: Simon & Schuster, 1982) 34–35, and Catherine A. MacKinnon, "Feminism, Marxism, Method, and the State: An Agenda for Theory," *Signs* 7.3 (1982): 526, have indicated similar reservations. However, Frank Lentricchia ("Reading Foucault [Punishment, Labor, Resistance]," *Raritan* 1.4 [1981]: 5–32; 2.1 [1982]: 41–70) has made a provocative effort to modify Foucaultian analysis, drawing upon Antonio Gramsci's analysis of hegemony in *Selections from the Prison Notebooks* (New York: International Publishers, 1971). See Foucault, *The Archaeology of Knowledge, Power/Knowledge,* ed. Colin Gordon (New York: Pantheon, 1980) esp. 92–108; and *The History of Sexuality,* vol. 1 (New York: Vintage, 1980) esp. 92–102.

7. This is not to discount the sufferings of other groups. But historically, the philosophical basis of Western racial discourse—which existed even before the European "discovery" of America—has been the equation of "good" and "evil" with light and darkness (or white and black). See Jacques Derrida, "White Mythology," *New Literary History* 6 (1974): 5–74; Winthrop Jordan, *White over Black* (New York: Norton, 1968) 1–40; and Cornel West, *Prophesy Deliverance* (Philadelphia: Westminster P, 1982) 47–65. Economically, the slave trade, chattel slavery, agricultural peonage, and color-coded wage differentials have made the exploitation of African Americans the most profitable form of racism. Finally, Afro-Americans have long been the largest American "minority" group. Consequently, the primacy of "the Negro" in American racial discourse is "overdetermined," to use Louis Althusser's term (*For Marx* [London: Verso, 1979] 87–126). The acknowledgment of primary status, however, is hardly a claim of privilege.

8. See Lawrence I. Berkove, "The Free Man of Color in *The Grandissimes* and Works by Harris and Mark Twain," *Southern Quarterly* 18.4 (1981): 60–73; Richard Gollin and Rita Gollin, "*Huckleberry Finn* and the

Time of the Evasion," *Modern Language Studies* 9 (Spring 1979): 5–15; Michael Egan, *Mark Twain's Huckleberry Finn: Race, Class and Society* (Atlantic Highlands, N.J.: Humanities P, 1977) esp. 66–102.

9. See Nat Hentoff's series of four columns in the *Village Voice* 27 (1982): "Huck Finn Better Get out of Town by Sundown" (May 4); "Is Any Book Worth the Humiliation of Our Kids?" (May 11); "Huck Finn and the Shortchanging of Black Kids" (May 18); and "These Are Little Battles Fought in Remote Places" (May 25).

10. *Mark Twain: A Biography* (New York: Harper, 1912).

11. See Arthur G. Pettit, *Mark Twain and the South* (Lexington: U of Kentucky P, 1974).

12. *I Hear America Talking* (New York: Van Nostrand Reinhold, 1976) 57.

13. *The Souls of Black Folk,* in *Three Negro Classics,* ed. John Hope Franklin (New York: Avon, 1965) 245.

14. (Boston: Beacon, 1962) 28.

15. See Ralph Ellison, "Change the Joke and Slip the Yoke," in *Shadow and Act* (New York: Random House, 1964) 45–59; Chadwick Hansen, "The Character of Jim and the Ending of *Huckleberry Finn,*" *Massachusetts Review* 5 (Autumn 1963): 45–66; Kenneth S. Lynn, *Mark Twain and Southwestern Humor* (Boston: Little, Brown, 1959).

16. See especially Daniel Hoffman, "Jim's Magic: Black or White?" *American Literature* 32 (Mar. 1960): 47–54.

17. Even the allegedly scientific works on the Negro focused on superstition as a definitive trait. See, for example, W. D. Weatherford, *Negro Life in the South* (New York: Young Men's Christian Association P, 1910); and Jerome Dowd, *Negro Races* (New York: Macmillan, 1907). No one has commented more scathingly on Negro superstitions than William Hannibal Thomas in *The American Negro* (1901; New York: Negro Universities P, 1969); by American definitions he was himself a Negro.

18. See Fredrick Woodard and Donnarae MacCann, "*Huckleberry Finn* and the Traditions of Blackface Minstrelsy," *Interracial Books for Children Bulletin* 15.1–2 (1984): 4–13.

19. Daniel Hoffman, in *Form and Fable in American Fiction* (New York: Oxford UP, 1961), reveals an implicit understanding of Jim's creativity, but he does not pursue the point in detail (331).

20. See Thomas Weaver and Merline Williams, "Mark Twain's Jim: Identity as an Index to Cultural Attitudes," *American Literary Realism* 13 (Spring 1980): 19–30.

21. See Lynn Altenbernd, "Huck Finn, Emancipator," *Criticism* 1 (1959): 298–307.

22. See, for example, Leo Marx, "Mr. Eliot, Mr. Trilling, and *Huckleberry Finn,*" *American Scholar* 22 (Autumn 1953): 423–40; and Neil Schmitz, "Twain, *Huckleberry Finn,* and the Reconstruction," *American Studies* 12 (Spring 1971): 59–67.

23. A number of critical works comment on Twain's religious views and the relation between his critiques of religion and racism. See Allison Ensor,

Mark Twain and the Bible (Lexington: U of Kentucky P, 1969); Arthur G. Pettit, "Mark Twain and the Negro, 1867–1869," *Journal of Negro History* 56 (Apr. 1971): 88–96; and Gollin and Gollin 5–15.

24. See Hoffman, *Form and Fable* 327–28.

25. I would like to thank my colleagues, David Langston and Michael Bell, for the helpful suggestions they offered me regarding this essay.

Blackface

and White

Inside

Ralph Ellison, writing in the mid-twentieth century, remarked about literary representations of black Americans, "Too often what is presented as the American Negro (a most complex example of Western man) emerges as an oversimplified clown, a beast or an angel. Seldom is he drawn as that sensitively focused process of opposites, of good and evil, of instinct and intellect, of passion and spirituality, which great literary art has projected as the image of man."[1] This beast/angel dichotomy points toward the untenable extremes that some black commentators have objected to in Twain's characterization of Jim. The essays in this section focus on the problems involved in the portrayal of Jim, and more generally on the limited view of African American humanity that Twain, to some degree, shared with his contemporaries. Of particular interest is the relation of Jim's conversations with Huck to the conventional dialogue of the Negro minstrel show—an entertainment in which mainly white actors put on elaborate clothing, blacked their faces, and enacted a routine of songs and jokes mostly at the expense of blacks.

Blackface minstrelsy was a popular entertainment in the nineteenth-century United States, and that popularity continued past the middle of the present century. As late as 1955 the NAACP had to protest plans for a minstrel show at a high school in Palo Alto, California; it was not until the 1960s that blackface was abandoned by marchers in the traditional Mummer's Parade held in Philadelphia each New Year's Day; and blackface routines continued even after that to be a staple of local amateur entertainments in the South. The presumed innocence of the racial caricature involved in blackface minstrelsy emblematizes the sort of blindness that has characterized white attitudes toward black people in America. The blackface mask worn by the minstrel-show entertainer is an appropriate symbol for the veil concealing black humanity that has begun to be lifted only during the last few decades.

Steven Mailloux says about the rhetorical structure of *Huckleberry Finn* that "the very staged debates that . . . [subvert] racism at one ideological level (blatant discrimination) work to reinforce it at another (cultural stereotype)."[2] Bernard W. Bell's essay, "Twain's 'Nigger' Jim: The Tragic Face behind the Minstrel Mask," explores both this dual effect of the minstrel ingredients in Twain's narrative and the corresponding ambivalence of Twain's own attitude toward blacks. Bell discusses Twain's development from early insensitivity toward slavery into a "desouthernized" New England–gentility abhorrence of the neglect and abuse of black Americans; but he also notes, quoting Twain's own remarks on the subject, Twain's lifelong enjoyment of blackface minstrelsy, which Bell terms "a national symbolic debasement of blacks." His discussion of *Huckleberry Finn* emphasizes Twain's unsettling return to the blackface stereotype in the novel's later chapters.

Fredrick Woodard and Donnarae MacCann, in their essay "Minstrel Shackles and Nineteenth-Century 'Liberality' in *Huckleberry Finn*," further document Mark Twain's enthusiasm for blackface minstrelsy and pursue his characterization of Jim and other black characters in *Huckleberry Finn* against the background of the minstrel-show "darky." Though conceding that Twain portrays Jim as good, generous, and humble, they rebut claims (such as those advanced by David Smith in this volume) for Jim's intelligence—the most important element necessary for establishing his humanity and the one, according to Woodard and MacCann, most conspicuously missing. Their discussion of Jim highlights the too-visible component of childishness in his personality—a mark of the white supremacy myth's view of blacks as an "infant race." The minstrel stereotype is, by their view, the single distinguishing component of "blackness" in Twain's portrayal; Jim is "white" (as expressed in Huck's "I knowed he was white inside") except for his minstrel-show-darky aspect. Jim as white can be a surrogate father to Huck, while as black he remains a one-dimensional buffoon. Woodard and MacCann point to *Tom Sawyer*

Abroad, a sequel to *Adventures of Huckleberry Finn,* as more blatant evidence of Twain's attitude toward Jim.

Betty H. Jones's essay, "Huck and Jim: A Reconsideration," traces the mythical/archetypal resonances in the story of Jim and Huck and their journey on the great river. Following the course of Huck's "mythic pattern of initiation," with its symbolic deaths and progressive rebirths, she casts him as the quintessential American boy (representative of the maturing country itself) seeking his proper identity. Characterizing Jim as the duped, abused, but noble innocent, she poses the question: Is our love for Jim matched by an equally profound respect? Her consideration of the question focuses on his dialectical relation to the often confused Huck, who, despite Jim's archetypal role as wise mentor and spiritual father, finds it difficult to see beyond the darky stereotype.

Taking his departure from W. E. B. Du Bois's description of the "double-consciousness" of blacks in the nineteenth-century United States, Rhett S. Jones, in his essay "Nigger and Knowledge: White Double-Consciousness in *Adventures of Huckleberry Finn,*" surveys a corresponding double view by whites of the same period: the theoretical black-person-as-chattel and the personally experienced black-person-as-person. Noting the strict denial—in both law and social practice—of racial mixing through intermarriage (or union outside marriage), he describes the false dilemma by which an individual was declared either black or white, with no acknowledged middle ground, and demonstrates the relevance of that denial to maintenance of the myth of black subhumanness (and, of course, white supremacy). Jones, seeing *Huckleberry Finn* as finally an "apologia for racism," proposes that Mark Twain recognized white double-consciousness but ultimately chose not to expose it in his novel. The ending of the novel, betraying Twain's own insights, becomes an object lesson in such betrayal.

James S. Leonard

Notes

1. Ralph Ellison, *Shadow and Act* (New York: Random House, 1964) 26.

2. Steven Mailloux, *Rhetorical Power* (Ithaca, N.Y.: Cornell UP, 1989) 85–86.

Twain's

"Nigger" Jim

The Tragic Face

behind the Minstrel

Mask

Bernard W. Bell

Is it racist trash or an American classic? A hundred years since the publication of *Adventures of Huckleberry Finn,* controversy still clouds the achievement of this tragicomic, satirical antislavery novel. Unlike nineteenth-century white readers and censors like the public library of Concord, Massachusetts, which condemned it as "trash and suitable for the slums," many modern-day black readers are less offended by the vulgarity and delinquency of Huck, the rebellious teenage narrator-protagonist, than by the minstrel image of Miss Watson's runaway slave, Jim, his companion in "crime" against the conventional morality, religion, and respect for property of the period.[1]

For some blacks the frequent use of the epithet "nigger" and the general ridicule of Afro-American character for the enjoyment of whites reflect only the blackface of white minstrelsy. Beneath the mask are the claims of white liberal scholars and commentators that Mark Twain, clearly a product of his time, place, and people, was, in the often-quoted phrase of his close friend William Dean Howells, a "desouthernized Southerner."[2]

Does the historical and literary evidence support the notion that America's most popular and representative nineteenth-century humorist and satirist escaped or outgrew the influence of the racial prejudice and discrimination endemic to the period? Born and bred in the antebellum Southwest, a volunteer in the Confederate militia, and an advocate of the delightful accuracy of minstrelsy, Twain, as we will see, struggles valiantly, like Huck, to reject the legacy of American racism and to accept his personal share of responsibility for the injustice of slavery, but never in *Adventures of Huckleberry Finn* does he fully and unequivocally accept the equality of blacks. "Writing at a time when the blackfaced minstrel was still popular, and shortly after a war which left even the abolitionists weary of those problems associated with the Negro, Twain," as Ralph Ellison noted in the 1950s during the public attack by blacks on the racial offensiveness of the book, "fitted Jim into the outlines of the minstrel tradition, and it is from behind this stereotype mask that we see Jim's dignity and human capacity—and Twain's complexity—emerge."[3] The portrayal of the complex humanity of Jim and Twain—the pernicious, tragic racism as well as the compassion behind their comic, occasionally ironic, masks—can best be fully understood and appreciated as an American classic rather than trash by interpreting *Adventures of Huckleberry Finn* in its sociohistorical as well as its literary context. Let us begin, therefore, with the racial climate in which Samuel Langhorne Clemens, alias Mark Twain, lived and wrote, and then examine the handling of point of view in the novel to discover the tragic face behind Jim's minstrel mask.

Twain's Socialization in the Ethics of Jim Crow

The major achievements of *Huck Finn* are its realistic and humorous portrayal of the moral hypocrisy of antebellum life along the Mississippi River and its satirical attack on slavery. What clouds this achievement is Twain's moral ambivalence about the humanity of blacks. The principal source of this ambivalence and the ethics that inform the novel is his boyhood experience with racism and slavery in Hannibal, Missouri, where his family settled in 1839, four years after his birth in Florida, Missouri. Although everybody in Hannibal was poor, Twain recalls in his autobiography, the small town "was a little democracy which was full of liberty, equality, and Fourth of July, and sincerely so, too; yet you perceived that the aristocratic taint was there."[4] The "aristocratic taint" in his own old Virginia and Kentucky family stock was mainly the legacy of his father, John Marshall Clemens—by profession a lawyer and by vocation a land speculator, storekeeper, justice of the peace, and slave owner[5]—whose declining fortunes led to the family's move from Tennessee to Missouri and ultimately resulted in bankruptcy. The paradox of Twain's memory of his Hannibal background, on the one hand, reveals his penchant as a storyteller to stretch the truth, and, on the other, suggests the conflict in his character between being a poor old southwestern river man and being a wealthy eastern writer, businessman, and world traveler. The paradox here "was mainly due to the circumstance that the town's population had come from slave states and still had the institution of slavery with them in their new home."[6]

Underscoring the fact that Twain's enlightened attitude "that slavery was a bald, grotesque and unwarrantable usurpation" came later in life is his confession that "in my schoolboy days, I had no aversion to slavery. I was not aware that there was anything wrong about it. No one arraigned it in my hearing; the local papers said nothing against it; the local pulpit taught us that God approved it; if the slaves themselves had any aversion to slavery they were wise and said nothing."[7] Explaining with apparently unintentional irony why "our slaves were convinced and content," he tells us in his autobiography that "there was nothing about the slavery of the Hannibal region to rouse one's dozing humane instincts to activity. It was the mild domestic slavery, not the brutal plantation article. Cruelties were very rare, and exceedingly and wholesomely unpopular. To separate and sell the members of a slave family to different masters was a thing not well liked by the people, and so it was not often done, except in the settling of estates."[8] Growing up in what was actually an antebellum slave state (thanks to the Missouri Compromise of 1820), the early Twain, in short, was no better or worse in his attitude and behavior toward blacks than other self-proclaimed benevolent white supremacists of his region and class.

When, then, did Twain become the desouthernized southwesterner or reformed midwesterner with southern values? Did leaving Hannibal in 1853 for New York arouse his "dozing humane instincts to activity"? Certainly not right away, for in a letter to his mother concerning the circumstances of free blacks he saw, the teenager writes: "I reckon I had better black my face, for in these Eastern States niggers are considerably better than white people."[9] After working for four years in the East and Midwest as a printer and occasional correspondent, Twain went south to New Orleans and became a riverboat pilot on the Mississippi. It was while visiting his hometown of Hannibal in 1861, he tells us in the semiautobiographical sketch "The Private History of a Campaign That Failed," that he joined the local Confederate militia as a second lieutenant. In neither the sketch nor this autobiography does Twain express any moral concern about his defense of slavery; instead, he humorously claims that he "resigned" after two weeks because he "was 'incapacitated by fatigue' through persistent retreating."[10] But in *Mark Twain and Southwestern Humor* Kenneth S. Lynn more accurately tells us:

> Not long after his enlistment, a hayloft in which he and some of his soldiers were sleeping caught fire, and Lieutenant Clemens was forced to jump for the barnyard below. In the fall, he painfully sprained his ankle and had to be put to bed. By the time he was up and about, he had had enough of fighting for a cause he only half-believed in, so that when his brother Orion . . . was appointed Territorial Secretary of Nevada, Twain leaped at the chance to secede from the Secession and go along as secretary to the Secretary.[11]

In *Mark Twain: Social Critic* Philip S. Foner also tells us that it was not antislavery sentiment but "a boil, a sprained ankle, and heavy rain" that hastened Twain's desertion from the Confederacy.[12]

When Twain went west in 1861, his experiences as a reporter, silver prospector, gold miner, and, later, world traveler certainly helped to democratize and deepen his humanity. But even after becoming a transplanted New Englander in 1871, publishing the deeply moving attack on the plantation tradition from the black perspective of Aunt Rachel in "A True Story" in 1874, observing firsthand that conditions were worse for blacks in the post-Reconstruction South in 1882, and developing around the same time a friendship with George W. Cable (a reformed southern writer who in 1865 moved to the more hospitable sociocultural climate of Northampton, Massachusetts), Twain never completely outgrew the racial prejudice and paternalism of his boyhood. Rather than an unequivocal commitment to egalitarianism, Twain's post-Reconstruction statement "that (bar one) I have no race prejudices, and I think I have no color prejudices nor caste prejudices nor creed prejudices. . . . All that I care to know is that a man is a human being—that is enough for me; he can't be worse" reveals the ambivalence and pessimism of his final years.[13] Behind the comic mask that Twain wears in his writings, in other words, is the complex humanity of a southwesterner whose ethics were shaped by the racism that defined the possibilities and limitations of democracy and freedom in nineteenth-century America.

Lamenting in 1906 the death of "the real nigger show—the genuine nigger show, the extravagant nigger show—the show which to me has no peer and whose peer has not arrived, in my experience,"

Twain writes: "To my mind it was a thoroughly delightful thing, and a most competent laughter-compeller and I am sorry it is gone."[14] He saw his first minstrel show in Hannibal in the 1840s. "It was a new institution," he reminds us. "In our village of Hannibal we had not heard of it before, and it burst upon us as a glad and stunning surprise." Sharing the commonplace notion of white contemporaries that their imitation of black character and culture was realistic as well as funny, he writes:

> The minstrels appeared with coal-black hands and faces and their cloth-ing was a loud and extravagant burlesque of the clothing worn by the plantation slave of the time; *not that the rags of the poor slave were burlesqued, for that would not have been possible; burlesque could have added nothing in the way of extravagance to the sorrowful accumulation of rags and patches which constituted his costume;* it was the form and color of his dress that was burlesqued. . . . *The minstrel used a very broad negro dialect; he used it competently and with easy facility and it was funny—delightfully and satisfyingly funny.*[15]

The buffoonery and extravagant comic arguments of Bones and Banjo, the stock minstrel characters, were believed to be particularly funny because of their assumed accuracy: "Sometimes the quarrel would last five minutes, the two contestants shouting deadly threats in each other's faces with their noses not six inches apart, the house shrieking with laughter all the while *at this happy and accurate imita-tion of the usual and familiar negro quarrel.*"[16] Since minstrelsy was essentially a national symbolic ritual of debasement of blacks for petty profit and for the psychological distancing of whites from their per-sonal responsibility in the tragic perversion of American principles, Twain's taste in humor reveals his socialization as an American, not merely as a southwesterner, in the ethics of white supremacy.

As an apprentice writer, Twain was also influenced by the offensive racism of southwestern humor. His notebooks reveal that he was familiar with Augustus B. Longstreet's *Georgia Scenes* (1835), John-son J. Hooper's *Some Adventures of Captain Simon Suggs* (1845), Jo-seph G. Baldwin's *Flush Times in Alabama and Mississippi* (1853), and George W. Harris's *Sut Lovingood Yarns* (collected 1867). These southwestern frontier humorists used coarse, violent humor in the oral tradition as an entertaining form of local color and irreverence for rank and respectability. The chief characteristics of their writing in-clude the use of frame stories, monologues, puns, eye dialect, con-

crete details, incongruity, gross exaggeration, understatement, caricature, anecdotes, tall tales, and sharp common sense.[17] "In the decade
of Dred Scott and bleeding Kansas," Lynn reminds us, "Southwestern jokes at the black man's expense reached an apotheosis of fury.
George Washington Harris' Sut Lovingood delighted in humiliating
and frightening slaves; while black men yelled with pain or terror, Sut
stood by and snickered."[18] Twain's offensive remarks in a series of
travel letters to the *Alta California* in 1869 about the odor of blacks
and his caricature of Blind Tom, the celebrated black pianist, as a minstrel are early evidence of this influence.[19] In the same year, however,
Twain wrote a satirical editorial in the *Buffalo Express* against the
lynching of blacks. Later, behind the ironic mask of Huck and the
comic mask of Jim, we sense Twain's continuing moral conflict in
acknowledging the humanity of blacks to a dual audience of white
readers of the post-Reconstruction South and North.

Twain's Relationship to His Audience, Huck, and Jim

One of the best ways to clear up the confusion about the nature of the
humanity behind the masks in *Huck Finn* is to address the three basic
questions concerning the vantage point from which an author tells his
story: (1) How is the story told? (2) When is it told? (3) Where does
the author stand in relation to his audience, narrator, and principal
characters? Quite clearly, the story of the friendship and flight to
freedom of a poor white boy and a runaway slave is told by a young,
first-person, naïve narrator-protagonist: the thirteen- or fourteen-
year-old "uncivilized" son of an antebellum frontier-town drunk.
This is immediately evident in the narrator's colloquial, direct introduction of himself in the opening chapter. By identifying himself as
one of the principal characters in *The Adventures of Tom Sawyer,* a
book by "Mr. Mark Twain . . . which is mostly a true book, with some
stretchers, as I said before," Huck, reinforcing the irony of Twain's
prefatory warning to readers searching for motive, moral, or plot in
the book, suggests that the narrative is merely a humorous sequel to
Tom Sawyer.

But the gradual development of Huck's ironic struggle to free
himself from the moral hypocrisy, romantic conventions, and racial
stereotypes of nineteenth-century America reveals a more serious,
essentially satiric thematic purpose, mode of characterization, and

structural design. Called a fool by Miss Watson because he does not believe that "a body can get anything they pray for," and "a numskull" by Tom Sawyer because he does not romanticize a Sunday-school picnic as "a whole parcel of Spanish merchants and rich A-rabs" (chap. 3), Huck struggles with the conflict between his ascribed identity as "poor white trash" and the affirmation of his essential humanity. Psychologically, the internalized community conventions are in conflict with his own natural impulses toward freedom, common sense, and compassion. He first tells us about this conflict and quest in the chapter suggestively titled "I Discover Moses and the Bulrushers": "The widow Douglas, she took me for her son, and allowed she would sivilize me; but it was rough living in the house all the time, considering how dismal regular and decent the widow was in all her ways; and so when I couldn't stand it no longer, I lit out. I got into my old rags, and my sugar-hogshead again, and was free and satisfied" (chap. 1). And then in the chapter "I Spare Miss Watson's Jim," we witness Huck's first dramatic evidence of sympathy for Jim when he promises not to turn him in: "People would call me a low-down Ablitionist and despise me for keepin' mum—but that don't make no difference. I ain't agoing to tell, and I ain't agoing back there anyways" (chap. 8).

As a naïve, unreliable narrator, Huck is unaware of the moral courage he demonstrates in his relationship with Jim, and, unlike the author and the modern reader, condemns himself for his inability to conform fully to the norms of the widow Douglas and Tom Sawyer, the representatives of conventional antebellum life along the Mississippi. As they escape (Huck from his father and the widow Douglas, and Jim from Miss Watson) down the Mississippi on a raft, Huck and Jim help and protect each other. The cornerstones of their friendship are, on the one hand, Jim's folk wisdom, woodsmanship, trust, and kindness, and, on the other, ironically, Huck's lying, cheating, and stealing. For black readers Jim's humanity is mainly affirmed by his natural desire for freedom to assert his manhood as a husband and father. Huck, however, wrestles with his conscience and responds ambivalently to Jim's humanity as they approach Cairo, the planned route north to freedom:

> Jim said it made him all over trembly and feverish to be so close to freedom. Well, I can tell you it made me all over trembly and feverish, too, to hear him, because I begun to get it through my head that he *was*

most free—and who was to blame for it? Why, *me*. I couldn't get that out of my conscience, no how nor no way. It got to troubling me so I couldn't rest; I couldn't stay still in one place. . . . I tried to make out to myself that *I* warn't to blame, because *I* didn't run Jim off from his rightful owner; but it warn't no use, conscience up and says, every time, "But you knowed he was running for his freedom, and you could a paddled ashore and told somebody." That was so—I couldn't get around that, noway. . . . I got to feeling so mean and so miserable I most wished I was dead. (Chap. 16)

Finally, in chapter 31, the climactic episode, Huck's moral ambivalence compels him to write and betray Jim to Miss Watson. This makes Huck feel "good and all washed clean of sin for the first time"; but before sending the letter, he recalls his relationship with Jim during their journey down the river. Then, remembering their good times together and Jim's consistent kindness toward him, he cannot go through with it: "I studied a minute, sort of holding my breath, and then says to myself: 'All right, then, I'll *go* to hell'—and tore it up." Most commentators cite this passage as the high point of Huck's moral triumph. They ignore or gloss over Huck's equal, if not more important, resolve, given Twain's belief in moral courage as independent action, "to work and steal Jim out of slavery again." Although Huck's moral resolve degenerates into burlesque under the influence of Tom's romantic escape plan for Jim in chapters 34–43, some modern black readers are more inclined to identify with Huck than with Jim. Ralph Ellison, for example, expressed the view of many when he wrote: "I could imagine myself as Huck Finn . . . but not, though I racially identified with him, as Nigger Jim, who struck me as a white man's inadequate portrait of a slave."[20]

Before looking more closely at the relationship of black readers to Jim and Twain, let us briefly address the significance of the time when Twain composed the story of Huck's adventures. Although the narrative present for the novel is some years before the end of slavery in 1865, Twain himself was writing in the post-Reconstruction period, when blacks were betrayed by the federal government and their lives were terrorized with impunity by white lynch mobs in order to promote white nationalism and industrial capitalism—a time which sets the stage not only for the unreliability of Twain's narrator but for his own ambivalence about what to do with free black men. The foregrounding of Jim's betrayal by Miss Watson and of his terrorization by a lynch mob on the Phelpses' farm signifies this political

reality and sociopsychological truth. "The sordid history of the Reconstruction with its betrayal and humiliation of the black man pours
into *Huckleberry Finn* at the end," Neil Schmitz notes, "inhibiting
Twain as Huck is inhibited."[21]

Knowing from external evidence that the novel was essentially
written in four sittings over a period of seven years (chapters 1–16 in
1876, chapters 17 and 18 between 1879 and 1880, chapters 19–21
between 1880 and 1883, and the remaining chapters in 1883),[22]
some black readers are at first intrigued but ultimately disappointed
by Huck's and Tom's imaginative embodiment of Twain's conflicting
realistic and romantic impulses toward his antebellum boyhood experiences in Hannibal, Missouri, and toward the Reconstruction and
post-Reconstruction experiences with free blacks. Most intriguing is
Twain's chief technical achievement: the effective use of the adolescent Huck as the center of consciousness in the book. As Ellison has
pointed out, "the historical and artistic justification for his adolescence lies in the fact that Twain was depicting a transitional period of
American life; its artistic justification is that adolescence is the time
of the 'great confusion' during which both individuals and nations
flounder between accepting and rejecting the responsibilities of adult-
hood."[23] That Huck succumbs to Tom's influence and flounders in
his responsibility as a friend to Jim in the final chapters of the novel is
painfully disappointing to many readers. This is a serious but hardly
fatal flaw in the novel; for rather than relying primarily on Huck's
summary and exposition of characters and events, Twain lets them
unfold before the reader like a drama or describes them in Huck's
vernacular in the natural sequence of his perceptions and memory of
them. Thus, Huck's psychological and moral struggle with slavery
and racism, especially his ambivalent response to Jim's humanity, is a
realistic dramatization of the tragicomic education of a poor young
white boy of his time, place, and class.

What, then, is Twain's relationship to his audience, Huck, and
Jim? Since most of Twain's books were sold "by subscription only,"
Twain, by circumstance and choice, wrote to appeal to the tastes of his
special primary audience. Hamlin Hill notes that "instead of the
urban, literature reader, the subscription book aimed at enticing the
common man, the masses, the rural, semi-literate, usually Midwest-
ern customer who had rarely bought a book before."[24] Twain's southern white stock, socialization in a border state, and literary apprenticeship in the southwestern tradition fostered a close racial, regional,

and class identification with this group of post-Reconstruction readers. It is important to remember that these readers were passive or
active participants in the rising tide of racial, political, and economic
oppression, terrorism, and exploitation that swept the nation in the
1870s and 1880s, depriving southern blacks of their civil rights and,
in many instances, their lives. These readers, many of whom, like
Twain, looked with nostalgia on the days before the war, expected a
mixture of sensationalism and moralizing. Explaining his choice of
this audience in a letter to Andrew Lang in 1890, Twain writes
defensively:

> The thin top crust of humanity—the cultivated—are worth pacifying,
> worth pleasing, worth coddling, worth nourishing and preserving with
> dainties and delicacies, it is true; but to be caterer to that little faction is
> no very dignified or valuable occupation, it seems to me; it is merely
> feeding the over-fed and there must be small satisfaction in that. It is not
> that little minority who are already saved that are best worth lifting at, I
> should think, but the mighty mass of the uncultivated who are under-
> neath. . . . Indeed I have been misjudged from the very first. I have never
> tried in even one single little instance to help cultivate the cultivated
> classes. I was not equipped for it, either by native gifts or training. And I
> never had any ambition in that direction, but always hunted for bigger
> game—the masses. I have seldom deliberately tried to instruct them but
> have done my best to entertain them.[25]

This passionate identification with the masses explains, in part,
Twain's apparent ambivalence toward the aristocratic pretensions of
the Grangerfords and toward the minstrel image of blacks in *Huckleberry Finn.*

While Twain's heart and guts moved him to identify with the
popular tastes of his subscription audience, his New England family
and friends encouraged him to appeal to the literary standards of the
cultivated. His marriage in 1870 to Olivia Langdon, the genteel, frail,
semiinvalid daughter of wealthy New York coal-mine owner and
philanthropist Jervis Langdon, opened the door to financial security,
the New England elite, and cultural ambivalence. Moving to Hartford, Connecticut, in 1871, he used the Langdon fortune to build
one of the largest, most fantastically designed and lavishly equipped
mansions in Nook Farm, a suburban community. His neighbors were
such genteel, middle-class, liberal writers as Harriet Beecher Stowe,
Charles Dudley Warner, and the Reverend Joseph Twichell; his close
friends were Twichell and the Bostonian (although, like Twain, orig-

inally a westerner) William Dean Howells, the most influential advocate during the age of realism of the genteel tradition in American letters. Howells and this Nook Farm community were, in effect, Twain's other audience.

Critics have frequently debated the influence that Twain's wife and friends, especially Twichell and Howells, had on his writing. "After my marriage," Twain confessed about his wife, "she edited everything I wrote. And what is more—she not only edited my works—she edited me."[26] Referring to her mother's censorship, Susy, his eldest daughter, wrote in her biography of the family:

> Papa read "Huckleberry Finn" to us in manuscript, just before it came out, and then he would leave parts of it with mamma to expergate [*sic*], while he went off to the study to work, and sometimes Clara and I would be sitting with mamma while she was looking the manuscript over, and I remember so well, with what pangs of regret we used to see her turn down the leaves of the pages which meant, that some delightfully terrible part must be scratched out.[27]

Still more influential as a literary adviser than his wife was Howells. In a letter to Howells, Twain wrote: "I owe as much to your training as the rude country job-printer owes to the city-boss who takes him in hand and teaches him the right way to handle his art."[28] Twain's secondary audience, then, as Michael Egan suggests,

> comprised the descendants of the original American revolutionary class, already beginning to sentimentalize their political heritage and edge towards conservatism and hypocrisy. Ten years earlier Twain had savagely attacked their dishonesties and double standards in *The Gilded Age*; by the time he came to write the later sections of *Huckleberry Finn*, however, he was merely their court-jester. This led . . . to pale burlesque and satire.[29]

The burlesque and satire in the early as well as the late sections of *Huckleberry Finn* illustrate Twain's relation to Huck and Jim. "Speaking through the mask of an 'irresponsible' boy," Lynn notes, "Twain was somehow able to 'let himself go' . . . with the result that Huck is the one Twain hero who is not shut out from the pageantry of life by his fear of being taken in by it."[30] Emotionally and philosophically, in other words, Twain is close to his naïve hero; but, as stated earlier, intellectually and morally he is, by virtue of Huck's ironic character, usually distant from him. Like Twain, Huck is unsentimental and uncultivated in behavior yet occasionally sensitive in his perceptions and use of the vernacular. Commenting on "the victuals" for supper at the widow Douglas's, Huck tells us, "there warn't really anything the matter with them. That is, nothing only everything was cooked by itself. In a barrel of odds and ends it is different; things get mixed up, and the juice kind of swaps around, and the things go better" (chap. 1). Later, in describing the Mississippi after escaping from Pap, he appeals winsomely for our understanding: "Everything was dead quiet, and it looked late, and *smelt* late. You know what I mean—I don't know the words to put it in" (chap. 7). Twain is sympathetic toward his protagonist as he underscores the hypocrisy of the widow by having Huck see her take snuff after refusing to let him smoke because "it was a mean practice and wasn't clean" (chap. 1). Huck's belief that "of course that [the snuff] was all right, because she done it herself" stresses his ironic role, for it is apparent here and throughout the narrative that the author and reader are more intellectually and morally aware of the hypocrisy of the respectable characters than is the protagonist.

But the author and his protagonist are kindred spirits in their ambivalence about the humanity and equality of blacks. In response, for example, to the tarring and feathering of the Duke and the King, the comic confidence men, Huck is moved to sympathy for them in chapter 33: "Well, it made me sick to see it," says Huck, "and I was sorry for them poor pitiful rascals. . . . It was a dreadful thing to see. Human beings *can* be awful cruel to one another." Yet earlier, when Aunt Sally Phelps asked if anybody was hurt on the boat that blew a cylinder, Huck's insensitivity to the humanity of blacks ("No'm. Killed a nigger") is as ironically racist as hers ("Well, it's lucky; because sometimes people do get hurt" [chap. 32]). Twain, like Huck, was a racist; yet both found themselves fighting nobly, though futilely, against the customs and laws of white supremacy. Even though while writing *Huckleberry Finn* Twain financed the college education of two blacks "as part of the reparation due from every white to every black man" and recommended Frederick Douglass to President-elect Garfield as marshal of the District of Columbia, the burlesque and satirical chapters showing Huck's participation— however reluctant—in Tom's bizarre plan to free Jim (whom Tom knows Miss Watson's will has already freed) from his imprisonment by the "kind and good" Phelpses provide more than ample evidence of this tragic flaw in Twain as well as in American character and culture.[31] On the one hand, these chapters are a satirical treatment of the romantic books on prison life and escape by Casanova, Cellini, Dumas, Carlyle, Dickens, and other writers—books which, as Walter Blair notes, few readers have recognized. On the other hand, they return to the same ignoble comic image of Jim that we have seen in chapters 2–8.

"The comedy," Blair continues, "is chiefly that of the Sut Lovingood school: hound packs streaming through Jim's cabin; menageries of bugs, spiders, caterpillars, and snakes discomforting Jim; snakes dropping from rafters onto Aunt Sally; butter melting atop Huck's head. Working notes show that Mark delighted in the elaboration."[32] Twain's training in the ethics of Jim Crow—evident in the influence of southwestern humor, his delight in minstrelsy, and traces of the paternalistic attitude toward blacks he knew on his uncle's Missouri farm—explains, in part, the tragic face of humanity behind Jim's comic mask. In his autobiography Twain nostalgically tells us about his "faithful and affectionate good friend, ally, and adviser . . . 'Uncle Dan'l,'" who was the model for Jim. In the manner of plantation-school writers like Joel Chandler Harris, whose Uncle Remus tales Twain also admired, he recalls Uncle Daniel as "a middle-aged slave whose head was the best one in the negro quarter, whose sympathies were wide and warm, and whose heart was honest and simple and knew no guile. . . . [H]e has endured . . . with the patience and friendliness and loyalty which were his birthright."[33] In giving imaginative shape to these memories of Uncle Daniel and appealing to the prejudices of his white readers, Twain creates the harmless, superstitious, childish character we first meet sleeping in chapter 2.

We are encouraged to laugh indulgently with the author at how Jim becomes a "monstrous proud," popular conjuror in the black community as a result of his interpretation of Tom's prank on him while he slept as the work of the devil and witches. Although Huck does not participate in the prank, he nevertheless concludes, with Twain's implicit agreement, that "Jim was most ruined, for a servant, because he got so stuck up on account of having seen the devil and been rode by witches" (chap. 2). In chapter 4 Twain uses eye dialect and the magical power of "a hair-ball as big as your fist, which had been took out of the fourth stomach of an ox" to burlesque Jim's prediction of Huck's fate with his father.[34] On one level, then, the bond between Huck and Jim is strengthened by their unsophisticated speech and mutual belief in the supernatural. On another, it is reinforced by such white paternalism as Huck's feeling, like Twain's for

Uncle Daniel, that Jim "had an uncommon level head, for a nigger" (chap. 14). Indeed, the highest praise that Huck can give Jim is that "he cared just as much for his people as white folks does for their'n. It don't seem natural, but I reckon it's so" (chap. 23). And after Jim sacrifices his freedom to save Tom's life at the end of the novel, Huck concludes that Jim is "white inside." For the reconstructed Twain as for Huck, in other words, the social relationship between blacks and whites during the post-Reconstruction era in its most benevolent form is that of noblesse oblige, a social bond of mutual love and loyalty between the master and slave classes, rather than that of a natural mutual respect for human rights and egalitarianism.

The ambiguity and ambivalence of Twain's relationship to Jim is vividly illustrated in chapter 15 when Jim violates the ethics of Jim Crow and noblesse oblige by reprimanding Huck for ridiculing him:

> When I got all wore out wid work, en wid de callin' for you, en went to sleep, my heart wuz mos' broke bekase you wuz los', en I didn' k'yer no mo' what become er me en de raf'. En when I wake up en fine you back agin, all safe en soun', de tears come en I could a got down on my knees en kiss' yo' foot I's so thankful. En all you wuz thinkin' 'bout wuz how you could make a fool uv ole Jim wid a lie. Dat truck dah is *trash;* en trash is what people is dat puts dirt on de head er dey fren's en makes 'em ashamed.

Here Jim's deep moral indignation surfaces from behind the comic mask which he wears defensively to conceal his true feelings and thoughts from Huck and other whites who pervert their humanity in demeaning or denying his. (The mask slips again when he vows to free his wife and children even if he must steal them.) Huck, in response, feels so bad that he "could almost kissed *his* foot to get him to take it back. It was fifteen minutes before I could work myself up to go and humble myself to a nigger—but I done it and I warn't ever sorry for it afterwards, neither." Huck's contrition here and his subsequent resolve not merely to go to hell but to steal Jim out of slavery represent Twain's moral identification with both Jim and Huck. For Ellison, "Huck Finn's acceptance of the evil implicit in his 'emancipation' of Jim represents Twain's acceptance of his personal responsibility in the condition of society. This was the tragic face behind the comic mask."[35] This perceptive interpretation certainly redeems narrative and author from being the trash that some would consign them to; for me and many other readers, though, Twain's tragic face is his failure of moral courage in reducing the complexity of Jim's assumption of manhood to a minstrel mask in the closing chapters. Jim's compromise of his desire for freedom, love of family, and self-respect in return for the forty dollars Tom gives him for cooperation in the burlesque escape plan is the tragic face behind his minstrel mask.

It is sad but true for many black readers that Twain's "Nigger" Jim is the best example of the humanity of black American slaves in nineteenth-century white American fiction. It is ironic, finally, as Ellison observed more than twenty-five years ago, that "down at the deep dark bottom of the melting pot, where the private is public and the public is private, where black is white and white is black, where the immoral becomes moral and the moral is anything that makes one feel good (or that one has the power to sustain), the white man's relish is apt to be the black man's gall."[36] Having boasted to Andrew Lang of writing for the belly rather than the head of the white post-Reconstruction masses, Twain—nostalgically and metaphorically—sells Jim's soul down the river for laughs at the end of *Adventures of Huckleberry Finn*.

Notes

1. Interview with John H. Wallace, Mark Twain Intermediate School, Fairfax County, Virginia. Quoted in "Nat Hentoff: *Huck Finn* Better Get out of Town by Sundown," *Village Voice* 4 May 1982. For the Concord Library censorship quotation, see Anne Lyon Haight, *Banned Books: Informal Notes on Some Books Banned for Various Reasons at Various Times in Various Places,* 3rd ed. (New York: R. R. Bowker, 1970) 57.

2. William Dean Howells, *My Mark Twain: Reminiscences and Criticisms,* ed. Marilyn A. Baldwin (Baton Rouge: Louisiana State UP, 1967) 30.

3. Ralph Ellison, "Change the Joke and Slip the Yoke," in *Shadow and Act* (New York: Random House, 1964) 50.

4. Albert Bigelow Paine, *Mark Twain's Autobiography* (New York: Harper & Brothers, 1924) 1: 120.

5. Justin Kaplan, *Mark Twain and His World* (New York: Simon & Schuster, 1974) 15.

6. Paine 1: 120.

7. Charles Neider, ed., *The Autobiography of Mark Twain: Including Chapters Now Published for the First Time* (New York: Harper, 1959) 6.

8. Paine 1: 123–24.

9. Quoted in Dixon Wecter, "Mark Twain," in *Mark Twain: A Profile,* ed. Justin Kaplan (New York: Hill & Wang, 1967) 20.

10. Neider, *The Autobiography* 102.

11. Kenneth S. Lynn, *Mark Twain and Southwestern Humor* (Boston: Little, Brown, 1959) 141.

12. Philip S. Foner, *Mark Twain: Social Critic* (1958; New York: International, 1975) 255.

13. Quoted in Foner 237. [The one "race prejudice" that Twain professed was against the French—ED.]

14. Bernard DeVoto, ed., *Mark Twain in Eruption: Hitherto Unpublished Pages about Men and Events* (New York: Harper & Brothers, 1940) 110, 115.

15. DeVoto, *Mark Twain in Eruption* 111; emphasis added. See also Robert C. Toll, *Blacking Up: The Minstrel Show in Nineteenth-Century America* (New York: Oxford UP, 1974).

16. DeVoto, *Mark Twain in Eruption* 113; emphasis added.

17. Walter Blair, *Native American Humor* (1937; San Francisco: Chandler, 1960) 62–101. A *frame story* is a story within another story, as in Chaucer's *Canterbury Tales*. *Eye dialect* is the pretended representation of uneducated speech through phonetic spellings ("uv," "mos'," "wuz," etc.) of what are, in some cases, normal pronunciations (e.g., "iz").

18. Lynn 104.

19. Lynn 145.

20. Ellison, "Change the Joke and Slip the Yoke" 58.

21. Neil Schmitz, "Twain, *Huckleberry Finn,* and the Reconstruction," *American Studies* 12 (Spring 1971): 65. For Schmitz, "Jim's situation at the end of *Huckleberry Finn* reflects that of the Negro in the Reconstruction, free at last and thoroughly impotent, the object of devious schemes and a hapless victim of constant brutality." Actually the survival strategies of black culture, as well as the Thirteenth, Fourteenth, and Fifteenth amendments and the Freedmen's Bureau, prevented blacks from being "thoroughly impotent" during Reconstruction. The political powerlessness and terrorization of blacks became acute during the post-Reconstruction period when, as Schmitz more accurately writes, "the Reconstruction was nullified, the ambitious programs of the Radical Republicans abandoned and the fate of the Negro restored to the keep of his former master, a fate manifest in the annual toll of lynchings" (60). See also Neil Schmitz, "The Paradox of Liberation in *Huckleberry Finn,*" *Texas Studies in Literature and Language* 13 (Spring 1971): 125–36.

22. Walter Blair, *Mark Twain and Huck Finn* (Berkeley: U of California P, 1960) 199.

23. Ralph Ellison, "Twentieth-Century Fiction and the Black Mask of Humanity," in *Shadow and Act* (New York: Random House, 1964) 33.

24. Hamlin Hill, "Mark Twain: Audience and Artistry," in *Mark Twain: Selected Criticism,* rev. ed., ed. Arthur L. Scott (Dallas: Southern Methodist UP, 1967) 287.

25. Bernard DeVoto, ed. *The Portable Mark Twain* (1946; New York: Penguin Books, 1979) 772–73.

26. Quoted in Van Wyck Brooks, *The Ordeal of Mark Twain* (1920; New York: E. P. Dutton, 1970) 136.

27. Charles Neider, ed. *Papa: An Intimate Biography of Mark Twain by*

Susy Clemens, His Daughter, Thirteen. With a foreword and copious comments by her father. Now published in its entirety for the first time a century later. (Garden City, N.Y.: Doubleday, 1985) 188–89.

28. Quoted in Brooks 153.

29. Michael Egan, *Mark Twain's Huckleberry Finn: Race, Class and Society* (1977; Atlantic Highlands, N.J.: Humanities P, 1978) 63–64.

30. Lynn 220.

31. Blair, *Mark Twain and Huck Finn* 323; Foner 282–83.

32. Blair, *Mark Twain and Huck Finn* 350.

33. Paine 1: 100.

34. Twain's introductory note that he "pains-takingly" represents "the Missouri negro dialect" as well as various others should be analyzed in the contexts of his belief in the authenticity of minstrelsy, his having been influenced by the eye dialect of southwestern humorists, his delineation of other blacks in the novel as comic servants, his own speech features, and all the distinctive grammatical, lexical, and phonetic features of nineteenth-century black Missouri speech—not merely in terms of Jim's pronunciation. See, for example, David Carkeet, "The Dialects in *Huckleberry Finn*," *American Literature* 51 (1979): 315–32.

In his three-page study of the representation of Jim's dialectical pronunciation, linguist James N. Tidwell admits that "Twain includes only two Negro language features in Jim's speech," yet he concludes that Twain was "sincere," "competent," and "accurate" in revealing "the salient low colloquial, Southern, and Negro features of Jim's speech" ("Mark Twain's Representation of Negro Speech," *American Speech* 17 [Oct. 1942]: 174–76). See also Summer Ives, "A Theory of Literary Dialect," *Tulane Studies in English* 2 (1950): 137–82; and David R. Sewell, *Mark Twain's Languages: Discourse, Dialogue, and Linguistic Variety* (Berkeley: U of California P, 1987) esp. chap. 5.

35. Ellison, "Twentieth-Century Fiction and the Black Mask of Humanity" 33.

36. Ellison, "Change the Joke and Slip the Yoke" 48–50.

Minstrel Shackles and Nineteenth-Century "Liberality" in *Huckleberry Finn*

Fredrick Woodard and

Donnarae MacCann

A crucial factor in Mark Twain's development of the character Jim in *Adventures of Huckleberry Finn* is that Twain conceived him with many of the same trappings attributed to blacks by other white writers in the late nineteenth century. This essential point—that Twain had problems with the characterization of the runaway slave—belongs at the center of *Huck Finn* criticism. Though Jim may reasonably be viewed as a model of goodness, generosity, and humility, he is characterized without an equally essential intelligence to buttress our claims for his humanity. Critics who wish, consciously or unconsciously, to maintain cultural control through a denial of this point fail to see in Jim a characterization imbued with the white supremacy myth of the time. Our basic argument in this essay is that even the most sophisticated reading today does not remove the shackles of the white supremacy presumption.

However, there is another point that warrants comment by way of introduction—namely, that *Huckleberry Finn* is Huck's story. It is told by a white adolescent, barely literate but nonetheless determined to shape an account of his adventures with Jim. As if the first paragraph of the story were not enough to warn the reader to be leery of the narrator and hence the trustworthiness of his point of view, the reader is forewarned in a headnote: "PERSONS attempting to find a motive in this narrative will be prosecuted; persons attempting to find a moral in it will be banished; persons attempting to find a plot in it will be shot." The forewarning is from Twain, of course; and it is a threat meant not so much to throw the reader off the course of motive, moral intent, or plot as, by indirection, to relieve the reader of any genteel preoccupation with such matters. Twain seems to suggest that the first sensible obligation is for the reader to experience the narrative, the very voice itself being the medium and the message. The current of the narrative voice, like the current of the river it resembles, meanders and is full of mean tricks. In short, the book is to be read for the pleasure of the voyage, and except for the mostly unwelcome (to the reader) intrusions of Tom Sawyer, Huck is the undisputed captain.

The history of Huck's story has created currents of its own as commentators have treated Twain's warning as an ironic invitation to take a plunge at every turn to determine what motives and meaning lie beneath the surface of one of the most troublesome novels about American civilization. That Huck's story is about freedom of one sort or another is an essential given. That the nature of that freedom is ambiguous, if not contradictory, remains a focus of debate. For some segments of American society, especially African Americans, the need for clarity, if not resolution, is urgent. Across the United States, blacks have felt the need to know why the generally lauded American "classic" has proved to be such a painful experience for their children in elementary and secondary school classrooms and in some college lecture halls. In the absence of satisfactory responses, parents, school boards, and librarians have continued to debate the question, not because censorship is an answer to the lack of secondary information to help teachers teach the work, but because they genuinely want to know for whom *Huckleberry Finn* is a classic.

For those of the academic literary establishment who "take both confidence and pleasure in deeming it a masterpiece of American literature,"[1] the question certainly must have a quality of the super-fluous. Yet neither the confidence nor the pleasure seems to have produced a body of critical literature that has paid adequate attention, beyond symbolic platitudes, to Twain's treatment of Jim, though the characterization of the black slave is at the heart of the debate. We have written elsewhere of Twain's use of minstrelsy to frame the humorous characterization of Jim.[2] Our position still holds: Twain's use of the minstrel tradition undercuts serious consideration of Jim's humanity beyond those qualities stereotypically attributed to the noble savage; and Jim is forever frozen within the convention of the minstrel darky. Even as one examines minstrel-like scenes for evidence that Jim may be acting the role of the trickster or shaman (as some contemporary critics have suggested),[3] the lingering effect of minstrelsy provides the frame of reference through which judgment of character is made.

One way to begin a new debate on the matter of literary convention and the depiction of Jim is to trace the limits of Twain's imagination as manifest in Jim's language and behavior throughout *Huckleberry Finn* (and its sequels). Such a reading must include discussion of the literary conventions and the intellectual currents of Twain's era.

Easily one of the most admirable scenes in the last fifth of the novel—the "evasion" section—is the one in which Huck and Jim persuade Tom that he should have a doctor look after his gunshot wound. On Jim's insistence, Huck is able to stand his ground against the whims of Tom:

> But me and Jim was consulting—and thinking. And after we'd thought a minute, I says:
> "Say it, Jim."
> So he says:
> "Well, den, dis is de way it look to me, Huck. Ef it wuz *him* dat 'uz bein' sot free, en one er de boys wuz to git shot, would he say, 'Go on en save me, nemmine 'bout a doctor f'r to save dis one'? Is dat like Mars Tom Sawyer? Would he say dat? You *bet* he wouldn't! *Well,* den, is *Jim* gwyne to say it? No, sah—I doan' budge a step out'n dis place, 'dout a *doctor;* not if it's forty year!"
> I knowed he was white inside, and I reckoned he'd say what he did say—so it was all right, now, and I told Tom I was agoing for a doctor. He raised considerable row about it, but me and Jim stuck to it and wouldn't budge. (Chap. 40)

That Jim has the courage and concern for human life to lead the way in securing medical attention for Tom (at the risk of his own freedom) earns interesting, albeit ironic, words of praise from Huck: "I knowed he was white inside." For all its ironic intent, Huck's praise speaks volumes about a persistent aura that surrounds Jim's goodness. In Huck's view such goodness is something other than Negro, nigger, black—all three of which are abstractions with no reference to being human. The closest textual container for Jim's goodness in *Huckleberry Finn* is, on the one hand, an abstraction of whiteness that is metaphysical, and, on the other, a set of values often regarded as women's values. To explore the latter would require an analysis of those values Huck acquires from Jim as compared to those associated with the widow Douglas, Judith Loftus, and Mary Jane Wilks.[4] But it must suffice to say for now that both Huck and Mark Twain have a frame of reference that makes Jim (slave or freedman) an invisible entity whose being we come to know as something other than what he is.

What all this means for our argument is that when Twain characterizes Jim as nonwhite in *Huckleberry Finn* and elsewhere, he does so in the literary convention that he felt best expressed the Negro character in its highest form of development: the antics of minstrelsy. Otherwise, Jim is characterized as though he were white.

By the 1880s, "blackface" minstrelsy had infiltrated the culture at the grass-roots level. Tom Sawyer comments in Twain's unfinished novel "Tom Sawyer's Conspiracy" that the family's "old nigger-show things" are up in Aunt Polly's garret. William Dean Howells, in *A Boy's Town,* explains that burnt-cork minstrel shows were among the games of neighborhood children, and that the blacking often smudged up their shirt-sleeves.[5] In the text of *Huckleberry Finn,* Twain makes one direct reference to "nigger shows" when Huck is bluffing his way through a conversation with the harelipped Wilks sister about his alleged life in England. Speaking of English servants, Huck says, "Why, Hare-l—why, Joanna, they never see a holiday from year's end to year's end; never go to the circus, nor theatre, nor nigger shows, nor nowheres" (chap. 26).

Elsewhere Twain provided readers with his general assessment of minstrelsy as "a thoroughly delightful thing," "a most competent laughter-compeller," and called the loud, on-stage confrontations in them an "accurate imitation of the usual and familiar negro quarrel."[6] This kind of assessment was widely shared. Sociologist Alan W. C. Green maintains that white audiences were so enthralled with this form of entertainment that "anyone after the early 1840s who wished to portray a humorous Negro on the stage had to conform to the minstrelsy pattern, and that included Negroes themselves."[7]

It is hard to ascertain why a comparison of Jim's antics and the farcical behavior of "stage Negroes" did not enter prominently into *Huckleberry Finn* scholarship as early as the 1950s, when Ralph Ellison made note of the similarities, or at least in the 1960s, when Donald B. Gibson elaborated this thesis further.[8] The "stage Negro's" typical banter about wife troubles, profit making, spooks, and formal education[9] is echoed in episodes in *Huckleberry Finn,* and their inclusion can be traced to a period when Twain was in the midst of planning a new tour of stage readings.[10] Jim gives his impression of

"King Sollermun" and his harem in a minstrel-like repartee (chap. 14), and his confusion about stock market profits is seen in a farcical account of how Jim's stock—his cow—failed to increase his fourteen-dollar fortune when he "tuck to specalat'n'" (chap. 8). Throughout the novel Jim is stupefied by information that Huck shares with him, as when they discuss Louis XVI's "little boy the dolphin." Huck's miseducation makes him the brunt of the humor here as much as Jim, but the reader is shown many sides of Huck's character, whereas Jim is usually either the total fool or the overgrown child. In episodes where he behaves as an adult, as when Jim chides Huck for "trashy" behavior after Huck tells Jim he has merely dreamed their fogbound separation, Twain often mixes Jim's befuddlements with his insights. If Jim is momentarily wise, it comes off as an accident because he is simultaneously the head-scratching darky. In the fog scene he puzzles, "Is I *me,* or who *is* I? Is I heah, or whah *is* I?" (chap. 15).

The swaggering buffoonery of the minstrel clown is represented early in the novel when Jim awakes and finds his hat in a tree (one of Tom's tricks), and then concocts a tale about witches and the devil. Tom has left a nickel on the kitchen table in exchange for some candles, but Jim claims that the devil left the money for him as a charm. Jim and the other slaves have the superstition-steeped minds that give the whole scene a minstrel flavor, a quality that cannot be explained away by concluding that Jim has been successfully hustling the other blacks. The notoriety and the five-cent piece that Jim ends up with (not to mention the counterfeit quarter that Huck gives him for telling his fortune from a hair ball) can be interpreted as successful con jobs on Jim's part only if we isolate these scenes from the many additional superstitious episodes in which no hustle can be inferred. For example, Jim thinks Huck is a ghost when he encounters him on Jackson's Island, and he believes that all the camping supplies have been acquired through witchcraft. Jim speaks to the ghost in a typical addle-brained manner: "I awluz liked dead people, en done all I could for 'em" (chap. 8).

David L. Smith is one of several commentators who argue that such details, especially the five-cent and twenty-five-cent windfalls, reveal Jim as more of a trickster than a stage darky.[11] He links Twain's caricature of Jim to frontier humor and its reliance on stock types. However, without denying a kinship between minstrel performers and frontier types (especially their urge to spin tall tales), one needs to make clear that Twain's references are far more likely to have come from the stage tradition. Furthermore, in stage readings Twain discovered that the exaggerated antics of minstrelsy were overwhelming crowd pleasers. To a fellow lecture circuit performer he said, "Try 'Readings.' They are all the rage now."[12] And to his wife, Livy, about his own reading of the farcical evasion sequence: "It is the biggest card I've got in my whole repertoire. I always thought so. It went abooming."[13]

Smith's interpretation does not consider the recurring examples of Jim's childishness—a characteristic of the stage caricature that undercuts Jim's sometimes convincing role as a parent figure. Jim is often scared stiff in contrast to Huck's calm, confident demeanor (as when the raft is lost at the site of a wrecked steamboat). When Huck reads from a history book, Jim's eyes "bug out," and when Huck sizes up the Duke and the Dauphin as humbug aristocrats, he assures us that "it warn't no use to tell Jim" (chap. 19). Infantile reactions on Jim's part are multiplied and intensified in the last fifth of the novel when he acquiesces completely to Tom's escape plan. Critical attention has been generally focused on Huck in this section because he appears to regress to Tom's moral plane. If attention were focused more on Jim, it would perhaps be recognized that Jim remains about the same—a victim and a playmate of children, a clown to be either admired or toyed with as the boys' maturity or lack of maturity dictates. Jim is Huck's toy now, as well as Tom's, and he gives no sign of perceiving himself as anything but a child among children until the scene in which Tom needs a doctor. Moreover, the implication of childishness and irresponsibility is reinforced as Jim watches complacently while another slave, Nat, is made the brunt of vicious, boyish tricks.

Here Jim shows little of the shrewdness Smith has noted earlier in the book. Yet a similar line of argument is taken by critic James M. Cox, who speculates that Jim's affectionate behavior toward Huck is really adroit hustling, as when Jim may suspect that Huck has decided to turn him in and he undermines that plan by calling Huck "honey," "friend," "de old true Huck," and "de on'y white genlman dat ever kep' his promise to ole Jim."[14] But if this is an instance of cleverly manipulating Huck, what can we say about the other scenes in which Jim showers Huck with endearments? There is no way to interpret those parallel scenes as examples of rewarding hustles. When Jim meets Huck at the Grangerfords' after they have been separated, Jim resembles a "mammy" stereotype clucking over her surrogate child, and the same can be said of other scenes of reunion. On the other hand, Jim's character transcends these plantation gestures when he is concretely helpful—for example, when he keeps Huck's night watch for him on the raft, when he conceals the identity of Pap's corpse, and when he comes out of hiding to assist Tom's doctor. On the last pages of the novel, these two sides of Jim—the clown versus the real father figure—are vividly juxtaposed. First Jim calls attention to "signs" and to the earlier minstrel-like dialogue about speculating and getting rich: "*Dah,* now, Huck, what I tell you?—what I tell you up dah on Jackson islan'? I *tole* you I got a hairy breas', en what's de sign un it; en I *tole* you I ben rich wunst, en gwineter to be rich *agin;* en it's come true; en heah she *is! Dah,* now! doan' talk to *me*—signs is *signs,* mine I tell you; en I knowed jis' 's well 'at I 'uz gwineter be rich agin as I's stannin' heah dis minute!" ("Chapter the Last"). Then Jim the humanitarian moves up-stage when Huck presses him for information about Pap: "Doan' you 'member de house dat was float'n down de river, en dey wuz a man in dah, kivered up, en I went in en unkivered him and didn' let you come in? Well, den, . . . dat wuz him" ("Chapter the Last").[15] Twain's ambivalence couldn't be clearer. Yet in the next published work about Huck, Tom, and Jim—*Tom Sawyer Abroad*—nothing is left of Jim but the clown.[16]

Examined as a whole, *Tom Sawyer Abroad* has a number of engaging moments as a satire on provincialism and a hymn to the "good life" (in this case, skimming across the Sahara in a balloon instead of down the Mississippi on a raft). However, the minstrel element mars the trip, as some Twain scholars concede. Kenneth S. Lynn writes that the Jim of *Huckleberry Finn* "is barely recognizable in the minstrel-show darky of the later book."[17]

Except for two characters in minor roles, the plot revolves around Tom, Huck, and Jim exclusively. And because there are fewer subplots than in *Huckleberry Finn,* and fewer thematic strands, Jim stands out vividly as a child among children, the stage role assigned to adult black males. Huck and Jim appear in the narrative as a "natural" twosome, sharing a common lack of schooling and a common adherence to folksy superstition, and lined up against Tom's bookishness and constant efforts to lord it over the "lunkheads." However, Huck's innate intelligence shines through his narration, especially in his graphic and often poetic descriptions of weather, landscapes, and the tragedies that overtake desert caravans. As for Tom, he is sometimes the nonsensical romancer and sometimes the unevenly educated provincial, but he nonetheless reveals in this book a body of geographical and literary knowledge that would probably be shared by many of Twain's readers. He is thus a character to identify with, whereas Jim is a character to laugh *at* and little more.

Jim comes across as the most immature member of the group. He loses his head in episodes with lions, mirages and other apparent apparitions, and tales of giants. He overreacts in the good times, too, as when a real oasis is spotted and when he catches his first glimpse of Egypt, the revered land of a fellow "Presbyterian," Moses. He is easily tricked by the children, as when they exploit his ignorance of fractions and dupe him into *choosing* to shovel a disproportionate share (four-fifths) of the sand that has collected in the balloon. One example of a minstrel-like monologue will suffice as an illustration of Jim's clowning in *Tom Sawyer Abroad*. He is explaining the Great Desert as one of the Lord's miscalculations:

> I b'lieve it uz jes' like when you's buildin' a house; dey's allays a lot o' truck en rubbish lef' over. What does you do wid it? Doan' you take en' k'yart it off en dump it onto a ole vacant back lot? 'Course. Now, den it's my opinion hit was jes' like dat. . . . He measure out some rocks en yearth en san', en stick 'em together en say 'Dat's Germany,' en pas'e a label on it en set it out to dry; en measure out some mo' rocks en yearth en san', en stick 'em together, en say, 'Dat's de United States,' en pas'e a label on it and set *it* out to dry. . . . Den he notice dat whilst He's cal'lated de yearth en de rocks jes' right, dey's a mos' turrible lot o' san' lef' over.[18]

Such a scene, compared with similar minstrel-inspired material in *Huckleberry Finn* and in "Tom Sawyer's Conspiracy," leads us to consider the Huck/Tom/Jim narratives as a unit in terms of their portrayal of Jim.[19] And the presence of some sympathy for Jim in each of these works is not surprising if we take into account the role of geniality in minstrelsy. According to Alan Green, the "stage Negroes" were intended to evoke a feeling of affection for a "permanently visible and permanently inferior clown who posed no threat and desired nothing more than laughter and applause at his imbecile antics."[20] Blacks had to be hilarious to white eyes, says Green, in order for whites to cease feeling guilt and anxiety.

Guilt has been mentioned by a number of historians as one of several impulses underlying the white supremacy myth. And there were few challenges to that myth in the intellectual circles of Twain's era. Even a cursory review of the intellectual climate reveals historians, scientists, artists, clergymen, and armchair anthropologists propounding tenets of white supremacy similar to those Twain adheres to in his fiction. One might say that Jim, in *Huckleberry Finn* and elsewhere, is a victim of white supremacist attitudes among liberal thinkers of the time. No aspect of the white supremacy myth is admirable; and though Twain transcends the posture of the true believer with respect to several aspects of the myth, there is no justification for glossing over its appearance in *Huckleberry Finn* and other works. *Huckleberry Finn* was written at a time when the federal troops were being removed from the South and the attempt at Reconstruction and democratic government had collapsed, leaving black people at the mercy of former masters, northern carpetbaggers, or the parvenu whites with whom they had competed for a place in the work force.

Without trying to establish a one-to-one link between Twain and the chief promoters of a nineteenth-century white superiority doctrine, we can ask: What was the general climate? What was in the air? According to George M. Fredrickson, southern clergymen in the 1880s "saw nothing in the development of an independent Negro religious life but emotional excess, moral decline, and a general falling away from the Christianity originally inculcated by whites on the slave plantations."[21] By 1889 historian Philip Alexander Bruce was arguing that the Negro race had degenerated since emancipation and would demonstrate increasing immorality, criminality, and, in particular, a dangerous lust for white women.[22] Bruce did not draw upon explicit Darwinian theories to make his case, but the concept of black degeneracy was amenable, as Fredrickson notes, to Darwinian explanations about natural selection and survival of the fittest, and the scientific community largely embraced those rationalizations.

In the literary field, Bruce's brother-in-law, Thomas Nelson Page, was sharply differentiating between plantation "darkies" and post-emancipation blacks, and making it clear that the benevolence he attributed to the former could not be passed down to the new generation—to the "lazy, thriftless, intemperate, insolent, dishonest [freed men and women] without the most rudimentary elements of morality."[23] Historian Rayford W. Logan carefully documents the prevalence of this kind of stereotyping and the biological inferiority myth in the literary products of the North as well as the South.[24]

In the field of anthropology, it was not until the 1930s that notions about blacks belonging to an "infant" race (thousands of years behind the "mature" white race) were becoming discredited in professional circles.[25] And some armchair anthropologists defined blacks as a unique species situated on a spectrum between anthropoids and humans. As a result of such beliefs, blacks were largely excluded from the political process and deemed incapable of participating in white-created political institutions. Black Codes, lynching, the interpretation of Reconstruction as a chaotic record of an inferior race—all these phenomena rested on the presumption that American civilization would rise or fall depending upon whether African Americans were successfully dominated.

In his essay "The United States of Lyncherdom," often pointed to as one of his most liberal pieces of writing, Twain indicates that he is not far removed from some of the main streams of thought, even while he places himself in the "liberal" camp. His essay condemns people who take the law into their own hands, but in referring to a specific case of alleged rape he presumes black guilt, and he alludes to presumed threats that whites experience at the hands of blacks. He writes of lynchings and their attendant publicity: "one much talked-of outrage and murder committed by a negro will upset the disturbed intellects of several other negroes and produce a series of the very tragedies [i.e., rapes of whites] the community would so strenuously wish to prevent; . . . in a word, the lynchers are themselves the worst enemies of their women."[26] Twain thus undercuts his plea for due process of law by implying an inherent basis for danger, a lurking "black peril."

On the other hand, he used *Huckleberry Finn* as a way to condemn slavery, and could therefore be said to have helped counteract the vindication of slavery that was gaining ground in post-Reconstruction history books. Yet again he makes his intent ambiguous. Jim is freed by the *slaver,* Miss Watson—an extraordinary sign of benevolence on Miss Watson's part since she has no way of knowing before she dies that Jim has not slain Huck, as many townsfolk believe and as evidence about Huck's disappearance indicates.

There is little question that Huck's story subverts several categorical, prevailing myths of Negro inferiority. That subversion is, of course, part of Huck's maturation, and it underscores Twain's proposition that individual experience neutralizes the forces of civilization that codify phenomena into a neat, symmetrical universe. Insofar as Huck's story dismantles that universe, particularly the socially constituted and sanctioned mythos of race, it outstrips other nineteenth-century examples. But at issue here is the limit of Huck's tale or the residue of the white supremacy myth that manifests itself in the characterization of Jim.[27] The problematical elements of Jim's character in *Huckleberry Finn* and *Tom Sawyer Abroad* are too thoroughly embedded in the convention of blackface minstrelsy for Twain to have made a literary gesture that carries far beyond the conventions of his own time. Consequently, the twentieth-century inheritors of this gesture, on reflection, must ask: Why does the apparent shift in individual attitude toward slavery and racism represented by Huck's story not extend to the literary convention in which Jim is framed?

Notes

1. James M. Cox, "A Hard Book to Take," in *One Hundred Years of Huckleberry Finn: The Boy, His Book, and American Culture,* ed. Robert Sattelmeyer and J. Donald Crowley (Columbia: U of Missouri P, 1985) 386.

2. Fredrick Woodard and Donnarae MacCann, "*Huckleberry Finn* and the Traditions of Blackface Minstrelsy," *Interracial Books for Children Bulletin* 15.1–2 (1984): 4–13; reprinted in *The Black American in Books for Children: Readings in Racism,* 2nd ed., ed. Donnarae MacCann and Gloria Woodard (Metuchen, N.J.: Scarecrow, 1985) 75–103.

3. [See the David Smith and Betty Jones essays for discussions of Jim as trickster and shaman, respectively—ED.]

4. See Nancy Walker's "Reformers and Young Maidens: Women and Virtue in *Huckleberry Finn*," in *One Hundred Years of Huckleberry Finn,* for a treatment of some women's issues.

5. (New York: Harper and Brothers, 1890) 105.

6. *Mark Twain in Eruption: Hitherto Unpublished Pages about Men and Events,* ed. Bernard DeVoto (New York: Harper, 1922) 113, 115.

7. Alan W. C. Green, "'Jim Crow,' 'Zip Coon': The Northern Origins of Negro Minstrelsy," *Massachusetts Review* 11 (Spring 1970): 394.

8. Ralph Ellison, "Change the Joke and Slip the Yoke," *Partisan Review* 25.2 (1958): 215–22; Donald B. Gibson, "Mark Twain's Jim in the Classroom," *English Journal* 57.2 (1968): 196–99, 202.

9. Examples of such minstrel routines can be found in manuals geared to the amateur and published well into the twentieth century. For example, see E. L. Gamble's *Gamble's Minstrel Book No. 2* (East Liverpool, Ohio, 1942).

10. In 1884 Twain adopted for the lecture circuit the format Charles Dickens used in public readings. His performance style became a mixture of telling and acting episodes from his books. See Justin Kaplan's *Mark Twain and His World* (New York: Simon & Schuster, 1974).

11. See Smith's essay, "Huck, Jim, and American Racial Discourse," in this volume (originally printed in *Mark Twain Journal* 22.2 [1984]: 4–12).

12. Paul Fatout, *Mark Twain on the Lecture Circuit* (Bloomington: Indiana UP, 1960; rpt., Gloucester, Mass.: Peter Smith, 1966) 190.

13. Franklin R. Rogers, *Mark Twain's Burlesque Patterns* (Dallas: Southern Methodist UP, 1960) 148.

14. Cox 392.

15. The difference between these two passages can be analyzed in relation to characterization and theme, but not in rhetorical terms because Jim's exaggerated dialect types him as a clown *whenever* he speaks. Twain's charm as a vernacular writer is a strength of *Huckleberry Finn,* but his densely packed deviations from standard orthography in dialogue attributed to blacks isolate them from the other homespun figures and their colloquialisms, and suggest ignorance of a different (and greater) dimension. [See the discussions of "eye dialect" in the introductory essay (Leonard and Tenney) and the Bernard Bell essay—ED.]

16. One of the most recent attempts to explicate *Huckleberry Finn* in relation to its finished and unfinished sequels is Henry Carr Phelps's unpublished dissertation "The Undiscovered Territory: Mark Twain's Later Huck and Tom Stories," U of British Columbia, 1983. Phelps focuses on the crisis of maturation in adolescent boys and hypothesizes that through contact with Jim, Huck becomes more responsible, courageous, and empathetic, while Tom is earmarked for this kind of personality development in two abortive sequels, "Tom Sawyer among the Indians" and "Tom Sawyer's Conspiracy." This theory appears largely speculative since, instead of carrying out such a plan, Twain brings Huck back down to Tom's level at the end of *Huckleberry Finn,* and Huck stays at that level in *Tom Sawyer Abroad* and in the completed chapters of "Tom Sawyer's Conspiracy." To surmise that Tom was on the verge of blossoming into greater maturity seems to be wishful thinking.

17. Kenneth S. Lynn, *Mark Twain and Southwestern Humor* (Westport, Conn.: Greenwood, 1972) 245.

18. Mark Twain, *The Works of Mark Twain: The Adventures of Tom Sawyer; Tom Sawyer Abroad; Tom Sawyer, Detective,* ed. John C. Gerber, Paul Baender, and Terry Firkins (Berkeley: U of California P, 1980) 310–11.

19. Twain drafted more than 30,000 words of the "Tom Sawyer's Conspiracy" manuscript, nearly as many as in the novel *Tom Sawyer Abroad.* Jim is again the patient simpleton, and Huck and Tom amuse themselves while risking Jim's dignity and even his life.

20. Green 395.

21. George M. Fredrickson, *The Black Image in the White Mind: The Debate on Afro-American Character and Destiny, 1817–1914* (New York: Harper Torchbooks, 1972) 259.

22. Fredrickson 259.

23. Fredrickson 260.

24. Rayford W. Logan, *The Betrayal of the Negro, from Rutherford B. Hayes to Woodrow Wilson,* enl. ed. (1954; New York: Collier, 1965) 242–75.

25. I. A. Newby, *Jim Crow's Defense: Anti-Negro Thought in America, 1900–30* (Baton Rouge: Louisiana State UP, 1965) 50–51.

26. Maxwell Geismar, ed., *Mark Twain and the Threes R's: Race, Religion, Revolution–and Related Matters* (Indianapolis: Bobbs-Merrill, 1973) 34.

27. While our focus has been on Jim's characterization, we should also point out that Twain includes gratuitous racist turns of phrase in both *Huckleberry Finn* and *Tom Sawyer Abroad*. These quips would not have surprised the minstrel enthusiasts or the dinner party audiences that Twain sometimes entertained with "nigger jokes." For example, in *Huckleberry Finn* Huck finds the lack of scruples in the Duke and the King amazing: "Well, if ever I struck anything like it, I'm a nigger." And in *Tom Sawyer Abroad*, "Tom went across Sahara and put his finger on it [a "treasure-hill"] as easy as you could pick a nigger out of a bunch of angels."

Huck and Jim

A Reconsideration

Betty H. Jones

In the contemporary climate of heightened awareness of the pride and sensitivity of ethnic minorities, it is not surprising that the figure of Jim in *Huckleberry Finn* should pose difficulties for many readers. The descriptions, events, and circumstances attending this black slave who shares much of Huck's experience along the Mississippi make Jim a problematic figure for black Americans as well as for many white readers. For though Jim possesses undeniable traits of nobility, far too often our admiration of him is tempered by the recognition (perhaps unwitting) that his is the nobility of the primitive—the intuitive, innocent child of nature. Surely we grow fond of him; perhaps we even love him. But does he command our full respect? The reader who responds to Jim's innate goodness may still desire to see it joined with cerebration. Thus, any consideration of Twain's masterpiece and Jim's role in it evokes a tension that may be left unresolved. Yet what is there to do about the troublesome, ambiguous responses Jim evokes in us?

To make sense of our contradictory responses, Jim must be recognized as a multifaceted character who fulfills many dramatic functions. In order to serve the necessities of Twain's moral vision, Jim must wear many hats, play many roles. There is a permissible but pronounced inconsistency in Twain's presentation of both Jim and Huck: their "characters" shift according to the immediate needs and intentions of the author. But Jim's multiple and shifting roles, and the moral significance of those changing roles, have been neither sufficiently noted nor understood.

Not fully aware of the satire in *Huckleberry Finn* and the various and manifold uses Twain's moral vision requires of Jim, some readers become disquieted, fearful that Twain shared the racist views of his society. Exactly the opposite is the case. The satirist enjoys the freedom to move his characters about at will—make them both targets of the satiric thrust and mouthpieces for the authorial voice. Characters may sometimes by victims and pawns; at other times they may be active agents. Ultimately, the satirist as social reformer will do with his characters whatever he needs to do to act as a corrective agent for the society he portrays. But some of the uses to which Twain puts the character Jim have caused readers to squirm in discomfort.

Jim's sometime role as minstrel-show buffoon, a role patently unacceptable to modern sensibilities, is a role people are likely to remember. The superstitious slave of chapter 2, who believes himself set upon and enchanted by witches who subsequently "rode him all over the State," leaves us with a strongly comic impression.* But the comic role blends with pity and sorrow as we respond to the naïve and child-like creature who can say with sincere gratitude to the foolishly romantic Tom Sawyer (who has concealed Jim's emancipation for the sake of a needless and dangerous "evasion"), "dey ain't *nobody* kin git up a plan dat's mo' mixed-up en splendid den what dat one wuz." Very much akin to this figure is the gullible and trusting Jim of chapter 15. In a scene informed by dramatic irony, by the discrepancies between our knowledge and his, we watch Jim subjected to the distortions of reality offered by a teasing, thoughtless Huck. The sadly comic victim who here is momentarily persuaded that he has dreamed his and Huck's separation in a terrible, all-pervasive fog, that he has dreamed Huck's near drowning, is for many the ultimate Jim in *Huckleberry Finn:* the duped, abused, but noble innocent.

But Jim is more than the good-hearted elder "boy" made a foil to the other boys, Huckleberry Finn and Tom Sawyer. In a way that elevates Jim and makes clear what Twain is really saying about racism in this pre–Civil War society, Jim's presence in *Huckleberry Finn* sets up mythic resonances that reverberate throughout the work. Indeed, part of Jim's real function is to contribute to and extend the mythic-archetypal patterns that operate just beneath the surface of Twain's text.

* [See David Smith's treatment of this episode for a discussion of its noncomic aspects— E D.]

A consideration of Jim's mythic role reveals that his occasional appearances as victim or buffoon are of the least importance to this work. More significantly, in his archetypal roles as both wise mentor and spiritual father to Huck—the quintessential American boy seeking his own identity—Jim plays a dialectical role of historic significance. Inasmuch as, allegorically speaking, Huck *is* his country, what happens to Huck is of interest to us all. In Huck's repeated assumptions of various identities, in his restless movements from place to place, in his efforts to find balance between the nightmarish, often corrosive experiences of shore life and the relative peace of life on the river, we see mirrored the conflicts and doubts of a young country struggling to come to terms with its history. If nature can offer only temporary refuge for young Huck, then the nation must come to terms with a postlapsarian world. Eden is lost forever.

Like Huck, who must learn to listen to and follow the dictates of his own conscience, America must release an imprisoned people. Huck's vacillations, his curious early inability to see beyond the social phenomenon or creation that is the "nigger" to the human being beneath the abstract term mimics the nation's denial of human rights to a portion of its people. Huck's role as initiate is to change, to grow, to go forward from the darkness of ignorance into the light of knowledge. His successful ascent into light will bode well for a nation soon to be dramatically divided by the question of slavery.

Twain's response to the urgent issues of his day is compelling but not always easy to understand. Twain chose to give the young white initiate an older black man as mentor. He uses the ancient archetypal symbolic patterns of the initiation rites to comment on the problems that beset his own times. As with all of the archetypal mentors who have preceded him, Jim's primary duty as mentor to the young initiate is to instruct, to guide him in his search for knowledge. Huck, like all young initiates, seeks knowledge of self, others, and his God. Jim's role is to ask the right questions of Huck, to provide him with situations that offer potential for knowledge, and to act always as a stable and consistent force of morality for him. Jim must guide Huck into the light while taking care that the journey is made gradually, in stages that prepare the initiate's consciousness. Twain's book proceeds in a series of revelations. Huck's movements between the shore and the raft allow him time to assimilate and internalize the often terrifying knowledge he gains on the shore. In like manner, Huck grows slowly into his recognition of Jim's humanity; Twain carefully chronicles Huck's progress in this regard.

If Jim's larger dialectical role is better understood, his presence in the novel is invested with significance of a higher order. Twain's intention is not to denigrate but to elevate. More attention should be paid to this aspect of Jim's presentation in Twain's towering work, for a fuller understanding of Jim's symbolic functions allows us to view the scenes with Jim as the victim or buffoon from another perspective. Clearly, whether Jim is deliberately or carelessly victimized, Twain as moralist is teaching by indirection. To bring vivid life to the cruelty of the folk along the shore is to allude to the spiritual waste places of the country. It would be folly on our part to conclude that the indignities Jim suffers affirm a racist code. Twain's method here is to suggest what *ought* to be by showing the ugliness of what *is*. In truth, Jim's suffering and pain are commingled with that of Twain, Jim's creator. Through the gritty realism of his work, Twain insists that the young nation look closely at itself, reexamine its own assumptions and goals.

Intermittently and briefly, Twain presents his ideal society more conventionally when we observe black and white existing harmoniously together in nature. Lyric scenes of Huck and Jim in peaceful, "cool and shady" woods, where rabbits, snakes, and other animals become curiously "tame," evoke images of Eden. The two cleanse themselves in the waters of the great river-god, waters symbolic of potential redemption and rebirth. Together, in perfect accord, they float down the river, riding the raft under a sky "speckled with stars." The raft provides a place "free and safe" and "comfortable." Scenes such as these remind us of the possibilities of beauty, truth, and grace in a society free of the oppressive burden of racism. That Twain repeatedly contrasts the terrifying experiences of shore life with the beauty of Huck and Jim at one with the natural world is a telling comment indeed on a society that would sanction the enslavement of a portion of its people. Floating along together, Huck and Jim are mentor and student, father and son.

They are linked in other ways as well. Both are children of nature, well versed in its ways. Emotionally compatible, both are superstitious, inventive, clever, patient, brave, and avowed realists in a world where romantic notions do not serve. Both realize the necessity of coming to terms with life *as it is lived*. While they share a common dream of freedom from the constraints of their society—Jim from slavery and Huck from "sivilization"—their dreams are born of harsh necessities, not the textbook romanticism of Tom Sawyer. Neither Huck nor Jim would be apt to say of the other, as Huck does of Tom Sawyer in chapter 41, "He had a dream . . . and it shot him." It is important to see that the many correspondences Twain establishes between Huck and Jim are crucial to the telling of this tale.

Symbolically, Huck's and Jim's dynamic, evolving relationship suggests the resolution of the nation's problems. A nation need not remain fixed in brutal, inhumane attitudes and forms of behavior. Like Huck and Jim, who frequently wash the mud from their bodies, the Adamic American state can acknowledge its loss of innocence, accept the claims of its history, and go forward into experience. As the friendship between Huck and Jim grows and develops, as they begin to constitute a family for each other, and particularly as Huck moves beyond the social category of "nigger," disdaining it for the abstraction that it is and realizing the full humanity of blacks as well as whites, the moral pattern of Twain's work becomes increasingly clear. We cannot understand Twain's moral intentions, however, unless we are attentive to the underlying mythic patterns and the various emotional and spiritual bonds that link Huck and Jim.

Early in the novel it is clear that Huck's real need is for a father. But it is also clear that he does not need the brutal, oppressive Pap. The reflective boy, who often sits alone to have "a long think" about his experiences, says of his father in chapter 3, "I didn't want to see him no more." News of his father's drowning momentarily allays his fears, but Huck's sensitivity to the signs and rhythms of nature alert him that a "drownded man don't float on his back, but on his face." And with the appearance of Pap's characteristic footprint in the snow, Huck's fears increase. He is swept by a curious, seemingly unconscious longing for death: "I felt so lonesome I most wished I was dead" (chap. 1). There is a prevailing and constant awareness of death: owls "who-who" about "somebody that was dead"; whippoorwills and dogs cry "about somebody that was going to die"; the wind makes "cold shivers" run over him; nights "grieve"; houses are "still as death"; ghosts "can't rest easy" in their graves. With these signs, Huck is amply forewarned of the reappearance of his abusive, drunken father, who will surely bring spiritual or physical death to the apprehensive boy. Nor surprisingly, Huck describes Pap in chapter 5 in images of death: "There warn't no color in his face . . . ; it was white; not like another man's white, but a white to make a body sick, a white to make a body's flesh crawl—a tree-toad white, a fish-belly white." Pap resembles a body found floating in water, a body from which life has long since departed.

If Pap's appearance foreshadows his actual death, yet when he is alive and confronting Huck he is a man filled with negatives and contradictions. Opposed to education, religion, and everything wholesome, he is a man in the service of death. He says indignantly to Huck, "Now looky here; you stop that putting on frills. I won't have it. I'll lay for you, my smarty; and if I catch you about that school I'll tan you good. First you know you'll get religion, too. I never see such a son." A man with private furies not explained in the novel, Pap is possessed by a fractious spirit all too familiar to Huck. Life with a man who thinks of fathering only in terms of ruthless power over his young has had much to do with rendering Huck the pensive, often melancholy creature he is. As Jim discusses Pap, based on the revelations of Jim's hair ball (chap. 4), he tells Huck, "Yo' ole father doan' know, yit, what he's a-gwyne to do. Sometimes he spec he'll go 'way, en den agin he spec he'll stay. De bes' way is res' easy en let de ole man take his own way."

Huck's worst fears are soon realized. In an ironic use of the ancient mythic pattern of initiation, in which the young hero is spirited away by older male relatives from the protective but ultimately constricting presence of the mother and other females, Pap kidnaps Huck, stealing him from the "sivilizing" influence of the widow Douglas and her sister. The conventional young hero is then sequestered in some remote location where *men* can dispense the knowledge and pose the challenges he needs to earn his identity, move from innocence to knowledge, and return to society with the hero's "boon": his transformed consciousness, his best self. Pap imprisons Huck in a remote log cabin and drives away all would-be liberators with a stolen gun. Pap alone will pass along the assumptions and values of his culture. And what values he expresses in his drunken tirade! After vitriolicly describing and railing against the well-dressed and well-educated "free nigger" from Ohio, and ranting briefly about the outrage of a black man voting, he concludes: "And to see the cool way of that nigger—why, he wouldn't a give me the road if I hadn't shoved him out o' the way. I says to the people, why ain't this nigger put up at auction and sold?—that's what I want to know. . . . Why, they said he couldn't be sold till he'd been in the State six months, and he hadn't been there that long yet." Lest anyone suppose that the racism in this passage reflects Twain as well as Pap, Huck's description of Pap as he delivers this diatribe should also be noted:

> Pap was agoing on so, he never noticed where his old . . . legs was taking him to, so he went head over heels over the tub of salt pork, and barked both shins, and the rest of his speech was all the hottest kind of lan-guage—mostly hove at the nigger and the govment, though he give the tub some, too. . . . He hopped around the cabin considerable, first on one leg and then on the other, . . . and at last he let out with his left foot all of a sudden and fetched the tub a rattling kick. But it warn't good judgment, because that was the boot that had a couple of his toes leaking out of the front end of it; so now he raised a howl that fairly made a body's hair raise, and down he went in the dirt, and rolled there. (Chap. 6)

The broad, farcical comic elements at work here speak for themselves. As a satirist who depends on an unstated but known norm, Twain can only assume that no reader will be persuaded by so ludicrous a figure as Pap; his racism is simply one more vile aspect of his nature. Obviously, Pap Finn is no fit spokesman for views Twain would endorse; rather, he and his racism are the target of a satiric attack.

What Huck must escape from is not only the cabin but also the degraded world it represents. When Pap eventually becomes "too handy with his hick'ry" (chap. 6), Huck determines to find a way out. Frightened severely by his drunken father chasing him with a knife, Huck, in an action of great symbolic importance, feigns his own death. Only the moonlight witnesses the young boy's rejection of bondage and his movement toward freedom (chap. 7). Like Moses, about whom he has recently learned from the widow Douglas, Huck must make a journey by water to escape captivity or death. Like Moses also, Huck cannot immediately assume his true name. Huck must live with false identities until he earns his rightful name and can serve as a moral standard for his people. The picaresque structure of Twain's novel accommodates itself to the series of journeys Huck must take, each bringing him closer to maturity.

It is interesting to note that Huck remains conscious of time as he moves from place to place. Even when he is on the water, he listens for the sound of clocks striking the hour (chap. 11). Again and again he stops and listens to hear what time it is. This awareness of time denotes Huck's unconscious desire to be fluid with time, to move, to progress. He senses that he must go forward. His series of journeys necessarily impels him through space and time. If Twain's moral vision is to be made abundantly clear, these are journeys that Huck must make. Huck's journeys on water take him to those moments when he is moved to protect and liberate Jim, to recognize Jim's humanity. When he does so, Huck's actions can serve as a moral alternative for his country. Ironically, Huck has decried the widow's efforts to go "a bothering about Moses." He could see no relevance in a man who "had been dead a considerable long time" (chap. 1). Yet the reader sees the parallels in the lives of these two figures so separated in space and time. Apart from their "escapes" on water, both must finally provide codes of ethics for their respective nations. And just as Moses led his enslaved people out of Egypt, Huck will violate a law that sanctions slavery and aid Jim in his quest for freedom. As Moses liberated the Israelites, Huck's actions serve as a moral standard that, if heeded, will free both the oppressed and the oppressor from the burdens of slavery. The allusions to Moses in chapter 1 permit us early recognition that *Huckleberry Finn* is a novel that must be understood in part from a mythical-archetypal perspective. With a mythic sensibility at work, we are particularly attentive to the following exchange, which takes place in chapter 2. Ben Rogers, one of Huck's cohorts, says at one point, "Here's Huck Finn, he hain't got no family. . . ." "Well, hain't he got a father?" says Tom Sawyer. Huck, indeed, has a father. But in Twain's ironic use of the archetypal abduction or isolation of the young initiate prior to his instruction in the forms of his new life, we know that Huck must escape from Pap, his biological but "false" father, to find the father who will instruct him truly, one who will instruct him with patience, generosity, and love. With Huck's escape from Pap, the stage is now set for the young white boy and the black slave, both fleeing oppression, to come together as a family, a newfound father and son.

After going through elaborate measures to simulate his own death (chap. 7), Huck prepares the way for his progressive rebirths. Once he is safe on Jackson's Island, he sees people searching for his body. In a novel where bodies floating in water are not rare sights, we are reminded of the exceeding dangers attendant upon Huck's journeys. The initiate must go through his perilous journey, his dark place; the possibility that he will not return is very real. Here, however, Huck finds refuge in nature. Like other young heroes who make the archetypal journey from innocence to experience, Huck is aided by a benevolent nature. With a safe harbor at hand, Huck is fed by literal bread upon the waters. He has only to set a line to catch all the fish he can eat. This temporary Eden is a source of delight in other ways as well to the young American Adam: "I was boss of it; it all belonged to me, so to say" (chap. 8). Significantly, it is here that Huck encounters Jim, who has also "lit out," because Miss Watson was about to sell him. Together the two assess their respective situations and explore the island.

Huck's instruction by his mentor begins almost immediately. Jim, as the ancient shaman, the high priest of the patent spiritualism, or "natural knowledge," that informs the work, teaches the young Huck how to read the signs and symbols of nature: "I had heard about some of these things before, but not all of them. Jim knew all kinds of signs. He said he knowed most everything." That Huck is an eager and enthusiastic student of natural lore comes as no surprise. We have already seen him attempt to ward off bad luck with salt thrown over his left shoulder (chap. 4); tie up a lock of his hair to keep witches away; turn around in his tracks three times and cross his breast each time to keep bad luck away (chap. 2); understand that "a drownded man don't float on his back, but on his face" (chap. 3); and receive what he needs from the river, whether it be motion, cordwood (chap. 7), or food (chap. 8). Their mutual superstitious bent and instinct for harmony with nature bind the pair together in a natural, unforced camaraderie. The accord between them is reflected in the serene figures they present in the larger serenity of nature.

Their shared experience in the woods enables Huck to discover other facets of Jim's nature, facets Huck would not otherwise have known. For example, Jim displays an innate dignity that Huck finds surprising in a black slave. Of his newfound freedom Jim says, "I's rich now, . . . I owns myself." Moreover, to a boy to whom "father" has meant only brutality and despair, Jim provides an alternative model of the older man. He is warm, compassionate, and at all times concerned for Huck's well-being. Immediately upon encountering Huck, Jim assumes the role he will fulfill from this point on. He becomes the "still point" of Huck's turning world, his personal refuge and safe harbor. Together, they make a home out of a huge cavern. Secure in their comfortable "house" against the furies of a thunderstorm, Huck says, "Jim, this is nice. . . . I wouldn't want to be nowhere else but here." Jim replies, "Well you wouldn't a ben here, 'f it hadn't a ben' for Jim. You'd a ben down dah in de woods widout any dinner, en gittn' mos' drownded, too, dat you would, honey" (chap. 9).

When the river brings a frame house floating past the island, the two go aboard. Huck sees something in a far corner that looks like a man, but Jim refuses to let Huck look because the dead man's face is "too gashly" (chap. 9). Only at the very end of the novel does Jim reveal that the dead man was Pap. Thus, Jim's role as father to Huck has begun just at the time when death has permanently extinguished the biological father-son relationship.

Jim's careful solicitude is consistent throughout the book, but unfortunately for Jim, Huck at this point has yet to attain his full moral stature. Still a boy, still aiming to play tricks on Jim for "fun," Huck is responsible for a snakebite that almost costs Jim his life. Only Jim's knowledge of natural lore—Jim in truth *is* a kind of shaman or medicine man—pulls him through. After Jim begins to recover, a repentant Huck assumes a girl's identity and goes ashore to seek information. In chapter 2 Huck has noted that the "new clothes" befitting his "sivilized" life were "all greased up and clayey." His disguise in female dress is representative of the many false identities he now must "try on" until he can mature and wear his own clothes, earn his own name. It is clear that Twain's use of symbolic clothing in these instances and elsewhere in the novel is thematically linked to the repeated symbolic deaths and rebirths Huck must undergo before he can finally become the true Huckleberry Finn, one with a new, altered, more expansive consciousness. But Huck's moral development could not take place without the ever-present stimulus and challenge provided by his friendship with Jim. Jim, then, is a moral *necessity* for Huck; in making Jim the instrument of Huck's development of moral consciousness, Twain confers significance of a high order on the black slave. Jim's role is to instruct or redeem, and this role elevates him. Those who are blind to Jim's role misread Twain. Far from affirming racist views, Twain's intention is to reveal racism for what it is: a refusal to acknowledge the humanity of a people.

In his excursion ashore Huck is a notable failure as a "girl," whether Sarah or Mary Williams, so he assumes still another identity, that of George Peters. Soon, "Sarah Mary Williams George Elexander Peters" hastens back to the island. His return marks a significant advance in the growing friendship between Huck and Jim. Landing on the island, Huck says, "Git up and hump yourself, Jim! There ain't a minute to lose. They're after us!" (chap. 11). Huck's instinctive use of the pronoun "us" here demonstrates his perception of himself and Jim as a team, or, more significantly, a family unit. From this point on in the narrative, Huck's use of the collective "we" far outweighs his use of the individual "I." Together they flee; together they exist in the serenity and beauty of the natural world. The harmony of their own relationship makes them at one with that world: "We catched fish, and talked, and we took a swim now and then to keep off sleepiness. It was kind of solemn, drifting down the big still river, laying on our backs looking up at the stars, and we didn't ever feel like talking loud, and it warn't often that we laughed, only a little kind of a low chuckle" (chap. 12).

Nature continues to provide the two with the food and shelter they need. In like measure, Jim continues to instruct Huck, providing the cautionary note he needs when the boy sometimes lapses into the romanticism more appropriate to Huck's friend, Tom Sawyer. Huck acknowledges that Jim "was right; he was most always right; he had an uncommon level head, for a nigger" (chap. 14). Huck's casual use of the word "nigger" here is stark evidence that the learning process he has undergone with Jim is far from complete. Before Huck's ritualistic immersions in water—his symbolic series of deaths and rebirths—can end, he must learn to test the cold abstraction of *that* word—Pap's word—against the intuitive truths of his own heart. But like America itself, Huck is in the process of becoming.

Back on the river again, headed for Cairo and freedom for Jim, Huck and Jim are separated in a symbolic, all-pervasive fog (chap. 15). Then, after much trouble and confusion, the two are reunited: "Goodness gracious, is dat you, Huck? En you ain' dead—you ain' drownded—you's back agin? It's too good for true, honey . . . you's back agin, 'live en soun' . . . thanks to goodness!" Jim's heartfelt joy here, however, is ignored by the boy who still must be educated as to the proper responses to love. Huck teases Jim unmercifully, temporarily convincing him that their separation was only a vivid dream, which Jim interprets symbolically. Full of thoughtless glee, Huck then asks Jim to interpret the significance of the branches and leaves that have fallen on the raft in its mad career downriver. Brought up short, Jim recognizes that he has been betrayed:

What do dey stan' for?, I's gwyne to tell you. When I got all wore out wid work, en wid callin' for you, en went to sleep, my heart wuz mos'

> broke bekase you wuz los', en I didn' k'yer no mo' what become er me en
> de raf'. En when I wake up en fine you back agin, all safe en soun', de
> tears come en I could a got down on my knees en kiss yo' foot I's so
> thankful. En all you wuz thinkin 'bout wuz how you could make a fool
> uv ole Jim wid a lie. Dat truck dah is *trash;* en trash is what people is dat
> puts dirt on de head er dey fren's en makes 'em ashamed.

Jim's moving and dignified response is not lost upon the young boy:

> It made me feel so mean I could almost kissed *his* foot to get him to take
> it back.
>   It was fifteen minutes before I could work myself up to go and
> humble myself to a nigger—but I done it, and I warn't ever sorry for it
> afterwards, neither. I didn't do him no more mean tricks, and I wouldn't
> done that one if I'd a knowed it would make him feel that way.

While Huck's response here reveals him to be still product enough
of his slaveholding society to render him capable of feeling superior
in rank and station to Jim, nevertheless he is, bit by bit, undergoing
a necessary sea change. It is a commonplace that metamorphosis is
the underlying principle of myth. And truth in this text, one so
charged with powerful mythic-archetypal symbols and patterns, lies
in change, process, and the evolution of character. As concerned
moralist, Twain traces Huck's metamorphosis slowly but steadily.

In fact, Huck's struggles toward moral stature are carefully documented by the author. Huck's vacillating about Jim's freedom is a case
in point. Although Huck has thought himself sympathetic to Jim's
desire for freedom, the closer they get to Cairo, the more anxious
Huck becomes. Twain vividly chronicles Huck's conflict:

> Jim said it made him all over trembly and feverish to be so close to
> freedom. Well, I can tell you it made me all over trembly and feverish,
> too, to hear him, because I begun to get it through my head that he *was*
> most free—and who was to blame for it? Why, *me.* . . . It got to troubling
> me so I couldn't rest. . . . I tried to make out to myself that *I* warn't to
> blame, because *I* didn't run Jim off from his rightful owner; but it warn't
> no use, conscience up and says, every time, "But you knowed he was
> running for his freedom, and you could a paddled ashore and told
> somebody."

If conscience has turned tyrant here, Huck's anxieties only increase
apace when Jim speaks of plans to steal his children back from their
owner. Huck is horrified by such talk; in his mind, Jim's children are

clearly the property of their white master. For the first time, Huck faces the knowledge that in helping Jim he has violated the laws of his society:

> It most froze me to hear such talk. He wouldn't ever dared to talk such talk in his life before. Just see what a difference it made in him the minute he judged he was about free. It was according to the old saying, "give a nigger an inch and he'll take an ell." Thinks I, this is what comes of my not thinking. Here was this nigger which I had as good as helped to run away, coming right out flat-footed and saying he would steal his children—children that belonged to a man I didn't even know; a man that hadn't ever done me no harm.
>
> I was sorry to hear Jim say that, it was such a lowering of him. (Chap. 16)

Clearly, Huck's inability to see that in a humane social order Jim's moral rights to his own children ought to supersede all other claims mark the young boy as the object of Twain's satiric thrust here. That Huck should think the noble Jim's desire to have a family life again is "a lowering of him" can only be read as ironic. Huck and, by extension, a slaveholding society that separates families at will are mercilessly attacked here.

Totally unaware of Huck's conflict, Jim looks ahead to the day when he can say, "I's a free man, en I couldn't ever ben free ef it hadn' ben for Huck; Huck done it." Jim assures Huck, "Jim won't ever forgit you, Huck; you's de bes' fren' Jim ever had; en you's de *only* fren' ole Jim's got now." But this only increases Huck's confusion. Paddling off to see if they have indeed reached Cairo, Huck has an opportunity to turn Jim in when he encounters two men in a skiff hunting runaway slaves. Irresolute at first, he finally moves firmly to protect Jim by stating that the man who has accompanied him on the raft is white. Huck's lie here represents a step in the growth of a moral conscience that has no antecedents in his life on the shore; rather, Jim and the values he has taught of the natural world are beginning to ascend here. Embellishing a strategic lie with his usual zest, Huck assumes yet another (temporary) identity: he invents a father critically ill with smallpox, a story he knows will keep the two gun-toting men from discovering Jim. But he is still torn as he returns to the raft,

> feeling bad and low, because I knowed very well I had done wrong. . . . Then I thought a minute, and says to myself, hold on,—s'pose you'd a done right and give Jim up; would you felt better than what you do

now? No, says I, I'd feel bad—I'd feel just the same way I do now. Well, then, says I, what's the use you learning to do right, when it's trouble-some to do right and ain't no trouble to do wrong, and the wages is just the same? I was stuck. I couldn't answer that.

Finding out soon afterward that he and Jim have actually gone *past* Cairo, the two commiserate silently together. United in their misery, they are united still further by fear when a steamboat, "looking like a black cloud with rows of glow-worms around it," bulges out "big and scary, with a long row of wide-open furnace doors shining like red-hot teeth" (chap. 16), and smashes through the raft. Immersed again in water, Huck must touch the bottom here if he is to escape the wheel. Significantly, Huck is fully submerged at this point, for he stays under the water at least a minute and a half. On breaking the surface he calls immediately for Jim, but receives no response. Nature continues to aid him by floating a plank in his direction; he seizes the plank and heads for shore.

After this archetypal encounter with the "dragon" and a ritualistic descent into darkness, Huck's ability to survive suggests that these are in truth life-bringing, not death-bringing, waters for the young initi-ate. Huck can be "reborn" endlessly as he struggles toward identity and full stature as a moral being. This time he will surface with yet another quickly assumed temporary identity. At the home of the sentimental but violent Grangerfords, he calls himself "George Jackson." That his interlude with this "mighty nice family," in this "mighty nice house" can only be temporary may be apparent even to Huck: soon after his arrival, he shows his characteristic attention to time. He is fascinated by the clock in the middle of the mantelpiece in the parlor. The clock has "a picture of a town painted on the bottom half of the glass front, and a round place in the middle of it for the sun." "It was beautiful to hear that clock tick," Huck says (chap. 17). The young initiate cannot stay here for long; he must be about the very important business of enacting for us his own, and his country's, maturation. Lest Huck become too enamored of his pleasant life with the Grangerfords, he might note that this beautiful clock does not keep perfect time. The reader is forewarned, then, that time is some-how distorted, out of joint, at this house.

The clock that commands Huck's attention ought to command ours as well for another reason: the pictures of the town and the sun painted on this clock conjoin the opposing values of the book. Huck's divided loyalties are thus brought before him. As successful initiate, one who earns his new name and rank by making crucial choices, Huck must finally decide between the values of the town, or the social world, and those of the sun, or the natural world. "Town" values would decree the noble Jim a "nigger," a word, category, and form of behavior derived entirely from the social world. But the world of the sun admits no distinctions between black "nigger" and white "man": a man is a man. "Sun" values permit Huck to listen to the intuitive promptings of his own heart; for the natural world proclaims the compelling truth that Jim is a man and his friend. Twain uses the clock as an important object to remind us of the definitive choice Huck has yet to make.

After Huck's almost idyllic stay here is abruptly terminated by the meaningless but nonetheless deadly feud between the Grangerfords and the Shepherdsons, in which he sees friends slaughtered in a bloody gunfight, he flees once more to the raft. Reunited again with Jim—"Laws bless you, chile, I 'uz right down sho' you's dead agin" (chap. 18)—Huck casts off the George Jackson identity and is reborn once more as he and Jim take off on the indestructible, seemingly magical raft. Safe on the water, the two decide that "there warn't no home like a raft. Other places do seem so cramped up and smothery, but a raft don't. You feel mighty free and easy and comfortable on a raft."

Huck undergoes still another ritual immersion shortly after the fleeing twosome encounter the fraudulent Duke and King. This time Huck must be brought into primeval contact with the purifying waters. While sleeping nude one night, he is washed overboard by a "regular ripper" of a wave (chap. 20). This involuntary immersion signals that Huck's experience with shore life will soon become potentially even more corrosive; his "education" will continue. Huck is being prepared for his final transformation. Later, on shore with the scheming Duke and King, Huck witnesses a transformation that, unknown to him, presages his own. At a circus, a so-called drunk commandeers a horse and ring. The crowd reacts violently at this intrusion of the drunken man who wishes to ride the circus horse. After many false starts and clumsy efforts to stay astride, the man suddenly and amazingly stands aloft on a horse "agoing like a house afire": "He just stood up there, a-sailing around as easy and comfortable as if he warn't ever drunk in his life—and then he begun to pull off his clothes and sling them. He shed them so thick they kind of clogged up the air, and altogether he shed seventeen suits. And then, there he was, slim and handsome" (chap. 22). Huck too must shed the false clothes a flawed social structure demands that he wear, until he can reveal the inner natural beauty of a fully developed moral nature.

In the meantime, Jim continues to instruct Huck. Jim points out that the reprehensible King and Duke are nothing but "regular rapscallions." Jim also continues to protect and care for Huck. On board the raft at night, Jim seldom calls Huck for his turn at watch, but takes his turn instead. And as he watches Jim grieve for his wife and children, Huck understands more and more that Jim is a *human* being. The child Huck says with amazement, "I do believe he cared just as much for his people as white folks does for their'n. It don't seem natural, but I reckon it's so. . . . He was a mighty good nigger, Jim was" (chap. 28). Huck's comment here reveals growth, but obviously his moral journey is not yet complete. Huck must "die" many times before he can be reborn into his new estate. After the long, potentially death-dealing saga with the thieving King and Duke at the Wilks farm ends with all the right identities and relations restored, Huck again cannot wait to quit the violence of shore life. But, reunited once more on the raft—"Out with you, Jim, and set her loose!"—Huck and Jim find themselves still saddled with the burden of their nefarious "royal" companions.

On a trip to shore one day, Huck seizes a chance opportunity to get rid of their unwanted companions (chap. 31). Racing joyfully back to the raft where Jim is hidden, Huck yells, "Set her loose, Jim, we're all right now!" But Jim is gone, and Huck is brokenhearted to learn that "them scoundrels" have betrayed Jim, sold him back into captivity for "forty dirty dollars." In considering what to do next, Huck again is beset by a conscience that stems from the social world. He cannot bring himself at first to write a letter to tell Miss Watson where Jim is because, once again, he is ashamed of the "low-down thing" he has done in helping Jim escape. At this point sorely troubled by his fear of eternal damnation for violating laws that were sanctioned by all the institutions of his society, Huck approaches his moral crisis. What shall the American Adam do? Huck tries to pray, "but the words wouldn't come"; and he understands why: "I knowed very well why they wouldn't come. . . . I was trying to make my mouth *say* I would do the right thing, and go and write to that nigger's owner and tell where he was; but deep down in me I knowed it was a lie—and He knowed it. You can't pray a lie—I found that out." In extremis, Huck makes a decision: he will write the letter. But this decision brings only temporary relief:

> I felt good and all washed clean of sin for the first time I had ever felt so in my life, and I knowed I could pray now. But I . . . got to *thinking over our trip down the river* [emphasis added]; and I see Jim before me, all the time, in the day, and in the night-time, sometimes moonlight, sometimes storms, and we a floating along, talking, and singing, and laughing. But somehow I couldn't seem to strike no places to harden me against him, but only the other kind. I'd see him . . . do everything he could think of for me, and how good he always was. . . . I happened to look around, and see that paper.

Huck's dramatic decision to "go to hell" rather than send the letter represents a triumph for the natural world. In tearing up the letter he strikes a blow for the inalienable right to be free. At this moment he serves as a moral standard for his country; he presents a righteous alternative to the inhumane system of slavery. That Twain renders both Huck's conflict and his ultimate decision so vividly is indication enough of his own position. America, to fully realize its own best self as a young nation struggling to move forward, must divest itself of the grievous burden of slavery. Twain is adamant and in no way ambiguous here. Racist notions and institutionalized oppression are wrong. If Huck's natural *goodness* here represents *wickedness* for the state, then the young initiate, who has just claimed his full estate as a man, decides he will "take up wickedness again, . . . and for a starter I would go to work and steal Jim out of slavery again." Huck has progressed far from the boy who once deplored a slave's intention to steal his children away from their owner. Repeated immersions in the healing, redemptive waters of the Mississippi have effected Huck's sea change. He is now willing to move forcefully to liberate his friend— the only true father he has ever known. Huck is now fully aware of the nature, validity, and strength of the bonds between himself and Jim. They are more than fellow seekers of liberty from the constraints of "town" life; nature has made them a family. Huck will respond with vigor to the urgent situation of his imprisoned "father."

Reinventing himself for the last time at the Phelps farm (where Jim is imprisoned), "born again" as Tom Sawyer, Huck seeks ways and means of releasing Jim. When he encounters the real Tom Sawyer (who momentarily thinks he has seen a ghost), Tom's offer to help

Huck steal Jim comes as a shock to Huck. While he can accept his own moral decision as coming from one who has long chafed at the restraints of the "sivilized" world, Tom has seemed to him the very epitome of one who dwells securely within the circle of the community. Only later does Huck find out that Tom has known all along that before she died, Miss Watson relented and freed Jim. Tom knows he is breaking no laws; and as he proceeds with his Byzantine plans to free an already freed slave, he becomes the target of Twain's satire.

Insisting on digging Jim out; importing spiders and rats for the cell; speculating about sawing Jim's leg off as part of the game; asking Jim to keep a prison journal in the "ink" of his own blood; stealing Aunt Sally's sheets, spoons, and candles and making her think she has imagined their loss: all these and other tricks inspired by Tom Sawyer reveal an author hard at work to excoriate those whose "head" wisdom dominates the wisdom of the heart. The romantic, bookish Tom loves *the idea* of freeing a slave, but Jim as a person has little reality for Tom. Huck is an often reluctant accomplice to Tom's elaborate schemes; but since he has assumed Tom's identity, he must humor Tom, or his entire plan to free Jim may collapse. Jim endures all of the needless indignities because he trusts Huck; Huck, in turn, genuinely admires Tom's intellect and ultimately trusts in Tom's plans.

After a needlessly convoluted, bizarre, but finally successful "escape," Huck is able to say to Jim, "Now, old Jim, you're a free man *again,* and I bet you won't ever be a slave no more" (chap. 40). True to his noble nature, however, Jim does not flee immediately because he is concerned about Tom, who has managed to get himself shot during the escape. Jim's loyalty to the foolish but wounded Tom leads to his recapture. A doctor present at the scene when Jim is retaken tells the angry captors about Jim's loyalty. To acknowledge and reward Jim's noble behavior, the men promise not to "cuss him no more." Again, Twain evokes our bitter laughter as he works to reveal the lilliputian moral instincts of the slaveholding society. Only after Tom's recovery does he reveal that Jim is indeed a free man: "Turn him loose! he ain't no slave; he's as free as any creatur that walks this earth." The final chapter of the book brings a necessary and welcome sight. Finally, Huck can say in a momentous and definitive action, "We had Jim out of the chains."

With the liberation of Jim, a series of parallel liberations takes place. Huck is liberated from his alienated, fatherless state, and liberated from solitariness. He now has a "father" who loves him unconditionally. There is no more need for him to spin his characteristic tale of the poor, fatherless boy alone in the world. Huck is now liberated also from his false identities. He has no more need to be Sarah/Mary Williams or George Jackson or Tom Sawyer. Further, he no longer needs to look to Tom Sawyer as his ideal of what a boy should be. The shrewd, resourceful, intuitive, healthy, and morally responsible manchild that is Huckleberry Finn can trust and believe in himself. He has earned his name. And finally, with Jim's liberation, Huck, as a model and type of his country, frees all slaves. Huck, and the action, can now go forward.

Huck's story springs from Mark Twain's anguished but loving look at his country. As Huck lights out for the Territory, he goes to inhabit a physical space that is but a parallel to his own new and expanded consciousness. The long sojourn on the river with Jim has allowed Huck to move beyond the empty abstraction of the word "nigger" to the recognition of a black man's humanity. Huck's transformation from boy to man, from one who accepts the dictates of a flawed social code to one who triumphantly aligns himself with the values of the natural world, represents Twain's best hope for a country that must give up its prolonged innocence and acknowledge the claims of history. In *Huckleberry Finn,* Twain challenges America to be better, to live up to its shining promise.

Nigger and Knowledge

White Double-Consciousness in *Adventures of Huckleberry Finn*

Rhett S. Jones

The Negro is a sort of seventh son, born with a veil, and gifted with second sight in this American world,—a world which yields him no true self-consciousness, but only lets him see himself through the revelation of the other world. It is a peculiar sensation, this double-consciousness, this sense of always looking at one's self through the eyes of others, of measuring one's soul by the tape of a world that looks on in amused contempt and pity. One ever feels his twoness,—an American, a Negro: two souls, two thoughts, two unreconciled strivings; two warring ideals in one dark body whose dogged strength alone keeps it from being torn asunder.

—W. E. B. Du Bois, *The Souls of Black Folk*[1]

While Du Bois seems to contradict himself—first observing that blacks have no true self-consciousness and then implying that they have a consciousness of themselves that differs from the white perspective on blacks—the frequency with which the passage is cited suggests that scholars have found it a persuasive one. Researchers in the social sciences, arts, and humanities accept the idea that black folk are able to view themselves now through the eyes of whites and now through the eyes of blacks. There appears, however, to be little recognition of the fact that the peculiar organization of American society around matters racial has produced a white double-consciousness as well as a black one.

White people have long viewed Afro-Americans in two different ways. From the beginnings of slavery in North America, it was to the economic advantage of Euro-Americans to define persons of African descent, if not as animals, then at least as less than full members of the human race—a perspective that enabled whites to barter and sell human beings in both Africa and America without serious pangs of conscience.[2] But while this viewpoint dominated the public arena and was supported by theologians, scientists, politicians, and philosophers, it never fully persuaded the mass of white Americans, who after all not infrequently left their children in the care of black folk. The stereotype of the "mammy" itself contradicted the idea that black people were incapable of thought and caring. After all, only a fool would turn her children over to the care of an animal, and white people did not count themselves fools.

Despite the resources invested by whites in proving to each other that black folk were not human, they never fully convinced one another. Writing in the early years of the nineteenth century, David Walker observed that in spite of all the racist rhetoric of whites, "there is a secret monitor in their hearts which tells them" blacks are human.[3] Whites have never been able to escape knowledge of black humanity but, given their hegemony, have been able to create a corpus of racist thought which defines blacks as inferior. Euro-Americans have moved back and forth between their two perspectives on Africanity, now seeing blacks as less than human, now recognizing their membership in the family of man.

White Double-Consciousness in Hemispheric Perspective

Adventures of Huckleberry Finn, by one of the nation's most distinguished authors, reflects and embodies white double-consciousness as Mark Twain shifts back and forth in his perspective on Jim and other blacks, now viewing them as full-fledged human beings, now regarding them as inferior creatures. Twain lived and wrote at the apogee of racist thought in the United States. During his lifetime, justifications for the enslavement, hatred, and exploitation of black and other colored peoples were given a final polish. The machine gun wiped out the last stubborn pockets of nonwhite resistance to white imperialism, forcing not only the Apache and Comanche of America's Southwest, but also the Ashanti of Ghana, the Araucanians of Chile, and other colored peoples around the globe to accept white rule. The British fought and won a war that enabled them to force the Chinese government to allow opium into China, and were soon to boast that the sun never set on the British Empire. The governments of Europe solemnly met and divided up Africa. Twain himself joined a Confederate militia unit, thereby offering his services to a government dedicated to maintaining the only slave system in North America. Rayford W. Logan describes the period between 1877 and 1901, during which time Twain's books won him a large following, as the "nadir" in the history of Afro-Americans.[4] The Ku Klux Klan reached its height during this era, and lynchings of blacks became commonplace.

The maltreatment of blacks in the nineteenth century, first under slavery and later under the rule of Jim Crow, was publicly endorsed by every major institution in the nation as the churches found biblical justifications for it, the courts repeatedly ruled that African Americans were not entitled to the protection of the Constitution, and businesses refused to employ blacks in any but the most menial capacities. Before Twain died, the newly emergent social sciences devised a number of ways to prove the inferiority of black folk.[5] Yet despite these public "proofs" repeatedly and often presented by powerful men in every walk of life, most whites were not able to escape knowledge of black humanity.

To fully understand white double-consciousness, it is necessary first to realize that while whites throughout the New World sought to control blacks and justify slavery, the solution reached in the United States, or, more correctly, in the thirteen British colonies that preceded its formation, was unique in the hemisphere. In the British settlements of North America, blacks were separated from whites in a pattern different from that which prevailed elsewhere in the Americas. This peculiar isolation of North American blacks is most clearly seen in the creation of what sociologist Harmannus Hoetink has termed a "two tier socio-racial structure," by which he means that only two racial groups were recognized in British North America, one white and one black.[6] In the rest of the hemisphere, at least three distinct racial groupings emerged: whites, mixed bloods, and blacks. The absence of a legally acknowledged, culturally legitimated mulatto caste meant that blacks and whites in British North America were separated from one another in a manner different from that of any other settlement in the colonial Americas. Historian Carl N. Degler has argued that the "mulatto escape hatch" that existed in Brazil and the Spanish-speaking Americas, enabling persons of mixed racial heritage to free themselves from the stigma of blackness, had no counterpart in English-speaking North America, where every person known to have an African ancestor was regarded as black.[7]

In the rest of the New World, the intermediate status of mixed bloods was written into the law, so that whites and blacks were forced to acknowledge their kinship to one another. The term "mulatto," found in so many laws, codes, and directives, underscored the fact that whites and blacks had not only social but sexual relations with one another. Spanish Americans also acknowledged the existence of ongoing relationships between blacks and Native Americans not only by passing numerous laws aimed at preventing such associations, but also by writing into the law the term "zambo," which identified a person of mixed African and Native American ancestry. While "zambo" is still in use in many parts of Latin America, there is no equivalent term in the United States. Its absence underscores the North American public position that Native Americans and Afro-Americans had neither sexual nor social relations; that no Indian ever slept with a black and therefore no term to identify their children was necessary. The term "mestee" was sometimes applied in colonial North America to refer to persons who were of mixed Native American and African ancestry, but it soon fell into disuse as whites found it to their political advantage to deny the existence of an Afro-Indian people. The term "mulatto," borrowed from the Spaniards, lingered longer than "mestee," but it has long ceased to have significant legal or cultural meaning. Mulattos are, for all practical purposes, regarded as black in the United States.

In contrast to the rest of the Americas, the United States established a public fiction that denied sexual and social contact among the races. The term "mestizo," which is applied to persons of mixed European and Native American ancestry in Mexico, Central America, and other parts of the Spanish-speaking Americas, has no counterpart in the United States. Mexico now celebrates itself as a mestizo nation, a country influenced by the best of the Native American and European cultures. In the United States, sexual relationships between Indians and whites are instead said to culminate in the birth of "half-breeds," who are, according to popular stereotype, dirty, drunken, degenerate persons—the untenable result of an "unnatural" mixing. The public fiction of racial purity facilitates the structural isolation of the races in the United States.[8] The absence of such terms as "mulatto," "zambo," and "mestizo" widens the gap among the races, suggesting that there has never been any meaningful contact among them and that each is therefore most comfortable in its own separate, segregated place. Admitting the existence of persons of mixed racial ancestry would force Euro-Americans who benefit from the present system to raise questions not only about their ancestry but also about the humanity of nonwhite peoples.

Twain wrote in the midst of this structural isolation. At one level *Adventures of Huckleberry Finn* simply reflects the public racial fiction of the time. Whites, blacks, and Indians all receive mention in the book, and there is seemingly in neither Twain's mind nor Huck's any doubt that they are three distinct peoples. There is nothing to suggest any meaningful contact among them in Huck's reflections as he accepts the white version of the meaning of blackness. But at another level Huck repeatedly encounters Jim under circumstances in which he is compelled to acknowledge Jim's humanity. Huck manifests white double-consciousness as he shifts back and forth between his own regard for Jim as a person and his understanding of the kind of person the society tells him Jim must be.

Huck and Jim live in a period when whites in the United States largely controlled blacks by means of slavery and by making the slaves, in the words of historian Kenneth M. Stampp, "stand in fear."[9] In contrast, whites in the Ibero-Americas early devised other means than slavery for controlling blacks. By the time Brazil formally abolished slavery, three quarters of the nation's black population were already free, although they remained subordinate to whites. Moreover, while Latin American whites had learned how to hide behind the corporate structures of church and state while exercising racial power, slavery in the United States was not only the central means of controlling blacks until the Civil War; it also rested on intimate, personal relationships. The North American slave was beaten, tortured, overworked, and maltreated not by some impersonal institution that administered estates on which hundreds of slaves labored, but by a single individual, the master, who more often than not owned only a few slaves and knew each one by name. Unlike the large plantations of Latin America, slavery in the United States was up close, personal, and intimate. In their day-to-day interactions with their black property, slave masters acknowledged black humanity, but they publicly denied that blacks were human. Although Huck Finn is not a slaveholder, he seldom criticizes the system that rationalized slavery. Yet he knows Jim and knows that Jim ill fits the stereotype of the ignorant darky. As the raft moves downriver, Huck shifts uneasily between the two layers of white double-consciousness. Now Jim is a person; now he is a nigger.

Huck Triumphant: The Exposure of Public Fictions

In denying Jim's humanity, Huck has the entire arsenal of nineteenth-century American culture on his side. This culture was organized so as to prevent whites from seeing how blacks suffered, and constructed so as to separate blacks from whites. When slave mothers wept as their children were sold away from them, the culture comforted white Americans by insisting that while the mothers seemed to be miserable, they were much like bitches deprived of their litter. The dog might miss them for a few days but soon forgot her pups. Because Euro-Americans, whether slaveholders or not, knew that black women were not bitches, they were far from convinced by such arguments; but at the same time they wanted to be convinced. Whites also knew, given the intimate association between the races, much about black life. While the structural isolation of the races provided whites with ready-to-hand explanations for the maltreatment of black folk, it did not fully prevent them from perceiving black suffering. But the culture itself, by insisting that blacks were a lesser breed of mankind, enabled whites to live comfortably with their knowledge of the pain of Afro-Americans. The public level of white double-consciousness—the level supported by culture and powerful institutions alike—helped Euro-Americans avoid reflecting on the conditions that produced black suffering.

When Jim meets Huck on Jackson's Island, the fugitive explains that he fled his mistress because she was considering the possibility of selling him down the river to New Orleans (chap. 8). Huck clearly understands that blacks in Missouri feared being sold downriver, since they believed slavery became ever harsher as one moved southward. When Huck later encounters the Duke and the King, who question him as to whether Jim might be a runaway slave, Huck replies, "Goodness sakes, would a runaway nigger run *south?*" (chap. 20). This answer satisfies the two scalawags, who likewise share the general white knowledge of the border state blacks' fear of the Deep South. Huck knows of this fear, but he does not spend much time thinking about it, and for an adventuresome, insightful boy, as quick with a lie as his Pap is with a bottle, Huck is curiously unable to come up with a plan that will enable Jim to move north rather than deeper into the South he so obviously fears. And Tom Sawyer, presumably every bit as knowledgeable of this black fear as Huck, the Duke, and the King, wants to take Jim all the way down to the mouth of the Mississippi, having "adventures" all the way ("Chapter the Last"). Tom knows Jim as a person, though he lacks the intimate knowledge of him that Huck has gained; and in regard to the fugitive's fear and feelings, the two boys are equally indifferent.

One of the ways in which whites avoided confrontation with the humanity of black folk was to see themselves as kind to Afro-Americans, focusing on their own feeling of being good, decent people rather than on the feelings of the enslaved blacks. This technique did not prevent white awareness of black suffering—that is, it did not prevent white double-consciousness—but it did to some degree enable Euro-Americans to drown out the human cries of black folk. According to Huck, Jim tells the two boys, "Uncle Silas come in every day or two to pray with him, and Aunt Sally come in to see if he was comfortable and had plenty to eat, and both of them was kind as they could be" (chap. 36). But Jim does not say that the Phelpses, who are repeatedly described by Huck as good, gentle, loving people, contemplated doing anything other than returning him to his owner. Aunt Sally "was kind" but not so kind as to release the fugitive, nor is there evidence that either of them ever asked Jim about his family or his life. There is also reason to question how kind they have been to Jim. Huck, although he finds Jim chained to a bed, does everything possible to present his captivity as a comfortable one, yet there are little indications that in perceiving the kind of treatment the Phelpses have given the runaway, Huck sees only what he wants to see. As part of his conception of Jim as a noble prisoner, Tom asks him to raise a flower in the cabin in which he is confined, but the bondsman replies that this will be difficult since the cabin does not get enough sunlight to make it possible to grow a flower (chap. 38). Have the kind Phelpses in their regular visits to pray with Jim not noticed how dark the cabin is, or did they just not care? The Phelpses take for granted the fact that Jim is chained to a bed in a dark cabin. The structural isolation of the races so characteristic of their time—and the time of Twain himself—prevents their full acknowledgment of Jim's humanity. In their case, white double-consciousness is truncated. The Phelpses visit Jim frequently, but he remains for them simply a runaway nigger whom they are obligated to return to his rightful owner.

They must know, given their frequent conversations with Jim, that he has feelings and even sufficient intelligence to benefit from the prayers he and Uncle Silas undertake together, but neither these feelings nor Jim's intellect matters to the Phelpses. Jim remains a nigger.

In Huck white double-consciousness is more fully developed. As one who is marginal to Euro-American society, Huck has a healthy suspicion of the culture that governs it, and he frequently reflects on the willingness of most whites to break the rules when it is in their interest. Unlike the Phelpses, he sees things more as they really are, so that when Tom proposes that Huck steal a slave girl's dress as part of the elaborate plot to help Jim escape, Huck frankly replies, "Why Tom, that'll make trouble next morning, because of course she prob'ly hain't got any but that one" (chap. 39). Huck, in attempting to bring Tom back to reality and to persuade him to simplify the escape plot, forces reality on his friend by insisting that stealing the only dress of a slave is bound to draw attention to the plan. Tom's arguments prove more persuasive than Huck's, and Huck steals the dress; but he has already demonstrated that he understands the deprivation to which blacks were subjected even on a small plantation run by such benevolent people as the Phelpses.

Much of the critical literature assigns Jim too large a role in changing Huck's attitude toward blacks, although it is true that the intimate association between the black man and the white boy as the raft drifts southward has an impact on Huck's ideas. But even before Huck encounters Jim on Jackson's Island, he is already an unconventional lad accustomed to thinking for himself. His experience with Jim merely sharpens his awareness of the contradictions of white double-consciousness as he moves back and forth between the public position on blackness and his personal conclusions.

Huck finds much to admire in Jim. He has any boy's admiration for the adult male who displays manual dexterity, knowledge of the physical world (both natural and built), and the ability to master inanimate objects. Huck describes with enthusiasm the improvements Jim makes on the raft (chap. 12). Although he is white, Huck is, after all, a boy who has learned much on his own (the instruction offered by Pap has seldom been systematic or even coherent), and he admires Jim's technical knowledge. But so, too, did most slaveholders of the time, who often publicly praised the physical achievements and manual dexterity of their slaves. Huck goes well beyond them, however, in recognizing Jim's humanity. Most whites knew blacks were human beings, but they well understood that to admit this fact would undercut not only slavery but also white hegemony. In Huck's time, in Twain's time, and in the present, whites are frequently unwilling to acknowledge black humanity, a reluctance understandable if they are to maintain their power. But Huck is not powerful; indeed—although he tends to downplay this reality—he is dependent upon Jim to help him escape the triple tyranny of community, the widow, and Pap. It is Jim who knows how to build a platform on the raft so as to keep their possessions dry, it is Jim who is knowledgeable of the customs of the river, and it is Jim who is able to establish connections between the behavior of animals and the actions of human beings. The two drifters need one another; Jim needs Huck's white skin and his ready quickness with the lie, while Huck needs the sure confidence Jim has in his own skills and the insight the runaway has into human behavior.

White double-consciousness was born of the awareness of Euro-Americans of their dependence on their slaves, and of their awareness, almost never publicly acknowledged, that without Afro-American labor, expertise, and intelligence America would have been a different and lesser place. The important difference between Huck and the mass of his fellow white Americans is to be found not only in the shrewd suspicion of self-serving public pronouncements, but also in his acknowledgment (however reluctant) of his need for Jim. Huck's youth and his dependence on Jim reverse the usual relationship between whites and blacks in the United States. Ordinarily it is blacks who are watchfully observant of whites, shrewdly calculating their moods and preparing to act in ways that will enable them to survive; the black double-consciousness of which Du Bois writes embodies this watchful reflectivity. Because Huck needs Jim, and because he is already a boy who peers beneath the surface, seeking to discern the workings below, Huck watches Jim, and in the course of his observations reaches conclusions about the fugitive which ill fit public pronouncements on blackness.

Huck finds Jim to be not a dull, dumb brute, but a sensitive human being, both loyal and loving. When, late in the novel, Tom Sawyer is wounded—justly so, one is tempted to add—in the execution of his elaborate, contrived plan to free Jim, the slave refuses to abandon the injured Tom. Huck says of Jim, "I knowed he was white inside" (chap. 40). Huck is not surprised that Jim is willing to put his freedom at risk in order to see that Tom receives the proper care, for he has every reason to know the stuff (which he ironically identifies as "whiteness") of which the slave is made.

While pretending to be asleep on the raft during the trip down the Mississippi, Huck observes and listens to Jim, who by reason of his flight has left his wife and his two children, Elizabeth and Johnny, behind. Says Huck: "I do believe he cared just as much for his people as white folks does for theirn. It don't seem natural, but I reckon it's so. He was often moaning and mourning that way, nights, when he judged I was asleep, and saying, 'Po' little 'Lizabeth! Po' little Johnny! it mighty hard; I spec' I ain't ever gwyne to see you no mo', no mo'!' He was a mighty good nigger, Jim was" (chap. 23). Huck's recognition of Jim's humanity is manifested in this scene in three ways. First, there is the game they play with each other in which Jim waits until he believes Huck is asleep before he gives vent to his sense of loss at being separated from his wife and children. As an adult, he realizes these are feelings Huck—whose own family consists solely of the cruel, drunken Pap—cannot understand or, more important, do anything about; as a boy himself, even though he is a white boy, there is nothing Huck can do to reunite a black family. Moreover, Jim has every reason to believe that Huck is already uneasy about helping him to escape, so the likelihood that the youngster would do anything to help Jim's family get out of bondage is remote. Second, Huck in his watchful observation of Jim is aware of the fact that Jim intends to spare him his agony. Finally, Huck recounts at some length Jim's story in which the slave berates himself for striking his four-year-old daughter, who had become deaf without his realizing it (chap. 23). It is difficult to imagine the Phelpses, for example, appreciating Jim's anger at himself. Huck does not quiz Jim, but watches him carefully and comes to understand that the runaway slave does indeed love his family much as any white person might.

Huck recognizes other positive human qualities in Jim: "I had the middle watch, you know, but I was pretty sleepy by that time, so Jim said he would stand the first half of it for me; he was always mighty good, that way, Jim was" (chap. 20); and, "I went to sleep, and Jim didn't call me when it was my turn. He often done that" (chap. 23). These observations refer to standing the watch on the raft; and while they reflect the natural willingness of a man to let a growing boy sleep, Huck gives no indication that he regards this act as an adult responsibility. Certainly Pap would not take pains to make certain his son got enough rest. Huck views Jim's treatment of him as a kindness based on their personal relationship. He is both grateful and appreciative.

Among the more interesting aspects of the relationship between the two is what Huck learns of black life beyond Jim as a result of their association. The double-consciousness of Euro-Americans made them not only aware of the existence of a black life on the other side of the wall racism had built, but suspicious and fearful of black plots. On the one hand, whites wished to believe that blacks were incapable of laying plans to attack whites, but on the other hand, what David Walker described as their "secret monitor" made them conscious of black cooperation and resistance. Through Jim, Huck is given a glimpse of this Afro-American cooperation. After Jim and Huck are separated, Huck takes up what turns out to be a temporary residence with the Grangerfords. A Grangerford slave, Jack, leads Huck to where Jim is hiding. Jim explains that he hid in the woods waiting for the opportunity to make contact with Huck, but, "Early in de mawnin' some er de niggers come along, gwyne to de fields, en dey tuck me en showed me dis place, whah de dogs can't track me on accounts o' de water, en dey brings me truck to eat every night, en tells me how you's a gitt'n along" (chap. 18). Huck shows no sur- prise, taking for granted the idea that slaves will aid a fugitive slave, and thereby demonstrating that whites fully understood that just as whites cooperated in maintaining slavery, so too did blacks work together in fighting it.

Huck agrees with Jim that Jack, who led him to Jim's hiding place, is "pooty smart," saying, "Yes, he is. He ain't ever told me you was here; told me to come and he'd show me a lot of water-moccasins. If anything happens, *he* ain't mixed up in it. He can say he never seen us together, and it'll be the truth." Huck does not seem to find this information surprising either, and he is familiar with the clever strat- egies used by blacks who engage in illegal activities. Both his own flight with Jim and the frank willingness of the runaway to share with him the secrets of black cooperation, then, give Huck a perspective on the black community that most whites did not personally experience, but he is not startled at what he finds. After all, white double- consciousness has prepared Huck to understand that blacks are peo- ple and behave quite differently from the empty-headed simpletons the culture insists they must be.

Huck is neither threatened nor frightened by this knowledge, in large part because, while his own experience with Jim leads him to reject the public fictions that make up one layer of white double-consciousness, these same experiences leave others intact. Huck really believes Jim loves him, and while most whites do not go so far as to believe that blacks love them, they find it difficult to acknowledge that blacks hate them; for in order to do so, they would have to accept, first, that they have done things to blacks that make them deserving of hatred, and, second, that blacks are sufficiently like themselves to return white hatred of blacks with black hatred of whites. The 1960s, a time in which many black Americans publicly stated, for the first time, their hatred for whites, was an era of rude awakening for many Euro-Americans. But in the era in which Twain lived and wrote, and in the time frame in which he places Huck, few whites were prepared to accept the idea that blacks might hate them. Huck believes him-self loved. After escaping from the Grangerford-Shepherdson battle, Huck rejoins Jim by running along the riverbank and jumping aboard the raft, where, "Jim he grabbed me and hugged me, he was so glad to see me" (chap. 18). Whenever Huck and Jim meet after a separation, Huck emphasizes how glad Jim is to see him, and how much Jim loves him. The boy is not, therefore, frightened by his knowledge of black cooperation, because he believes that blacks have so much love for whites that they will do them no serious harm. This attitude is maintained despite Huck's knowledge of the terrible things whites do to blacks.

Moreover, Huck, like most Euro-Americans of his time, wants to believe not only that Jim loves him but that the fugitive slave ac-knowledges the superiority of white folk. After listening to Tom's elaborate plot for Jim's escape from the Phelps cabin, "Jim he couldn't see no sense in the most of it, but he allowed we was white folks and knowed better than him; so he was satisfied and said he would do it all just as Tom said" (chap. 36). The two factors taken together—the belief that blacks love whites and the belief that blacks accept the idea that whites are superior—make whites comfortable, first, at the social level. Huck, after all, does not fear attack by Jim, or other black Americans, because they love and admire white Americans. Sec-ond, these two beliefs make whites comfortable at the psychological level because they need feel no guilt for what they say about Afro-Americans or do to them. Some scholars have suggested that blacks pretended to accept these beliefs in order to manipulate and influence white folk.[10] Whether or not this hypothesis is correct, Twain presents, through Huck, the belief that blacks admire, accept, and love whites.

Huck also says a great deal about black stupidity. After Huck and Jim meet on Jackson's Island, the boy shows Jim the supplies he has brought with him and goes on to say, "the nigger was set back considerable, because he reckoned it was all done with witchcraft" (chap. 8). It is Nat, however, not Jim, who provides Twain with his best opportunity to demonstrate the superstitious credulousness of blacks. Nat is the slave on the Phelpses' plantation charged with the responsibility of bringing food to Jim. Tom and Huck are given numerous opportunities to bamboozle this dumb darky who believes in witches, ghosts, and other supernatural figures, and who is made to disregard the evidence of his own senses (as in chaps. 34 and 36). Perhaps the most racist aspect of this entire episode rests on the idea that two white boys—clever lads to be sure—are able to convince a full-grown man that he does not see what his eyes tell him he surely sees. It is also difficult to believe that Jim, despite his loyalty to Huck and, to a lesser extent, Tom, does not talk with Nat, tell him that here are two boys up to tomfoolery, and that Nat should simply go along with their juvenile plans. But no matter how carefully Twain's text is read, there is no suggestion that Nat and Jim have such a discussion, nor is there any indication that two adult black men would talk seriously with one another about the antics of white boys. This failure even to hint at talks between Nat and Jim is particularly striking in light of the fact that Huck (and Twain) have earlier conceded knowledge of cooperation between blacks.

Jim Diminished: The Triumph of Public Fictions

Throughout the novel Twain moves Huck back and forth between the two levels of white double-consciousness, as Huck now accepts the public pronouncements on blackness and now reaches his own conclusions concerning the nature of black folk. In the final analysis, however, Huck, for all his shrewd, sharpened insight, accepts the teachings of the society of which he is a part. Twain seems simply unable to accept the humanity of Jim or, by extension, the humanity of Afro-Americans. Huck and Twain are aware of the misrepresentation of black people and black life in the United States, but neither of them is willing to confront racist lies head-on. For black people and for those sympathetic to their long struggle for fair treatment in North America, *Adventures of Huckleberry Finn* spirals down to a dispiriting and racist close. The high adventures of the middle chapters, Huck's admiration of Jim, Jim's own strong self-confidence, and the slave's willingness to protect and guide Huck are all, in some sense, rendered meaningless by the closing chapters, in which Twain turns Jim over to two white boys on a lark.

Tom and Huck treat Jim as a toy as they follow Tom's complicated script for the liberation of a prisoner. From chapters 34 to the end of chapter 40, Twain lets Tom and Huck toy with Jim, and while it is possible to readily accept Tom's perspective on Jim as "nigger," for Tom Sawyer comes off as an insensitive, self-centered prig, it is depressing to find Huck so willing to fall in with Tom's game. Huck, after all, knows Jim, believes in him, loves him, and has knowledge of Jim's love for his family. But Huck never confronts Tom, *never* says: "I have traveled downriver with this man for miles, we have had many adventures, I have apologized to him, he has let me sleep when I should have been awake, and while he thought I was asleep, he has lamented the loss of wife and children." Huck *never* says, "This is my friend. I will not allow you to toy with him and his determination to be free." Huck never mentions Jim's family in his many talks with Tom. Instead, Huck accepts Tom's perspective and that of Euro-American culture. Jim is returned to the status of "nigger." Huck tells Tom:

> I don't care shucks for the morality of it, nohow. When I start in to steal a nigger, or a watermelon, or a Sunday school book, I ain't no ways particular how it's done, so it's done. What I want is my nigger; or what I want is my watermelon; or what I want is my Sunday school book: and if a pick's the handiest thing, that's the thing I'm agoing to dig that nigger or that watermelon or that Sunday school book out with; and I don't give a dead rat what the authorities thinks about it, nuther. (Chap. 36)

Huck thereby reduces Jim to the level of watermelon and Sunday-school text, regarding all three as objects to be manipulated by a shrewd white boy. While this speech may be principally intended as a rhetorical ploy to persuade Tom, it nonetheless casually dismisses all the good times he and Jim have had.

Twain at this point has clearly made a decision in favor of racism.

While the middle part of the book celebrates and acknowledges the growing friendship between white boy and black man, in the last part Twain thinks it important that Jim be shoved back into his place. Twain accomplishes this end in two ways: first, he makes Huck's character over in such a way that the youngster is made to forget, or at least deemphasize, the warm companionship between boy and slave; second, he has Huck support the certainty of the good white folk of Arkansas that slavery is right, proper, and just. Put in a slightly different way, Twain opts to make Huck side with the powerful against the powerless.

Tom Sawyer is the mechanism by means of which Huck finally comes to reject Jim's humanity, as Twain effectively demonstrates that most whites accept the public fiction that blacks are inferior after being persuaded by other whites. Huck has come to know a black person in a way the structural isolation of the times has prevented Tom from doing, but he readily accepts Tom's evaluation of Jim's worth. Huck clearly recognizes in the voice of Tom the voice of the white establishment and expects his friend to be antiblack. When Tom agrees to help Jim escape, Huck is shocked, observing, "I'm bound to say Tom Sawyer fell, considerable, in my estimation. Only I couldn't believe it. Tom Sawyer a *nigger stealer!*" (chap. 33). When Huck later learns that Tom has agreed to help Jim escape only because Tom knows that Jim has already been freed, a weight is taken off his mind since Huck has long been worrying about how Tom "*could* help a body set a nigger free with his bringing-up" (chap. 42). The runaway boy thereby demonstrates that he understands the larger cultural forces—Tom's "bringing-up"—that have led Tom to his attitude toward blacks. Earlier in the novel Huck is willing to confront these forces, as when he tells Jim he will not turn him in: "People would call me a low-down Ablitionist and despise me for keeping mum—but that don't make no difference" (chap. 8). Here is a clear example of white double-consciousness, for Huck indicates that he understands the attitude of whites toward fugitive slaves and then consciously defies it. He does not, however, maintain this defiance, as he later surrenders his knowledge of Jim's humanity and allows Tom to play with his friend as though he were a toy.

Huck's final repression of what might be called the experiential aspect of white double-consciousness, as opposed to its public component, comes as no real surprise, though a black reader naturally hopes this unconventional white boy will be sufficiently independent to overcome racism. But Huck has never been fully at ease with his recognition of Jim's humanity. His knowledge of Jim clashes too sharply with public declarations on the nature of blackness. It is perhaps too much to expect that one young boy would be capable of confronting and defying the values of his time. Huck is uneasy about Jim's comments as the raft comes over closer to Cairo, Illinois, and to freedom:

> He was saying how the first thing he would do when he got to a free State he would go to saving up money and never spend a single cent, and when he got enough he would buy his wife, which was owned on a farm close to where Miss Watson lived; and then they would both work to buy the two children, and if their master wouldn't sell them, they'd get an Ab'litionist to go and steal them.
>
> It most froze me to hear such talk. . . . Here was this nigger which I had as good as helped to run away, coming right out flat-footed and saying he would steal his children—children that belonged to a man I didn't even know; a man that hadn't ever done me no harm.
>
> I was sorry to hear Jim say that, it was such a lowering of him. (Chap. 16)

Early on in the novel, Huck has no conception of Jim as a person, much less of Jim as a man who naturally wants not only to escape from slavery himself but to help his wife and children out of bondage as well.

Later, as Huck wrestles with the decision of whether or not to write Miss Watson and let her know where Jim may be found, he confronts the same forces as he sets his own knowledge of Jim over against the racist teachings of Euro-America. The boy drafts the letter to Miss Watson but tears it up, declaring in an oft-cited passage, "All right, then, I'll *go* to hell." There is no reason to doubt Huck's courage, so it comes as no surprise to see that he is prepared to confront eternal hellfire—the place which, as a branch of Euro-American Christianity made clear, was the certain destination of whites who helped slaves escape from their masters—but his willingness to do so has little to do with Jim and his needs, and everything to do with Huck and his. In a long monologue as he reflects on the mailing of the letter, Huck covers familiar ground as he reviews Jim's love for him, Jim's humanity, and, most important, the ways in which Jim has served Huck (chap. 31). He concludes that Jim has done a great deal for him, but in none of his reflections does he consider Jim's own needs, much less those of his wife and children.

Huck's failure to confront Jim's needs as an adult male makes manifest Twain's genius. Twain has made Huck *a boy, not a man,* and therefore, as pointed out earlier, vulnerable and dependent on the black fugitive. Out of his dependence on the runaway slave, Huck develops insight into the meaning of race that no adult white male—who would have dominated Jim and not been dominated by him—could possibly have developed. By making Huck a boy, Twain has made clear the nature of slavery and race relations in the antebellum period. Whites know they need blacks and know that blacks are human, but they also know it ill serves them to acknowledge either their need for blacks or black humanity. Huck comes close to acknowledging both the humanity of Jim and his personal dependency on him, but Twain is simply too much a man of his time to permit his youthful protagonist to fully expose the nature of black-white relations. Huck sides with Tom, Tom represents white supremacy, and Jim is forgotten. The novel dwindles down into a depressingly mealy-mouthed apologia for racism.

Tom insists that Jim must have rats, snakes, and spiders in his cabin in order to become a proper prisoner, and goes on to argue that if Jim will allow the creatures to be placed in his cabin, they will have "a noble good time." Jim replies, "Yes, *dey* will, I reck'n, Mars Tom, but what kine er time is *Jim* havin?" (chap. 38). Huck signals his acceptance of the public fiction that makes up one level of white double-consciousness by ignoring Jim and siding with Tom. Instead of speaking up on his friend's behalf, he busily works to help Tom introduce vermin into Jim's cabin. And later, when Jim stays behind to help the doctor nurse Tom, who has been wounded in the escape attempt, and the doctor praises Jim for doing so, Huck is pleased and "hoped they was going to say he could have one or two of the chains took off, because they was rotten heavy, or could have meat and greens with his bread and water, but they didn't think of it" (chap. 42). Huck *thinks* of it but does not speak up for Jim. He—and Twain—have made their choice. Huck represses what he knows of Jim and accepts what society teaches him.

Nor does Huck find Tom's future plans for Jim bizarre, though they clearly represent the dreams of a racist white boy who has succeeded in denying his knowledge of black life. Had the escape been successful, Tom had planned "for us to run him down the river, on the raft, and have adventures plumb to the mouth of the river, and then tell him about his being free, and take him back up home on a steamboat, in style, and pay him for his lost time, and write word ahead, and get out all the niggers around, and have them waltz him into town with a torch light procession, and a brass band, and then he would be a hero, and so would we" ("Chapter the Last"). Leaving aside the inherent cruelty of withholding from a slave the knowledge that he is free and taking even a freed black ever deeper into the South, Tom's plans show little regard for reality. The idea that whites would allow an escaped fugitive to return to his home with a torchlit ceremony and a brass band is as absurd as the idea that blacks would be foolish enough to publicly celebrate his return. Neither idea shows much recognition of the realities of American life. They make about as much sense as Tom's other suggestion that the "three slide out of here, one of these nights, and get an outfit, and go for howling adventures amongst the Injuns, over in the Territory, for a couple of weeks or two" ("Chapter the Last").

Huck Diminished: Twain's Support for Racist Fictions

But by the time these concluding statements appear in the novel, it is abundantly clear that Twain has made his choice, and little additional evidence is necessary to make the point that Tom Sawyer has racist conceptions of black life. In the closing passages of the novel Twain once again brings the elements of white double-consciousness together as Jim is provided one last chance to demonstrate his humanity. After some prodding by Huck, Jim admits that he has kept from the boy the fact of his father's death. When he saw the naked body of a dead man in a disreputable house floating down the river, Jim's first impulse was to protect Huck from the sight; and when on examining the body he discovered it to be Pap, his second impulse was to protect the boy from this knowledge as well (chap. 9). This final indication of the essential kindness of Jim has little impact on Huck, who in the closing paragraph is careful to tell the reader all about Tom and himself, including Aunt Sally's plans to adopt him. But the reader who is interested in learning what Jim intends to do, how he intends to rejoin his family, and what plans he has for freeing them is left in the dark when Huck flatly concludes, "There ain't nothing more to write about." Huck is not interested in the fate of Jim—much less that of his family—nor is Tom; nor, evidently, was Twain.

In his widely read study of race relations in the United States,

Swedish sociologist Gunnar Myrdal argued that white Americans felt guilty about their treatment of blacks, and that this guilt would eventually lead to the improvement of race relations.[11] Myrdal was severely criticized by black scholars who insisted whites felt no particular guilt for the things they had done and were doing to Afro-Americans. In the wake of widespread urban riots in the 1960s, the National Advisory Commission on Civil Disorders seemingly sided with these blacks, observing in its report: "What white Americans have never fully understood—but what the negro can never forget—is that white society is deeply implemented in the ghetto. White institutions created it, white institutions maintain it, and white society condones it."[12] White double-consciousness suggests that most whites are indeed aware—some, like Huck, by virtue of experience—of black suffering. Moreover, almost all whites are aware, also by virtue of personal experience, of the humanity of black folk. But set over and against this knowledge is not only the power of the state—what some students of race relations are coming to call institutionalized racism—but also a public fiction that insists blacks are less human than whites. To the extent they are able to repress their personal knowledge of the humanity of blacks and accept this public fiction, whites are able to escape the guilt suggested by Myrdal.

Mark Twain clearly reveals knowledge of the two different levels of white thought concerning blacks. *Adventures of Huckleberry Finn* also reveals Twain's knowledge of Euro-American double-consciousness in other areas of life, as he repeatedly allows his favored characters to show a healthy disdain for some of the most celebrated public fictions of the era.

But Twain finally proves unwilling or unable to reveal the cruel contradictions of racism. He makes Jim into a man—a gentle, caring man who gives affection and guidance to a boy who has not known much of either. Like any boy his age, Huck assigns himself the central role in moving the raft downriver, but the careful reader will see that it is Jim, not Huck, who provisions the raft, recovers it, keeps it seaworthy, and advises the boy on moral and social issues. Moreover, Jim seldom contradicts or chastises Huck, sensing that he needs both love and support. Huck begins by viewing Jim as a nigger, moves through a period in which he admires and respects him, and ends by again regarding Jim as a nigger. Jim does nothing to diminish his humanity while Huck passes through these phases. Twain is fair and makes it clear that Huck's willingness to allow his friend to become a toy in a game organized by the selfish, insensitive Tom has nothing to do with the fugitive's behavior. It is Huck who makes the decision to accept the public fiction concerning blacks.

It therefore may be profitless to debate whether or not Twain was a racist. His white double-consciousness enabled him to see Jim now as human, now as nigger. Jim emerges, briefly, as fully human in the book, but Twain then shoves him back into the role of nigger. The continuing controversy over the book is not fueled primarily by its abundance of racist statements; far more virulent ones may be found in far more recent novels which remain unchallenged on the shelves of the nation's libraries. Rather, those (scholars, librarians, teachers, parents, and students—whether black or white) who object to *Huckleberry Finn* are venting their sense of betrayal that a man of Twain's genius, who so clearly perceived the racist public fictions that so dominated the nineteenth century, decided at a crucial moment to accept them.

Adventures of Huckleberry Finn must remain on the bookshelves. Twain would no doubt be delighted to learn that he is still making folks angry eight decades after his death, but this anger should encourage additional studies of the man and his work rather than spiteful, petty attacks aimed at taking his books off the shelves. In particular, understanding is needed of Twain's willingness to diminish Huck rather than allow the boy to reveal the silliness, ugliness, and cruelty of racism. Huck, a shrewd, reflective, watchful boy, is bound, or so it seems in the early chapters, to topple this idiotic idol as he and Twain have, between them, kicked over so many others. Twain stops Huck. But in order to do so he must snatch from the boy his insightful, original view of the world and place him in thralldom to foolish, stupid Tom, who can do no better than copycat the ideas of others. Readers have a right, therefore, to be angry at Twain not only for what he does to Jim but for what he must do to Huck—arguably his most magnificent creation—in order to return Jim to the status of nigger. Readers have a right to feel betrayed at this perversion of Huck, this sacrifice of him on the high altar of racism at which so many Euro-Americans worship.

This anger at Twain should not be turned outward at Twain's books, but rather inward in an effort to understand why Twain was willing to betray Jim, Huck, his readers, and his own insight rather than let Huck go on in his exposure of racism. Why did Twain stop Huck? *Huckleberry Finn* must remain available to the reading public so that people can continue to read the novel, get angry, feel betrayed, and eventually find an answer. In so doing, they may find clues that will help explain why so many of Euro-America's most distinguished novelists have found it possible to accept or ignore racism, despite their awareness of the ugly things it does not only to the souls of black folk but to those of whites as well. At a time when both political and literary forces seem determined to turn the nation's attention away from the racist maltreatment of black people and to focus blacks' attention on "true scholarship"—the study of white people and their public fictions—Twain deserves a careful reading as a white person who almost, but not quite, publicly emancipated himself from racism. He and his books call out for reflective, careful study, not angry efforts to prohibit the readings of his work.

Notes

1. (1903; Greenwich, Conn.: Fawcett, 1961) 16–17.
2. Useful perspectives on this are found in Gustavus Myers, *History of Bigotry in the United States* (1943; New York: Capricorn, 1960); Barry N. Schwartz and Robert Disch, *White Racism: Its History, Pathology and Practice* (New York: Dell, 1970); and Stanley Feldstein, ed., *The Poisoned Tongue: A Documentary History of American Racism and Prejudice* (New York: Morrow, 1972).
3. *David Walker's Appeal to the Coloured Citizens of the World,* introduction by Charles M. Wiltse (1829; New York: Hill & Wang, 1965) 61.
4. Rayford W. Logan, *The Betrayal of the Negro* (New York: Collier, 1965). Interestingly, the original title of the book, first published in 1954, was *The Negro in American Life and Thought: The Nadir, 1877–1901,* which better suggests the low ebb of black fortunes in the period.
5. See Rhett S. Jones, "Proving Blacks Inferior, 1870–1930," *Black World* 20 (1971): 4–19.
6. Harmannus Hoetink, *The Two Variants in Caribbean Race Relations* (New York: Oxford UP, 1967).
7. Carl N. Degler, *Neither Black nor White: Slavery and Race Relations in Brazil and the United States* (New York: Macmillan, 1971).
8. The meaning and consequences of the term "structural isolation" are explored in a series of articles by Rhett S. Jones. See "Understanding Afro-American Thought: Can the Black Writer Help?" *Studies in Black Literature* 7 (1976): 10–15; "Structural Isolation, Race, and Cruelty in the New World," *Third World Review* 4 (1978): 34–43; and "Structural Isolation and the Genius of Black Nationalism in Colonial America," *Colby Library Quarterly* 15 (1979): 252–66.
9. Kenneth M. Stampp, *The Peculiar Institution: Slavery in the Ante-*

Bellum South (New York: Vintage, 1956). See especially chapter 4, "To Make Them Stand in Fear."

10. There is a considerable literature on blacks who pretended affection for whites in order to gain their own ends. See, for example, Gilbert Osofsky, ed., *Puttin on Ole Massa* (New York: Harper & Row, 1969); and Ina Corrine Brown, *Understanding Race Relations* (Englewood Cliffs, N.J.: Prentice-Hall, 1973).

11. *An American Dilemma: The Negro Problem in Modern Democracy* (New York: Harper, 1944).

12. *Report of the National Advisory Commission on Civil Disorders* (New York: Bantam, 1968) 2.

Huck Finn in the Twentieth Century

The place of *Adventures of Huckleberry Finn* in the literary canon has been assured in the twentieth century by the commendations of canonized critics such as T. S. Eliot and Lionel Trilling, by Ernest Hemingway's claim that it is the source for "all modern American literature," and by the continued semi-mythical status of both Huck and his author. Familiarity with the novel is a sine qua non of "cultural literacy," and most Americans who have an opinion on the matter are likely to think of it as unim-peachably wholesome. For some, however, as Julius Lester suggests, the novel delves too intimately into both past abuse in the form of black slavery and current unresolved difficulties faced by the descendants of those slaves—descendants who are today still struggling to attain social equality in the United States.

Lester's essay, "Morality and *Adventures of Huckleberry Finn*," derives much of its rhetorical vigor from the racial overtones of an incident that happened when he stopped at Hannibal, Missouri, intending to visit Mark Twain's boyhood home. His description of the event and reaction to it intertwine with his assessment of *Huckleberry Finn* in a way that seems emblematic of the blending of textual and extratextual in the controversies surrounding Twain's novel. Lester's encounter with the racial situation in twentieth-century Hannibal also plays interestingly off a passage not mentioned in his essay from *Life on the Mississippi*, in which Twain alludes to his own return to Hannibal: "On my way through town to the hotel, I saw the house which was my home when I was a boy. At present rates, the people who now occupy it are of no more value than I am, but in my time they would have been worth not less than five hundred dollars apiece. They are colored folk."[1] Lester freely concedes that he has spent little time with the text of *Huckleberry Finn* (having not even read it until recently), but his anecdotal approach captures something of the emotional and rhetorical force of contemporary objections to the novel, reminding us of the many bitter reasons for resentment which cloud the context of the novel's creation in the late nineteenth century and still affect its reception in the late twentieth.

Two points of fact should be mentioned regarding Lester's essay. The first has to do with his complaint that "Miss Watson's will frees Jim but makes no mention of his wife and children." This objection misses the textual fact: as Twain's narrative makes clear (chap. 16), Miss Watson did not own Jim's wife and children. But Lester's rhetorical point is on target in that, as Charles Nilon's essay suggests, the absence of any apparent concern by Jim for his family at the time of his release from slavery (in contrast to earlier expressions of concern) seems a curious and significant omission. And as Lester says (and Betty Jones's essay concurs), the freeing of Jim himself seems an unlikely benevolence for an unenlightened white slave owner who may believe that Jim has murdered Huck Finn. The second matter involves Lester's contention that the entire journey downriver is implausible since Jim could simply have crossed the river to the free state of Illinois. A number of critics, including Nilon and Carmen Subryan in this volume, point out that crossing to Illinois did not by any means put a fleeing slave out of jeopardy because fugitive slave laws (see the introduction to "Jim and Huck in the Nineteenth Century") were in force and were actively prosecuted in Illinois.[2] On the other hand, at least one recent critic, Harold Beaver, taking these laws into account, agrees with Lester that crossing into Illinois would have been the sensible thing:

> The whole adventure only makes boyish sense. Despite the river's current, Jim might have risked swimming the quarter mile channel from Jackson's Island to the Illinois shore. By . . . law, it is true, he would have been subject to arrest and (on conviction) indentured labour. Without freedom papers, that is, he would still have been on the run. Rewards were offered from way beyond the Ohio which made returning runaways profitable business. But the risks of going down-river seem far greater. Even if Huck and Jim had located the southern tip of Illinois and turned east up the Ohio river, what then? They could not go against the

current. So they planned to take a *public steamboat*. . . . A 14-year-old boy and "his Negro" were to sail openly past slave territory on the Kentucky side!³

Lester's essay affords a sense of the way in which the novel's overtly racist context remains relevant to the hurt and anger resulting from black experience in twentieth-century America. Equally important, he makes a more general connection between Huck's escapist concept of freedom and the social malaise that results when a puerile avoidance of social responsibility is valorized.

Charles Nichols, in "'A True Book—With Some Stretchers': *Huck Finn* Today," agrees with Lester that Jim's and Huck's journey downriver is hopeless from the beginning, but he finds Twain's treatment of that hopeless quest successful both in satirizing false values and in presenting, through the relationship between Jim and Huck, a hopeful vision of the possibility of human brotherhood. Describing the Mark Twain of 1885 (the year of the novel's American publication) as a man in vigorous rebellion against the "tribal gods" (religious, political, and economic) of American society, he focuses on the ironic distance between Huck Finn and Mark Twain and on Twain's thematically purposeful filling of that gap as Huck's "developing moral sense" rejects his society's false gods in favor of a more thoroughly humanized perspective.

Arnold Rampersad, in "*Adventures of Huckleberry Finn* and Afro-American Literature," surveys the influence of the novel on Afro-American fiction, which he describes as predominantly "practical, skeptical, human-centered, and secular." Rampersad discusses the importance of Twain's placing a black character and his culture in the context of freedom and identifies the novel's exposure of societal myths, particularly those related to the "moral inversion" present in a slave society, as an influential example for black writers. But he also notes that Afro-American fiction has generally not, at least until very recently, followed Twain's example in the use of such stylistic devices as first-person narrative, dialect, and child narrators, or such themes as genuine male bonding and man's relation to nature.

Kenny J. Williams's "*Adventures of Huckleberry Finn;* or, Mark Twain's Racial Ambiguity" considers the figure of Jim as an expression of Twain's ambivalence toward racial issues. Clearly, Jim is noble and life affirming (in contrast to Huck's fascination with the subject of death), but at the same time he is degraded by the pervasiveness of racial epithets of which he either is or could be the subject. Following the clue of such "mixed signals" on race, Williams discusses the way in which Twain's novel reflects the racial ambivalence of nineteenth-century American society as a whole, and speculates that perhaps the novel reveals more about racial attitudes than many Americans in the twentieth century want to know. Regardless of the racial feelings that impelled Twain in the writing of *Huckleberry Finn,* she terms the result a "classic statement that weighs the nation in the balance."

James S. Leonard and Thomas A. Tenney

Notes

1. Quoted in Lucinda H. MacKethan, "Huck Finn and Slave Narratives: Lighting out as Design," *Southern Review* 20 (April 1984): 250.

2. For an indication of Twain's knowledge of the Fugitive Slave Act, see the Nick Karanovich entry in "For Further Reading," in this volume.

3. Harold Beaver, *Huckleberry Finn* (London: Allen & Unwin, 1987) 51.

Morality

and *Adventures*

of Huckleberry Finn

Julius Lester

I don't think I'd ever read *Adventures of Huckleberry Finn*. Could that be? Every American child reads it, and a child who read as much as I did must have.

As carefully as I search the ocean floor of memory, however, I find no barnacle-encrusted remnant of Huckleberry Finn. I may have read *Tom Sawyer,* but maybe I didn't. Huckleberry Finn and Tom Sawyer are embedded in the American collective memory like George Washington (about whom I know I have never read). Tom and Huck are part of our American selves, a mythologem we imbibe with our mother's milk.

I do have an emotional memory of going to Hannibal, Missouri, with my parents when I was eight or nine, and visiting the two-story white frame house where Mark Twain lived as a boy—where Huck and Tom lived as boys. In the American collective memory, Twain, Huck, and Tom merge into a paradigm of boyhood which shines as poignantly as a beacon, beckoning, always beckoning to us from some paradise lost, albeit no paradise we (or they) ever had.

I remember that house, and I remember the white picket fence around it. Maybe it was my father who told me the story about Tom Sawyer painting the fence (if it was Tom Sawyer who did), and maybe he told me about Huckleberry Finn, too. But it occurs to me only now to wonder if my father ever read Twain's books—my father born in Mississippi when slavery still cast a cold shadow at brightest and hottest noon. And if he did not read Twain, is there any Lester who

did? Probably not, and it doesn't matter. In the character of Huckleberry Finn, Twain evoked something poignant and real in the American psyche, and now, having read the novel, I see that it is something
dangerously, fatally seductive.

In the summer of 1973 I drove across country from New York
City, where I was living, and returned to Hannibal to visit that two-
story white house for the first time since childhood. It was mid-
afternoon when I drove into Hannibal, planning to stay in a motel
that night and spend the next morning leisurely going through the
Twain boyhood home. As I walked toward the motel desk, there was
a noticeable hush among the people in the lobby, and I perceived a
tightening of many razor-thin, white lips. I was not surprised, therefore, when the motel clerk said there were no vacancies. The same
scenario was repeated at a second and third motel. It was the kind of
situation black people know all about and white people say is merely
our imaginations, our hypersensitivity, our seeing discrimination
where none exists. All I know is that no motel in town could find a
room for me and that as I got into the car and drove away from
Hannibal, another childhood memory returned. It was my father's
voice reminding me that "Hannibal is rough on Negroes."

That's the kind of thing that can happen to a black person when
the American collective memory subsumes black reality, when you
remember Huck shining brightly and forget to keep an eye on what
(or who) may be lurking in the shadows.

I am grateful that among the many indignities inflicted on me in
childhood, I escaped *Huckleberry Finn*. As a black parent, however, I
sympathize with those who want the book banned, or at least removed from required reading lists in schools. While I am opposed to
book banning, I know that my children's education will be enhanced
by not reading *Huckleberry Finn*. It is, in John Gardner's phrase, a
"well-meant, noble sounding error" that "devalue[s] the world."[1]

That may sound harsh and moralistic, but I cannot separate literature, no matter how well written, from morality. By morality I do not
mean bourgeois mores, which seek to govern the behavior of others
in order to create (or coerce) that conformity thought necessary for
social cohesion. The truly moral is far broader, far more difficult, and
less certain of itself than bourgeois morality, because it is not concerned with the "what" of behavior but with the spirit we bring to our
living, and, by implication, to literature. Gardner put it this way: "We

recognize true art by its careful, thoroughly honest research for and analysis of values. It is not didactic because, instead of teaching by authority and force, it explores, open-mindedly, to learn what it should teach. It clarifies and confirms. . . . [M]oral art tests values and rouses trustworthy feelings about the better and the worse in human action."[2]

It is in this sense, then, that morality can and should be one of the criteria for assessing literature. It must be if a book is to "serve as the axe for the frozen sea within us," as Kafka wrote. *Adventures of Huckleberry Finn* is not the axe; it is the frozen sea, immoral in its major premises, one of which demeans blacks and insults history.

Twain makes an odious parallel between Huck's being "enslaved" by a drunken father who keeps him locked in a cabin and Jim's legal enslavement. Regardless of how awful and wrong it is for a boy to be held physically captive by his father, there is a profound difference between that and slavery. By making them into a parallelism, Twain applies a veneer to slavery which obscures the fact that, by definition, slavery was a horror. Such a parallelism also allowed Twain's contemporaries to comfortably evade responsibility and remorse for the horror they had made.

A boy held captive by a drunken father is not in the same category of human experience as a man enslaved. Twain willfully refused to understand what it meant to be legally owned by another human being and to have that legal ownership supported by the full power of local, state, and federal government enforcement. Twain did not take slavery, and therefore black people, seriously.

Even allowing for the fact that the novel is written from the limited first-person point of view of a fourteen-year-old boy (and at fourteen it is not possible to take anything seriously except oneself), the author must be held responsible for choosing to write from that particular point of view. If the novel had been written before emancipation, Huck's dilemma and conflicting feelings over Jim's escape would have been moving. But in 1884 slavery was legally over. Huck's almost Hamlet-like interior monologues on the rights and wrongs of helping Jim escape are not proof of liberalism or compassion, but evidence of an inability to relinquish whiteness as a badge of superiority. "I knowed he was white inside," is Huck's final assessment of Jim (chap. 40).

Jim does not exist with an integrity of his own. He is a childlike person who, in attitude and character, is more like one of the boys in Tom Sawyer's gang than a grown man with a wife and children, an important fact we do not learn until much later. But to Twain, slavery was not an emotional reality to be explored extensively or with love.

The novel plays with black reality from the moment Jim runs away and does not immediately seek his freedom. It defies logic that Jim did not know Illinois was a free state. Yet Twain wants us not only to believe he didn't, but to accept as credible that a runaway slave would drift *south* down the Mississippi River, the only route to freedom he knew being at Cairo, Illinois, where the Ohio River meets the Mississippi. If Jim knew that the Ohio met the Mississippi at Cairo, how could he not have known of the closer proximity of freedom to the east in Illinois or north in Iowa? If the reader must suspend intelligence to accept this, intelligence has to be dispensed with altogether to believe that Jim, having unknowingly passed the confluence of the Ohio and Mississippi Rivers, would continue down the river and go deeper and deeper into the heart of slave country. A century of white readers have accepted this as credible, a grim reminder of the abysmal feelings of superiority with which whites are burdened.

The least we expect of a novel is that it be credible—if not wholly in fact, then in emotion; for it is emotions that are the true subject matter of fiction. As Jim floats down the river farther and farther into slave country, without anxiety about his fate and without making the least effort to reverse matters, we leave the realm of factual and emotional credibility and enter the all-too-familiar one of white fantasy in which blacks have all the humanity of Cabbage Patch dolls.

The novel's climax comes when Jim is sold and Tom and Huck concoct a ridiculous scheme to free him. During the course of the rescue, Tom Sawyer is shot. Huck sends the doctor, who cannot administer to Tom alone. Jim comes out of hiding and aids the doctor, knowing he will be recaptured. The doctor recounts the story this way:

> so I says, I got to have *help*, somehow; and the minute I says it, out crawls this nigger from somewheres, and says he'll help, and he done it, too, and done it very well. Of course I judged he must be a runaway nigger, and there I *was!* and there I had to stick, right straight along, all the rest of the day, and all night. . . . *I never see a nigger that was a better nuss or faithfuller* [emphasis added], and yet he was resking his freedom to do it, and was all tired out, too, and I see plain enough he'd been worked main

hard, lately. I liked the nigger for that; I tell you, gentlemen, a nigger like that is worth a thousand dollars—and kind treatment, too. . . . there I *was*, . . . and there I had to stick, till about dawn this morning; then some men in a skiff come by, and as good luck would have it, the nigger was setting by the pallet with his head propped on his knees, sound asleep; so I motioned them in, quiet, and they slipped up on him and grabbed him and tied him before he knowed what he was about, and we never had no trouble. . . . the nigger never made the least row nor said a word, from the start. He ain't no bad nigger, gentlemen; that's what I think about him. (Chap. 42)

This depiction of a black "hero" is familiar by now since it has been repeated in countless novels and films. It is a picture of the only kind of black that whites have ever truly liked—faithful, tending sick whites, not speaking, not causing trouble, and totally passive. He is the archetypal "good nigger," who lacks self-respect, dignity, and a sense of self separate from the one whites want him to have. A century of white readers have accepted this characterization because it permits their own "humanity" to shine with more luster.

The depth of Twain's contempt for blacks is not revealed fully until Tom Sawyer clears up something that has confused Huck. When Huck first proposed freeing Jim, he was surprised that Tom agreed so readily. The reason Tom did so is because he knew all the while that Miss Watson had freed Jim when she died two months before.

Once again credibility is slain. Early in the novel Jim's disappearance from the town coincided with Huck's. Huck, having manufactured "evidence" of his "murder" to cover his escape, learned that the townspeople believed that Jim had killed him. Yet we are now to believe that an old white lady would free a black slave suspected of murdering a white child. White people may want to believe such fairy tales about themselves, but blacks know better.

But this is not the nadir of Twain's contempt, because when Aunt Sally asks Tom why he wanted to free Jim, knowing he was already free, Tom replies: "Well that *is* a question, I must say; and *just* like women! Why, I wanted the *adventure* of it" (chap. 42). Now Huck understands why Tom was so eager to help Jim "escape."

Tom goes on to explain that his plan was "for us to run him down the river, on the raft, and have adventures plumb to the mouth of the river." Then he and Huck would tell Jim he was free and take him "back up home on a steamboat, in style, and pay him for his lost time." They would tell everyone they were coming and "get out all the niggers around, and have them waltz him into town with a torchlight procession and a brass band, and then he would be a hero, and so would we" ("Chapter the Last").

There is no honor here; there is no feeling for or sense of what Gardner calls that which "is necessary to humanness." Jim is a plaything, an excuse for "the *adventure* of it," to be used as it suits the fancies of the white folk, whether that fancy be a journey on a raft down the river or a torchlight parade. What Jim clearly is not is a human being, and this is emphasized by the fact that Miss Watson's will frees Jim but makes no mention of his wife and children.

Twain doesn't care about the lives the slaves actually lived. Because he doesn't care, he devalues the world.

> Every hero's proper function is to provide a noble image for men to be inspired by and guided by in their own actions; that is, the hero's business is to reveal what the gods require and love. . . . [T]he hero's function . . . is to set the standard in action . . . the business of the poet (or "memory" . . .) is to celebrate the work of the hero, pass the image on, keep the heroic model of behavior fresh, generation on generation.[3]

Criticizing *Adventures of Huckleberry Finn* because of Twain's portrayal of blacks is almost too easy, and, some would add sotto voce, to be expected from a black writer. But a black writer accepts such arrogant dismissals before he or she sits down to write. We could not write otherwise.

But let me not be cynical. Let me allow for the possibility that what I have written may be accepted as having more than a measure of truth. Yet doesn't *Huckleberry Finn* still deserve to be acknowledged as an American classic, eminently deserving of being read?

The Council on Interracial Books for Children, while highly critical of the book, maintains "that much can be learned from this book—not only about the craft of writing and other issues commonly raised when the work is taught, but also about racism. . . . Unless *Huck Finn*'s racist *and* anti-racist messages are considered, the book can have racist results."[4] While it is flattering that the council goes on to recommend one of my books, *To Be a Slave,* as supplementary reading to correct Twain's portrayal of slavery, racism is not the most insidious and damaging of the book's flaws. In its very essence the book offends that morality which would give "a noble image . . . to be inspired and guided by." If it is the hero's task "to reveal what the gods require and love," what do we learn from *Adventures of Huckleberry Finn?*

The novel's major premise is established in the first chapter: "The widow Douglas, she took me for her son, and allowed she would sivilize me; but it was rough living in the house all the time, considering how dismal regular and decent the widow was in all her ways; so when I couldn't stand it no longer, I lit out. I got into my old rags, and my sugar-hogshead again, and was free and satisfied" (chap. 1). Civilization is equated with education, regularity, decency, and being "cramped up," and the representatives of civilization are women. Freedom is old clothes and doing what one wants to do. "All I wanted was a change, I warn't particular" (chap. 1).

The fact that the novel is regarded as a classic tells us much about the psyche of the white American male, because the novel is a powerful evocation of the *puer,* the eternal boy for whom growth, maturity, and responsibility are enemies. There is no more powerful evocation in American literature of the eternal adolescent than *Adventures of Huckleberry Finn.* It is a fantasy adolescence, however. Not only is it free of the usual adolescent problems caused by awakening sexuality, but also Huck has a verbal adroitness and cleverness beyond the capability of an actual fourteen-year-old. In the person of Huck, the novel exalts verbal cleverness, lying, and miseducation. The novel presents, with admiration, a model we (men) would and could be if not for the pernicious influence of civilization and women.

In its lyrical descriptions of the river and life on the raft, the novel creates an almost primordial yearning for a life of freedom from responsibility:

> It was kind of solemn, drifting down the big still river, laying on our backs looking up at the stars, and we didn't ever feel like talking loud, and it warn't often that we laughed, only a little kind of low chuckle. We had mighty good weather, as a general thing, and nothing ever happened to us at all. (Chap. 12)

> Sometimes we'd have that whole river all to ourselves for the longest time. Yonder was the banks and the islands, across the water; and maybe a spark—which was a candle in a cabin window—and sometimes on the water you could see a spark or two—on a raft or a scow, you know; and maybe you could hear a fiddle or a song coming over from one of them crafts. It's lovely to live on a raft. We had the sky, up there, all speckled with stars, and we used to lay on our backs and look up at them, and discuss about whether they was made, or only just happened. (Chap. 19)

It is in passages such as these that the book is most seductive in its quiet singing of the "natural" life over the life of "sivilization," which is another form of slavery for Huck. It is here also that the novel fails most profoundly as moral literature.

Twain's notion of freedom is the simplistic one of freedom from restraint and responsibility. It is an adolescent vision of life, an exercise in nostalgia for the paradise that never was. Nowhere is this adolescent vision more clearly expressed than in the often-quoted and much-admired closing sentences of the book: "But I reckon I got to light out for the Territory ahead of the rest, because aunt Sally she's going to adopt me and sivilize me, and I can't stand it. I been there before."

That's just the problem, Huck. You haven't "been there before." Then again, neither have too many other white American males, and that's the problem, too. They persist in clinging to the teat of adolescence long after only blood oozes from the nipples. They persist in believing that freedom from restraint and responsibility represents paradise. The eternal paradox is that this is a mockery of freedom, a void. We express the deepest caring for this world and ourselves only by taking responsibility for ourselves and whatever portion of this world we make ours.

Twain's failure is that he does not care until it hurts, and because he doesn't, his contempt for humanity is disguised as satire, as humor. No matter how charming and appealing Huck is, Twain holds him in contempt. And here we come to the other paradox, the critical one that white Americans have so assiduously resisted: it is not possible to regard blacks with contempt without having first so regarded themselves.

To be moral. It takes an enormous effort of will to be moral, and that's another paradox. Only to the extent that we make the effort to be moral do we grow away from adolescent notions of freedom and begin to see that the true nature of freedom does not lie in "striking out for the territory ahead" but resides where it always has—in the territory within.

Only there does one begin to live with oneself with that seriousness from which genuine humor and satire are born. Twain could not explore the shadowy realms of slavery and freedom with integrity because he did not risk becoming a person. Only by doing so could he have achieved real compassion. Then Jim would have been a man and

Huck would have been a boy, and we, the readers, would have learned a little more about the territory ahead which is always within.

Adventures of Huckleberry Finn is a dismal portrait of the white male psyche. Can I really expect white males to recognize that? Yet they must. All of us suffer the consequences as long as they do not.

Notes

1. John Gardner, *On Moral Fiction* (New York: Basic Books, 1978) 8.
2. Gardner 19.
3. Gardner 29.
4. Anon., "On Huck, Criticism, and Censorship" (editorial), *Interracial Books for Children Bulletin* 15.1–2 (1984): 3.

"A True Book—

With Some Stretchers"

Huck Finn Today

Charles H. Nichols

The power of *Huckleberry Finn* lies in the way it dramatizes the contradictions in nineteenth-century America. It is a society where respectable Christians, bred on the democratic teachings of the Constitution, abuse children, shoot their neighbors in mindless feuds, rob and cheat those weaker than themselves, and enslave the black population. The young Huck confronts a baffling and oppressive prospect.

The moral issues at the heart of the novel are developed by a "transvaluation of values." The conflict in the mind of a fourteen-year-old boy is essentially the conflict in Twain's own consciousness. *Huckleberry Finn,* Twain pointed out in a notebook, is "a book of mine where a sound heart and a deformed conscience come into collision and conscience suffers defeat."[1] In allowing himself to be the mere funny man of the Gilded Age, the tycoon of the publishing business, the emasculated writer whose wife watered down his sharpest effects with her "editing," Mark Twain was, like Huck, false to his own best impulses and saddled with a "deformed conscience."

Twain conveys this sense of conflict, contradiction, paradox, and ambivalence through irony and satire. As he says in *The Mysterious Stranger,* the human race, "for all its grotesqueries and absurdities and shams has one really effective weapon—laughter. . . . Power, money, persuasion, supplication, persecution—these can lift at a colossal humbug—push it a little—weaken it a little, century by century; but only laughter can blow it to rags and atoms at a blast. Against the assault of laughter nothing can stand" (chap. 10). The design of *Huckleberry Finn* is artistically sure, centered in the consciousness of

Huck, who, with his slave companion, is pitted against the "respectable" people of the Mississippi Valley: Miss Watson, the Grangerfords, and the Phelps family. In his ungrammatical, dialectal speech he overturns conventional, smug standards of life and punctures the inflated moral claims of Miss Watson. One of Huck's malapropisms (adopted in naïve acceptance of the King's satirical conversion) unmasks the "Duke of Bridgewater," who becomes the "Duke of Bilgewater." His description of the posturings of the King and the Duke robs them of all credibility. Exaggeration, incongruity, and bathos turn Pap and Emmeline Grangerford into grotesques. The swaggering boasts of Pap, the town drunkard, reveal at a stroke the absurdity of his prejudices: "When they told me there was a State in this country where they'd let that nigger [professor] vote, I drawed out. I says I'll never vote agin" (chap. 6). Such uses of irony make us sensitive to the complexity of the challenges of life and aware of the inevitability of struggle and pain.

The genius of the author is best exemplified in the portraits of Huck and Jim. The story is told not only from Huck's point of view, but also in his own language. Mark Twain described Tom Blankenship, the original of Huck Finn, this way: "He was ignorant, unwashed, insufficiently fed; but he had as good a heart as ever any boy had. His liberties were totally unrestricted. He was the only really independent person—boy or man—in the community."[2] Huck—a boy of good heart and basic good nature—is shown to be sensitive to the outrageous inhumanity of the Mississippi townspeople, yet also obviously a product of their moral teaching. The book is the account of his moral struggle as he comes to recognize the humanity of the slave Jim. These two outcasts, Huck and Jim, embody the theme on which the book's significance depends, namely, the human quest for freedom and integrity.

Huck's and Jim's quest for liberty is, of course, from the outset a hopeless venture. Paradoxically, in their flight from slavery and convention, they miss their chance to leave the Mississippi at Cairo, Illinois, where they had planned to "sell the raft and get on a steamboat and go way up the Ohio amongst the free states, and then be out of trouble" (chap. 15). Passing Cairo in the night, they continue to drift with the current more deeply into bondage down the river, culminating in Jim's eventual consignment to the Phelps farm and slavery by the King and the Duke—by which, more clearly than before, we realize that he has been subject to one kind of bondage or another throughout his lifetime. The dramatic tension of the novel is maintained by the constant danger of recapture, their isolation and loneliness, and the persistent threat of death—and offset by their determined survival and their growing affection for one another. The pattern of the novel, as Warren Beck writes, "turns on an equilibrium of opposites: escape and confrontation, evasion and commitment and fantasy and reality, and thereby achieves its logical symmetry and aesthetic unity."[3]

Controversy arose over *Huckleberry Finn* soon after its publication in 1885. It was condemned as coarse, ungrammatical, and profane. It was rightly perceived as an attack on the values of genteel America—its pseudoaristocratic pretensions, its primitive religion, and its absurd boasts of Confederate "honor." Mark Twain summed up the reactions of the censors sardonically: "When Huck appeared, 21 years ago, the public library of Concord, Massachusetts flung him out indignantly, partly because, after deep meditation and careful deliberation he made up his mind on a difficult point, and said that if he'd got to betray Jim or go to hell, he would go to hell—which was profanity, and those Concord purists couldn't stand it."[4] Indeed, by 1885 Mark Twain was in furious rebellion even against our tribal gods—Christianity, democracy, and progress. The book makes fun of prayer and churchgoing, parodies Shakespeare, and unmasks the claims of white supremacists. Its satirical mode forces us to recognize the inconsistencies in our moral consciousness.

The objections of many modern readers to *Huckleberry Finn* arise from the picture it presents of the antebellum southern mind. But the book's values supersede its racist and inhumane details. Its larger meaning for America outshines its author's ambivalence in race relations. It is my contention that *Huckleberry Finn* is an indispensable part of the education of both black and white youth. It is indispensable because (1) it unmasks the violence, hypocrisy, and pretense of nineteenth-century America; (2) it reaffirms the values of our democratic faith, our celebration of the worthiness of the individual, however poor, ignorant, or despised; (3) it gives us a vision of the possibility of love and harmony in our multiethnic society; and (4) it dramatizes the truth that justice and freedom are always in jeopardy. The modern novel, says Milan Kundera, presents the world to the reader as a question. Good writing not only reflects experience; it adds to life *more* life. *Huckleberry Finn* is instinct with life. We can all profit by wrestling with the issues the book raises.

Huck Finn, the son of the town drunkard, is caught between a rock and a hard place. Beaten, abused, and half starved by Pap, a disreputable and violent man, he escapes briefly to the smothering restrictions of the sanctimonious Miss Watson, the woman who owns the slave Jim. Leo Marx reminds us, "Miss Watson . . . is the Enemy. She pronounces the polite lies of civilization that suffocate Huck's spirit. The freedom which Jim seeks, and which Huck and Jim temporarily enjoy aboard the raft, is accordingly freedom *from* everything for which Miss Watson stands."[5] Like Miss Watson, the Grangerford family represents the best of the Old South's society, the world created by the image of Sir Walter Scott's heroes. Dressed in spotless white linen suits, Grangerford "was a gentleman all over." His deceased daughter, Emmeline, had aspirations to poetry and art. But the Grangerfords carry on a violent feud with their neighbors in which two of them are killed. In terror, Huck and Jim flee to their raft. ("There warn't no home like a raft, after all.") Colonel Sherburn, another pasteboard figure of a gentleman, shoots the innocent Boggs in cold blood and defies the mob to lynch him. But it is the two bums and con men, the King and the Duke, who provide the most distressing examples of human depravity. They sell Jim and leave Huck sad and angry "because they could have the heart to serve Jim such a trick as that, and make him a slave again all his life, and amongst strangers, too, for forty dirty dollars" (chap. 31). Yet it is when Huck sees the King and the Duke in tar and feathers driven out of town on a rail that he sums up his dreadful experience: "human beings *can* be awful cruel to one another" (chap. 33).

The vigorous satire and realism of the novel do not obscure Mark Twain's idealism, his faith in natural goodness. Huck Finn and Jim in their flight from Pap and Miss Watson are seeking the American dream. Huck identifies with the young "Moses of the Bulrushers," who will lead his people out of Egypt. The boy and the slave on their raft have turned their backs on an oppressive civilization. They are now open to every natural and healthy instinct and caught up in the tides of the great river, which symbolizes the boundless possibilities of the human spirit. In their contacts with the people of the towns in the valley, and in their collisions with the traffic on the river, they provide moral insights into mid-century America. As in Gogol's use of the satirical perceptions of Chichikoff in *Dead Souls,* the battle is joined between freedom and slavery, art and profit, life and death. No literary work of the nineteenth century, save *Moby Dick,* is more vital to an understanding of American aspirations and values. The reference to Moses suggests the biblical dimensions of the historic struggle of a people through bondage and travail to the Promised Land.

The heart of *Huckleberry Finn* is, of course, the developing moral sense of the boy Huck. This growth depends upon his recognition of the humanity of the slave Jim. When he first meets Jim on Jackson's Island, he patronizes him as an ignorant and superstitious slave but profits by Jim's knowledge of woodlore and the means of survival. He soon recognizes that he has found another father, a friend and protector. The bond that grows between them is stronger than any human connection Huck has known before. A modern reader is immediately aware of the stereotype of minstrelsy that Twain has used in creating the character of Jim—the absurd dialectal speech, the superstition, the obsequious servility. Jim does indeed, as Ellison puts it, represent "a lost fall in Twain's otherwise successful wrestle with the ambiguous figure in blackface.[6] Yet we must not overlook the author's most powerful evidences of Jim's humanity. He is loyal to his friends and those who love him. He is devoted to his family and his handicapped daughter. He runs away from his owner, Miss Watson, when he realizes she plans to sell him down the river for eight hundred dollars, but risks his liberty to protect the wounded Tom Sawyer. He is, above all, a man with a good heart. Mark Twain's deep conviction is that kindness and compassion are the highest moral values. Huck Finn, reared in a slaveholding community, must struggle mightily against its horror of abolitionism. Conscious of his love for Jim and his indebtedness to him, he is finally ready to be damned for his friend. "All right, then, I'll *go* to hell," he says at the climax of the novel.

American literary critics are almost of one mind in condemning the last twelve chapters of the book. After the splendid account of the risks taken by a boy and a runaway slave for freedom and independence, we are confronted by the foolish games of Tom Sawyer, who plays fast and loose with a man's liberty, and the "benevolence" of Miss Watson, who is, after all, a slaveholder. Jim's freedom is attributed to the very people who enslaved him, and the author appears to "portray defeat in the guise of victory." But it is my view that the denouement must be seen as another of Twain's ironic reversals. "Justice is always in jeopardy and truth walks amid hourly pitfalls." By 1885 Mark Twain was well aware how little freedom had been achieved by the Emancipation Proclamation and Reconstruction.

The Old South's ex-Confederates did everything possible to keep the blacks enslaved. The ending of the book is Twain's satire on the extremes to which the defeated Confederacy went to keep the black population enslaved.[7]

Huckleberry Finn represents the brief flowering of Mark Twain's dream of brotherhood. His experience as a southerner in nineteenth-century America produced a writer of tangled contradictions and caused his career to end in bitterness and cynicism, for Twain was profoundly convinced that slavery, racism, violence, and imperialism, unchecked, would destroy the future of the human race. As W. E. B. Du Bois wrote, color would be the most urgent issue of the twentieth century.

In his attempt to explain his late arrival at the Phelps farm, Huck tells Aunt Sally the lie that leaps again into the heart of the drama:

> "We blowed out a cylinder-head."
> "Good gracious! anybody hurt?"
> "No'm. Killed a nigger."
> "Well, it's lucky; because sometimes people do get hurt." (Chap. 32)

The steamboat, the accident, and the man supposedly killed are imaginary, part of the big lie Huck is telling to get himself accepted by Aunt Sally. But he hesitates to talk of casualties, since deaths of whites would surely be investigated. So he says, "No'm. Killed a nigger," pretending to adopt the standards of his society, where a black man is regarded as a commodity. Aunt Sally then underscores the inhumanity of the slaveholding society by rambling on about the sad fate of a *white* man killed in a similar accident: "He turned blue all over and died in the hope of a glorious resurrection." The death of a "nigger" evokes no comment at all from this sentimental, seemingly warmhearted woman.

The irony here is surely plain to any literate reader. In dealing with *Huckleberry Finn* in the classroom, a teacher is morally obligated to deal candidly and honestly with slavery, discrimination, and the status of Afro-Americans in America. The vexed question of Twain's own attitude need not lessen the value of this exercise. For the emergence of Samuel Clemens, son of a slaveholder and himself, briefly, a Confederate soldier, into a literary figure of international reputation and a champion of the rights of freedmen is an instructive paradigm for all Americans. John Marshall Clemens, Sam's father, flogged slaves and sold a black servant for ten barrels of tar worth forty dollars. A slave owned by Twain's uncle furnished the model for the slave Jim in *Huckleberry Finn*. The Civil War caused Samuel Clemens some anguish, but he soon deserted his irregular unit and eventually became staunchly pro-Union. He enjoyed the benefits of the Gilded Age as a Whig and a rising author who married into eastern wealth and respectability. Although he was the humorist who enjoyed "nigger jokes," he protested against lynching and racial discrimination. He paid a black student's way through Yale Law School and championed both Frederick Douglass and Booker T. Washington's Tuskegee Institute. By the end of the century he was protesting American imperialism abroad.

Yet Twain remained throughout his career a bundle of contradictions. As Arthur Gordon Pettit wrote:

> Out of patience with his times, he nonetheless enthusiastically embraced the "sivilisation" that Huck Finn lit out from. Fond of imagining a day when Americans were not mad about money, he wanted to be rich: he had lofty conceptions about the simple life but no gift for living it. Deeply distraught over the business ethics and machine madness of the Gilded Age, he patented at least four inventions, considered some shady business enterprises and, throughout his life, tended to humanize machines and to mechanize people. He was alternately an eccentric and a conformist, a Christian and an atheist, an imperialist and an isolationist, an outspoken patriot and a disillusioned expatriate who spent a quarter of his adult life abroad. At once the idol of the common man and the pet and protégé of the plutocracy he championed labor unions and hobnobbed with Standard Oil moguls, endorsed the Russian Revolution and accepted barrels of Scotch whiskey from Andrew Carnegie.[8]

Huckleberry Finn brings alive our enduring sense of what America means to all the struggling and suffering peoples of the earth. In the character of the slave Jim, Twain embodied natural goodness and a love of liberty: "He said if he ever got out [of bondage] this time, he wouldn't ever be a prisoner again, not for a salary." In the relationship between Huck and Jim, Twain dramatized our persistent hope of brotherhood. We do well in studying Mark Twain to bear in mind William Dean Howells's advice: "I warn the reader that if he leaves out of the account an indignant sense of right and wrong, a scorn of all affectation and pretense, an ardent hate of meanness and injustice, he will come infinitely short of knowing Mark Twain."[9]

Notes

1. Unpublished Notebook 28a (I), typescript, p. 35 (1895), Mark Twain Papers, Bancroft Library, University of California, Berkeley.

2. *Mark Twain's Autobiography,* 2 vols., ed. Albert Bigelow Paine (New York: Harper & Brothers, 1924) 1: 174.

3. "Huck Finn at Phelps Farm: An Essay in Defense of the Novel's Form," *Archives des Lettres Modernes* 13–15 (1958): 7.

4. *Autobiography* 2: 333.

5. "Mr. Eliot, Mr. Trilling, and *Huckleberry Finn,*" *American Scholar* 22 (Autumn 1953): 423–40; reprinted in *Adventures of Huckleberry Finn,* ed. Bradley et al. (New York: Norton, 1977) 339.

6. "Change the Joke and Slip the Yoke," in *Shadow and Act* (New York: New American Library, 1966) 61–71.

7. See John Hope Franklin, *Reconstruction: After the Civil War* (Chicago: U of Chicago P, 1961); and Rayford Logan, *The Betrayal of the Negro from Rutherford B. Hayes to Woodrow Wilson* (New York: Macmillan, 1970).

8. *Mark Twain and the South* (Lexington: U of Kentucky P, 1974) 6–7.

9. "Mark Twain," *Century Magazine* 24 (Sept. 1882): 782; reprinted in *My Mark Twain* (New York: Harper & Brothers, 1910) 141.

Adventures

of Huckleberry Finn

and Afro-American

Literature

Arnold Rampersad

Whenever *Adventures of Huckleberry Finn* is the topic of discussion, we are likely to hear and read a great deal about Ernest Hemingway's remark on the primary place of the book in the history of modern American literature. Hemingway's observations can be found, of course, in *Green Hills of Africa:* "All modern American literature comes from one book by Mark Twain called *Huckleberry Finn.* If you read it you must stop where the nigger Jim is stolen from the boys. This is the real end. The rest is just cheating. But it's the best book we've had. All American writing comes from that. There was nothing before. There has been nothing as good since."

Although the exact meaning of the remark is not altogether clear (at least to me), we can assume that Hemingway saw Mark Twain's novel not merely as a great work in itself—a milestone in American fiction—but also as a great influence on the writers who came after it, even if these writers were unable to surpass *Huckleberry Finn* in the quality of their fiction. (I take Hemingway to mean "fiction" when he wrote "literature.") As much as he also admired Stephen Crane and Henry James, Hemingway obviously thought of *Huckleberry Finn* as the fountainhead of inspiration for American fiction—or the fiction up to October 1935, when the remark was first published. Certainly, Hemingway's biographer Carlos Baker, in his critical study *Hemingway: The Writer as Artist,* proceeded from a careful noting of this remark to a discussion of some of the similarities and differences between Mark Twain's prose style and that of Hemingway.

Whatever Hemingway meant precisely, the wisdom of his placing

Huckleberry Finn in the most honored position in the history of the national literature has seldom been questioned. Nor do I want to question it here. But does Hemingway's remark also hold true for the relationship between *Adventures of Huckleberry Finn* and black American fiction? In what way or ways is Afro-American fiction descended from, or indebted to, Mark Twain's highly influential novel? In what way or ways are this novel and black fiction importantly different? Any attempt to find answers to these questions probably should proceed in as casual a manner as that of Hemingway's observation, in spite of its surface dogmatism. Casually or formally, however, such an attempt might help us to understand a little more about both *Adventures of Huckleberry Finn* and the fictional works of black Americans. And, although it is not my concern here at all, the attempt might also cast some light on the ongoing controversy about the suitability of the book for use by young black readers. (In this respect, it might be useful to point out once again that the term "Nigger Jim," as used by Hemingway and many other American writers, is not to be found anywhere in Mark Twain's writing; it was apparently a figment of Albert Bigelow Paine's imagination—one that struck a responsive chord in Hemingway and many other white Americans.)

Adventures of Huckleberry Finn differs from the bulk of black American fiction, it seems to me, in certain quite specific ways. In the first place (though by no means the most important one), Twain's use of a first-person narrator—a device popular in white American fictions as distinctly different as *Moby Dick, The Blithedale Romance, The Great Gatsby,* and *The Sun Also Rises*—has few counterparts in black American fiction. Until very recent times, only three black American novels of consequence stood out as using the autobiographical mode: James Weldon Johnson's *The Autobiography of an Ex-Colored Man* (1912), Chester Himes's *If He Hollers Let Him Go* (1946), and Ralph Ellison's *Invisible Man* (1952). Why should this be so? If the black American writer has resisted an autobiographical approach to fiction, perhaps the reason may be found, ironically, in the fact that, from the first slave narratives through Washington's *Up from Slavery* (1901), Du Bois's *Dusk of Dawn* (1940), Langston Hughes's *The Big Sea* (1940), and *The Autobiography of Malcolm X* (1964), autobiography has been the single most important literary genre for black Americans. Moreover, the black definition of autobiography has almost always stressed either its moral and confessional tradition or its quasi-moral function in recording the search of the individual and his race for freedom.

Surrounding black autobiography, then, has been a respect for its orthodox definition that has probably discouraged experimentation with the form, especially of the notoriously irreverent sort that served Mark Twain so well in *Huckleberry Finn*. The link between black autobiography and the quest for freedom probably has tended to forbid cavalier approaches to the notions of authorial truth and authenticity—notions that Twain mocked in the second sentence of his narrative with Huck's jaunty remark about Mr. Mark Twain telling "the truth, mainly."

A second, related difference lies in the unbroken relationship in *Huckleberry Finn* between autobiography and dialect, linked by Mark Twain to comprise almost certainly the most remarkable single structural element of his book. In so doing, he endowed dialect with a degree of prestige unheard of in black fiction until recent times. Examples in recent black fiction of the combining of autobiography and dialect in Twain's manner are Alice Childress's *A Hero Ain't Nothin' but a Sandwich* (1973), whose thirteen-year-old narrator is Huck's age and even of his temperament; Al Young's *Sitting Pretty* (1976), whose hero has more than once been compared with Huck by reviewers; and Alice Walker's best-seller *The Color Purple,* whose heroine, Celie, whether or not Walker herself would like the notion, is definitely a black country cousin of Huck Finn. The autobiographical approach in black fiction, interestingly, has coincided with the rise to prominence of women's fiction, where the device seems particularly comfortable; as, for example, in Louise Meriwether's *Daddy Was a Number Runner* (1970).

In his ambition to elevate the prestige of dialect, as announced in the famous note preceding the novel about the "shadings" of dialect (they had "not been done in a hap-hazard fashion, or by guess work; but pains-takingly, and with the trustworthy guidance and support of personal familiarity with these several forms of speech"), Mark Twain has had very few serious followers in black fiction. For all the celebrated daring of the writers of the Harlem Renaissance in the 1920s, black dialect remained so much seasoning in the speech of characters developed by such writers as Rudolph Fisher, Wallace Thurman, Langston Hughes, and Claude McKay, and was virtually shunned in the work of other writers such as W. E. B. Du Bois, Jesse Fauset, and Nella Larsen. This fact is particularly noteworthy because entire poems were written in honest black dialect by such fine poets as Langston Hughes and Sterling Brown, and, earlier, Paul Laurence

Dunbar, who published four novels in addition to his poetry. Moreover, Hughes and Zora Neale Hurston collaborated between 1929 and 1930 on a play entirely in dialect, *Mule Bone*. Only writers of fiction stood back from making that complete commitment to dialect without which the epochal success of *Huckleberry Finn* would have been impossible. In the 1930s Richard Wright employed dialect, but again in spare and, according to Hurston in her review of *Uncle Tom's Children* (1938), inept fashion. Hurston herself, the undisputed master of black dialect by virtue of her southern upbringing and her Barnard training as a folklorist, came closest in the 1930s to rendering full tribute to the language of American blacks in *Their Eyes Were Watching God* (1937). But while her characters speak something else, her narrator in the novel speaks standard English, or slips occasionally into a folk-influenced form of educated English. Almost fifty years later, Alice Walker, conscious of an indebtedness to Hurston, perhaps also consciously would take the final step with Celie in *The Color Purple*. In 1943, however, Langston Hughes began building perhaps the best achievement in the fictional use of dialect by a black author when he created in the *Chicago Defender* his extremely popular character Jesse B. Semple, or "Simple," who would converse comically there for over twenty years, in thick dialect, with Hughes's educated and very dull narrator. The books that resulted between 1950 and 1965 (*Simple Speaks His Mind, Simple Takes a Wife, Simple Stakes a Claim, Simple's U.S.A.,* and *The Best of Simple*) were all very well received by critics, who persisted in pointing out, to the Missouri-born Hughes's great satisfaction, the similarities between his work and that of Mark Twain. Ironically, in 1962, at the request of Cyril Clemens, Hughes wrote a brief tribute to the late Ernest Hemingway for the *Mark Twain Journal*.

Daring to entrust his tale to a young, essentially illiterate boy, Mark Twain was confident that countrified speech, far from being a millstone dragging down his fiction, would serve to free his young hero's unvarnished poetic sensibility and rich folk utterance. In contrast, few black writers historically have dared to entrust their tales to members of the black folk or the black masses. Their approach has been one to which Henry James would have granted approval—and writers as different as Wright and Baldwin have admitted the crucial influence of James. Few have dared to entrust their tales to anyone other than a narrator as intellectually and linguistically refined as themselves, someone capable of mediating between the presumably

"soiled" black subject, on the one hand, and the ideal, highly bourgeois, and almost entirely white readership expected, on the other.
One reads a document such as Richard Wright's "Blueprint for Negro
Writing," in which he stresses the importance of folk expression as
part of the culture of the black masses, but one looks in vain through
his several novels and stories for a release of folk expression comparable to that of Mark Twain in his greatest work.

In another related area of difference, no significant black writer has
dared to completely entrust his or her story to a child, as Mark Twain
did in *Huckleberry Finn*. In general, the black writer has been reluctant
until recently even to approach serious fiction from a child's point of
view. Alice Childress comes to mind again, and Tony Cade Bambara
in parts of *Gorilla, My Love* (1972). Of older writers, only Langston
Hughes with *Not without Laughter* (1930) emerges as an important
black novelist who hazarded (certainly the approach is risky) a major
statement about Afro-American reality by filtering it through the
consciousness of a black child. Richard Wright effectively attempts
something similar in his short stories "Big Boy Leaves Home" and
"Almos' A Man," but on a far smaller scale, and one that emphasizes
violence and fear. Among more recent works, James Baldwin's *Go Tell
It on the Mountain* (1953) also exemplifies this interest in the young,
though John Grimes's consciousness is but one mediating aspect of
Baldwin's novel; moreover, it is difficult to conceive of John Grimes
as a child. In black American fiction in general, however, children are
seldom seen and even less frequently heard. Or to put it another
way—black fictionalists seem to believe that the social reality they
describe, and in which their people historically have lived, has never
given them leave to depict young lives relatively free from pain, an
exemption on which the depiction of the beauty and dignity of
childhood probably depends. A paradox remains: scenes of childhood have always been very important in black autobiography; but
nineteenth-century black fiction, for example, is virtually devoid of
images of black children.

Similarly, the phenomenon of adult fiction readily accessible to
young readers, of which *Huckleberry Finn* remains perhaps the best
example, also belongs to the white, but not the black, world of fiction.
The intelligent, well-prepared young American grows up on adult
fiction that is also in part palatable to the young—*Huck Finn*, *The Red
Badge of Courage*, *Moby Dick* (in some abridged version), *Two Years
before the Mast*, the Leatherstocking stories, and so on. The black child

has no alternative canon drawn from his or her own writers. The main reason, of course, is that most of these books were written several generations ago, when blacks were recent ex-slaves or only a generation removed from slavery, and when standards of fiction were different; notably, they were written in a time when escapist fiction enjoyed perhaps its greatest prestige. For blacks, escape from slavery was always appealing; but the aim then and later almost always was to escape *into* the whole society, not away from it. The chains that traditionally have bound the black individual in white America before and after slavery have also circumscribed black fiction, forbidding almost all venturing, or adventuring, that does not lead seriously to black freedom. In Chesnutt's *House behind the Cedars* (1900), reading escapist or adventurist fiction leads only to trouble for the black dreamer. Wright's first story, the escapist "Voodoo of Hell's Half Acre," enraged his domineering grandmother (as he mentions in *Black Boy* [1945]). The black writer disciplined himself or herself to write about the search for freedom.

But a fiction about bondage and freedom (in particular, one about slavery itself) might be precisely the kind of story from which one is inclined to shelter black children. One does so to protect them, in their more susceptible periods of growth, from even the knowledge of extreme human cruelty; in some respects, the controversy over the word "nigger" in *Huck Finn* is an excellent example of such protectionism. The treatment of slavery within the context of adventure has been successfully realized, from the general point of view, in certain works by white writers, but precisely because the slaves were not white. Two works stand out here: *Huck Finn* itself, and Harriet Beecher Stowe's *Uncle Tom's Cabin*. It is surely instructive that neither has achieved unqualified success, to say the least, among black readers. The slave Jim, noble for a while, becomes an object of burlesque before Twain's fiction is complete; in the case of *Uncle Tom's Cabin,* the name of its black hero quickly became a byword among blacks for unmanly compromise.

Much adventuring is written by men for the little boys supposedly resident in grown men, and to cater to their chauvinism. In this respect *Huck Finn* is an extremely American narrative, and also akin to the bulk of black fiction, which until recently was written mostly by men. The importance of the bond between males in *Huck Finn* is reflected in most male black fiction but negatively so, mostly as antifeminine behavior and values. Genuine male bonding is not correspondingly prominent; perhaps the truth is that black fiction, as compared to white, is in general relatively loveless.

Another important area of difference between *Huck Finn* and black fiction concerns the propriety of comedy in a fiction about race. Zora Neale Hurston possessed a rich comic talent, probably the richest in black fiction, and one very much in the Mark Twain tradition. But unlike Mark Twain, in writing comically about blacks Hurston notably avoided the topic of race. Just as the black story has been perceived as too grim to accommodate easily either children or modes of adventure pleasing to the young, so too has it resisted treatment by way of comedy, which is one of the principal glories of *Huckleberry Finn*. Slavery, many blacks would say, is no laughing matter. And yet comedy and slavery have a limited but definite coexistence in the history of black writing. One sees comic depictions of slave life in the dialect verse of black poets such as Daniel Webster Davis and James Carrothers, who were prepared to assist in propagating the myth of a golden age of slavery fostered by white writers as different as Thomas Nelson Page and Joel Chandler Harris. But if black poets were at one point content to serve such a point of view, black fictionalists were almost always opposed to doing so. Charles Chesnutt is perhaps the only black writer of fiction to approach the depiction of slavery with a marked degree of humor and irony. In fact, he writes not of slavery but of neoslavery, the historical aftermath of slavery; moreover, his Uncle Julius laughs, but he also connives and wins. Bent on a degree of real subversion, Mark Twain understood the subversive power of comedy; but it is an aspect of his book that few black writers have paralleled before the current generation. Not the last reason for the primacy of *Invisible Man* among black fictions is its rich comic detail, an aspect that links it to some of the writing of Chester Himes and to the most innovative recent black fiction—that of Ishmael Reed in particular, as in *Mumbo Jumbo* (1972), and of William Melvin Kelley, as in *dem* (1967). Of *Huck Finn,* however, one should remember one thing here; much of the humor is at Jim's expense. Huck and Tom are the tricksters; Jim is largely one of the tricked.

Another, perhaps more decisively important, way in which *Huck Finn* goes against the grain of black fiction is in its typically American "twinning" of white and dark-skinned characters to suggest an ideal American hero who combines the best qualities of the white and some darker race in a merger of complementary abilities and values.

This device, analyzed most famously by Leslie Fiedler a generation ago, and present in varying degrees in the works of Cooper, Melville, Twain, and Stephen Crane, is even more dominant in the iconography of popular culture, as seen in figures such as the Lone Ranger and Tonto, Mandrake and Lothar, Tarzan and his apes, Han Solo and Chewbacca, and even in the "twinning" of various white and black performers, invariably male, in television and motion pictures. In rare instances the device has been used to find a vehicle for a gifted black "star" (probably paralyzed in his career because of racism); in general, however, the motivation remains largely the same as that behind Cooper, Melville, and Mark Twain—a sense of a black or Native American familiarity with Nature, noble in essence and finally inaccessible to the white man.

Black writers of fiction have had little time for this oblique approach to characterization and to the problem of race, just as black readers and audiences have probably reacted to such "twinnings" mostly with distrust and annoyance. The black or Indian character, whatever the degree of his "nobility" and his other gifts, is almost inevitably secondary in importance to the white hero. He is only an acolyte in the ritual of American absolution from sin—when he isn't the sacrificial victim. The device allows little flexibility in this aspect of its essence. In *Huck Finn,* Mark Twain exalts Jim—just beyond the level of a white boy—but finally cannot allow him to remain exalted. Jim then becomes little more than a plaything, like a great stuffed bear, for the white boys over whom he once stood morally.

Finally, very few black writers, if any, have been teased by the great question of Nature and its relationship to humanity, which I take to be at the heart of Mark Twain's depiction of the river in *Adventures of Huckleberry Finn.* Whether one sees the river, according to the debate now some forty years old, as a god or as a morally neutral agency, certainly the Mississippi rolls through Mark Twain's novel as a constant reminder of an ultimate force beyond human beings, a force identifiable not merely with the God of Christianity but with Nature itself. The presence of the river and the boy's response to it form the main element by which Mark Twain's fiction deepens philosophically, or perhaps thickens atmospherically. Huck's moral questionings sound and resound in the presence of the river, which represents in this novel the elevating form of the absolute. By contrast, however, black fiction has been notably practical, skeptical, human-centered, and secular. Nature is invoked not as ultimate cause but largely for dramatic effect. Appearing to have ultimate, magical properties in, say, the opening of Hughes's *Not without Laughter,* where a tornado sweeps us into a boy's world (see also Gordon Parks's *The Learning Tree* [1963]), Nature soon loses its shamanlike authority and becomes ultimately subservient to social action. Richard Wright dusts off effects borrowed from the stockroom of literary naturalism for use in *Lawd Today, Uncle Tom's Children, Native Son,* and *Black Boy,* but Nature is finally overridden and reduced, put in its place by the questions of power and politics, history and civil liberties, that have of necessity dominated black thinking.

We have seen that in certain of the areas discussed above, such as the use of folk material, dialect, comedy, and the autobiographical mode, *Adventures of Huckleberry Finn* clearly anticipated eventual trends in black fiction—even if, for much of black literary history, its example went largely ignored. But in what respects was the primacy of Mark Twain's novel relatively immediate, and how was Mark Twain himself very close to the general intentions of the black writer?

The first area concerns the placing of the issue of black character and culture squarely in the context of the search for freedom. Obviously the strategy, or the vision, did not originate with Mark Twain, but with other black writers, on the one hand, and with literary abolitionism, epitomized by Harriet Beecher Stowe, on the other. But Mark Twain wrote as a southerner in a period of intense reaction against blacks; he clearly conceived of his book as, in part, a blow against white reactionary attitudes, against the rising walls of segregation, against lynching, and against the slanderous imputation that blacks were less than human and therefore should be treated with prejudice. Whatever the limitations in his depiction of Jim (and they are considerable), Mark Twain made it clear that Jim was good, deeply human, loving, and anxious for freedom. It is a reflection on American culture that such an approach should be historic.

A related aspect of the novel is its exposure of the South, and to some extent American culture as a whole, as gullible, irrational, violence-prone, mob-threatened, and profoundly hypocritical in touting its possession of superior values. This is a world from which Mark Twain's alienated young, white narrator recoils finally in something like horror, and in comparison to which black Jim, in his patience and love, appears to be positively noble. The acts of exposing the falseness of white and, in particular, southern claims to "civilization" and of resisting the allegation of intrinsic black inferiority have been among the principal concerns of black writers of fiction almost from the beginning of the literature. Except perhaps for Martin R. Delany in his *Blake; or, The Huts of America* (1861–62), Mark Twain went further than any black writer of the nineteenth century, further even than Sutton Griggs in *Imperium in Imperio* (1899), in that he not only repudiated white claims to superiority by virtue of possessing a genuine civilization but depicted those claims as ludicrous.

But the most important way in which *Adventures of Huckleberry Finn* predicts later black fiction is in Mark Twain's depiction of a moral dilemma, or moral inversion, as being at the heart of southern, and by inference American, society. The consequence of slavery and racism is an apparently permanent inversion of moral order, so that right becomes wrong and wrong becomes right; and the individual of consequence, like Huckleberry Finn, follows the instincts of his heart at peril not only to his place in society but also to his own sanity. The man—and it is almost always a man, except in dramas of "passing"— who allows himself to become caught in this dilemma rather than accept the moral disorder masquerading as moral law marks himself as a candidate for existential loneliness or alienation, and probably a violent fate. He or she easily becomes an outsider, like Richard Wright's incoherent, brutish Bigger Thomas, or his more urbane Cross Damon in *The Outsider;* or the embittered and suicidal Richard and Rufus of Baldwin's *Go Tell It on the Mountain* and *Another Country;* or Ralph Ellison's far more charming but nonetheless wildly disoriented hero in *Invisible Man.* In some key respects Huck is one of those white Biggers whom Wright, to his amazement, discovered in the world outside the South, as he revealed in his essay "How Bigger Was Born"; these were persons cut off somehow from their cultures and potentially lethal in their attitudes toward society. Only Huck Finn's white skin and his youth have saved him so far from a bloody fate, although Twain surrounds him with a frightening, signifying level of violence, including Huck's gruesome "murder" of his own self. Bigger could have learned from Huck: "I took the axe and smashed in the door—I beat it and hacked it considerable, a-doing it. I fetched the pig in and took him back nearly to the table and hacked into his throat with the axe, and laid him down on the ground to bleed—I say ground, because it *was* ground—hard packed and no boards" (chap. 7). Cross Damon, Wright's hero in *The Outsider,* "kills" himself as Huck did, and watches his own funeral.

But an important difference must be noted. Mark Twain depicted white Huck, but not black Jim, as being torn and alienated; he left it to black writers, or to a more polemical, if less gifted, white writer such as George Washington Cable in *The Grandissimes,* to show what happens when a member of Jim's race acquires Huck's disruptive alienation. This is a crucial point in evaluating the political and racial force of the book: Mark Twain does not suggest that Jim can catch Huck's dangerous virus. More important than the ending, about which everyone writes, this may be the major compromise in *Huck Finn.* Assuredly Twain knew that Huck's attitude could be contagious, and that blacks had more reason than whites to be alienated and angry.

The historic black statement of the condition ascribed in embryo to Huck—but in its black mutation—would come from *The Souls of Black Folk* (1903), in which W. E. B. Du Bois identifies the core of the black American psychology as comprising "two souls, two thoughts, two unreconciled strivings . . . in one dark body, whose dogged strength alone keeps it from being torn asunder." Du Bois's book included, among the essays, a short story in which the conflict is dramatized; the result is a blow struck by a black man against a white—one of the earliest of such acts in black fiction—and the resulting death of the white man and the black hero. Du Bois's book has long been recognized as the most influential single volume in black literature, at least until the appearance of Wright's *Native Son* in 1940. If all Afro-American literature comes from any one source, that fountainhead is most likely *The Souls of Black Folk,* which the authoritative James Weldon Johnson declared in *Along This Way* (1933), published two years before Hemingway's *Green Hills of Africa,* to have had "a greater effect upon and within the Negro race in America than any other single book published in this country since *Uncle Tom's Cabin.*"

In spite of the crucial differences between *Souls* and *Huck Finn,* however, I would venture to say that very near to the fountainhead (nearer than any other work of fiction, including *Uncle Tom's Cabin*) must be *Adventures of Huckleberry Finn.* Although many of the writers of fiction acknowledged the intellectual supremacy of Du Bois, and had little or nothing to say about Mark Twain, it is difficult to miss the affinity between them and the author of *Huckleberry Finn*—especially if one compares Twain with other American masters of fiction such as the much-admired James, or Howells, or Melville, or Sinclair Lewis, or Hemingway himself. In his stress on folk culture, on dialect, and on American humor, Mark Twain anticipated Dunbar, Hughes (who lauded Twain in an introduction to *Pudd'nhead Wilson*), Hurston, Fisher, Thurman, Ellison, Gaines, Childress, Reed, and Alice Walker; in his depiction of alienation in an American context, prominently including race, Twain anticipates other aspects of most of these writers' work and also that of Richard Wright, Chester Himes, Ann Petry, James Baldwin, and Toni Morrison.

In *Adventures of Huckleberry Finn,* Mark Twain flinched before the potentially dangerous confrontation of these two major aspects of his work—its democratic folk and racial features, and its depiction of the alienation and moral disorder endemic to southern and even American culture. Such a confrontation, which in effect (certainly from a black point of view) is akin to a synthesis of Twain and Du Bois, or of *Huckleberry Finn* and *The Souls of Black Folk,* had begun to take place when Hemingway made his celebrated comment in 1935. One sees the meeting in the works of the maturing William Faulkner, who had published *Light in August* three years before and would publish *Absalom, Absalom!* a year later; and, importantly, in the fledgling efforts of the young Richard Wright, still struggling in 1935 to find his own fictive voice.

Adventures of Huckleberry Finn; or, Mark Twain's Racial Ambiguity

Kenny J. Williams

No matter what we may wish to tell other nations about ourselves and our American Dream, the ambivalence of many Americans toward matters of race relations remains a factor that is often used to illustrate the hypocrisy of the professed creeds of the United States. If a literary classic is a work that transcends its time and is relevant for the present, the racial implications of *Adventures of Huckleberry Finn*—negative though they are in some respects—may be of value in understanding American civilization. Not only did Mark Twain include overt and subliminal commentary on his own day, but he also displayed the uncertainties that have marked the so-called American dilemma. As we continue to extol the virtue of our democratic experiment to others, the world may well point to our "classic" as evidence of our inherent hypocrisy.

The greatness of *Adventures of Huckleberry Finn* has been accepted without much question. To identify its apparent weaknesses subjects the critic to charges of undue sensitivity or literary naïvete, but one does not have to be particularly knowledgeable, for example, to realize that a slave seeking freedom would hardly travel southward on the Mississippi River. Yet Twain apologists claim that such a concern for historic validity denies the power and license of literary imagination. That additional aspects of this realistic novel tax a reader's credulity can be dismissed by those who remind others of Twain's early notice: "PERSONS attempting to find a motive in this narrative will be prosecuted; persons attempting to find a moral in it will be banished; persons attempting to find a plot in it will be shot." In the end, many considerations of the novel's shortcomings fade before the discussions of its "greatness."

From Ernest Hemingway's declaration ("all modern American literature comes from [it . . . and] it's the best book we've had") to the numerous studies of the novel, *Adventures of Huckleberry Finn* has indeed become part of the folklore of American culture. Throughout the years critics have cited such elements as Twain's deviation from a genteel tradition that had become artistically stifling in the latter part of the nineteenth century and his picaresque use of the Mississippi River that stresses the symbolic role of that river in American life. Others have pointed to the novel's exploration into such abstract principles as loyalty, morality, freedom, alienation, conscience, and noncompliance with unjust laws to prove its merit. Furthermore, in its use of the vernacular, the work unwittingly fulfills Noah Webster's eighteenth-century observation that a national literature would not be created until American English was accepted as an artistic medium. All of these characteristics suggest that the novel is an outstanding one.

Twain's chronicle of the adolescent Huck Finn, however, was not without its detractors and doubters even from the beginning. Perhaps no work in American literature has been banned as consistently or frequently. Initially, its very points of greatness bothered many. Early arbiters of taste thought stories should be didactic and uplifting. They insisted that tales display a respect for a commitment to the genteel tradition. Huck was viewed as an inappropriate hero. His language— filled with slang and irreverent allusions, with no regard for the rules of grammar—left much to be desired. He was disrespectful of adults and seemed to have little interest in telling the truth. No wonder the prim Louisa May Alcott complained: "If Mr. Clemens cannot think of something better to tell our pure-minded lads and lasses he had better stop writing for them."

Interestingly, but not unexpectedly, Twain's early critics and readers were not greatly concerned about the racial implications of the novel. The Philadelphia Centennial of 1876 had ushered in a new spirit among America's visual artists, who recognized not only a need for a continued representation of American subjects but also an obligation, despite the immediate social and political problems, to present in a visual manner the possibilities of American democracy. For many of them this meant delineations of the newly freed slaves; nevertheless, even the most tolerant American artists and audiences have had difficulty in dealing with certain phases of our national life, despite ardent attempts. In the nineteenth century most Americans were more comfortable with the literary portraits drawn by the popular writers and practitioners of the plantation tradition than with any attempt at greater realism. Twain chose to resurrect the antebellum period; and although the picture of the imagined happy and contented slaves is augmented by the freedom-seeking Jim, the other slave characters who infrequently appear seem shadowy reminders of an unaltered plantation tradition.

That there is still some discomfort with Twain's novel is evident from the nature of its defenders and assailants. The focus has shifted. It is Jim, rather than Huck, who now presents the problem for some readers. Certain questions naturally arise. Did Twain use the slave figure in a pejorative way that would have satisfied his audience? Is Jim simply an embodiment of the popular minstrel tradition, or is he in reality an example of "the noble savage"? While apologists for the novel insist on Jim's "nobility," the fact remains that there were (and still are) acceptable racial stereotypes that appealed (as they do today) to the American public.

Given the racial climate of the late 1870s and 1880s, with its uncontrolled animus, one might wonder what Twain hoped to accomplish. Second-guessing authors has become big business in academe; finding evidence to support various theories is never difficult. And academicians are not alone in these exercises. The history of book promotion and banning demonstrates that there are those who—like literary critics—select certain aspects of a work to condemn or praise the entire production. Certain works and authors especially lend themselves to misreadings, reinterpretations, and thinly veiled inquiries, and this has often led to overt and covert censorship. And so it has been with *Adventures of Huckleberry Finn*.

The earliest censors, who believed the novel would corrupt the young, have been replaced by later ones who claim the book is racist and degrading. Needless to say, dealing with *Adventures of Huckleberry Finn* on racial grounds creates its own dilemma. To suggest anything on that subject is to run the risk of treading on sensitive ground. One can be accused of narrowness, meanness of spirit, and being amenable to censorship. But to attempt to use the novel as a lesson in tolerance also seems to avoid the central issue in view of the excessive use of the word "nigger" by all of the characters, including Jim. (Those who have counted the word's appearance maintain that it occurs between 160 and 200 times.)* The fact that current editors often explain at length that the term was not as pejorative as modern readers imagine because it was a commonly used designation for slaves in the 1830s and 1840s does little to lessen its impact. Nor does it give comfort to those students, parents, school boards, and other organizations that question the use of the book in public schools. Clearly, the novel presents a problem for those youngsters who have not had a chance to think through the subtleties of racial epithets. Thus, for many readers there is an implied racism in the novel that does not disappear even when Twain advocates insist the work is a "classic" which should be read.

Some parents and school boards have assumed that deleting the novel from required reading lists is one viable option. In 1984, for instance, efforts were made in Springfield, Illinois, to ban the book from the high school curriculum. By implication there seems to be an acceptance of the notion that to require students to read the novel is to perpetuate its presumed derogatory point of view. Those who would ban it have accepted the argument that students will be embarrassed, hurt, or otherwise damaged. Those who oppose such action assume that blacks can and ought to "understand" the use of a term that is categorized as vulgar and offensive when applied to a Negro.

Implicit in many of the discussions of the novel are some unasked questions about the author. Whether or not Twain was a racist is a moot point that need not be addressed, although it is amazing to note the number of times readers find it necessary to assert with conviction that he was not. (Some critics apparently believe that saying so is sufficient to dispel any such notion.) I still remember one of my teachers who discussed Jim by explaining, uncomfortably, that Twain paid the tuition of some Negro students who attended Yale University. I could never understand the relationship between Jim and those unnamed students, but I suppose it must have had something to do with what Huck might have called "conscience"—Twain's and my teacher's.

I suspected even then that—given the time, the conditions, and his background—Twain's racial attitudes probably did not vary appreciably, at least publicly, from the dominant ones of his day. That he may have become a concerned paternalistic figure like his friend

* [A recently compiled concordance of *Huckleberry Finn* sets the figure even higher: a total of 213 occurrences for all forms of the word—ED.]

William Dean Howells or that he was to examine slavery sharply and critically in *The Tragedy of Pudd'nhead Wilson* (1894) does not alter the fact that the young Mark Twain served as a Confederate irregular. No matter what he used as a later explanation, his separation from that service had more to do with his desire to go west than with any strong commitment or switch of loyalties. His knowledge of race, furthermore, was probably limited to a particular group. There is no reason to suppose he would have known much about such men and women as Maria Stewart, William Hamilton, Joseph Coors, or James Forten. The Missouri of Mark Twain was a cultural world apart from that of John Jones, the Chicago multimillionaire who was making his mark in the financial empires of the Midwest. But in the final analysis it is the novel—not Twain—that must be reviewed.

If one assumes that the literary classics of a nation represent the ideals, unspoken values, and psychology of a people, *Adventures of Huckleberry Finn* presents some fascinating ambiguities. On one level, there is the possibility of viewing the novel in terms of the Emersonian doctrine of self-reliance, the freedom of the spirit, the dignity of humanity that cannot be enslaved, and the ultimate note of optimism that emphasizes the ability "to light out for [new] Territory ahead of the rest." Yet the novel gives mixed signals on matters of race. The slave characters are, for the most part, undeveloped stereotypes who perform within the mandates of the plantation tradition. Mention of a free black appears in the context of Pap's diatribe against the "govment." While sophisticated readers may dismiss Pap as one of the "ornery" ones, the fact remains that he repeats a widely held denigration of blacks by those who objected to a Negro's dress, education, right to vote, and claims to freedom. The history of American race relations reveals that Pap was not alone in such complaints. Furthermore, the people of the novel are essentially the poor whites and rogues of the Mississippi Valley. Colonel Sherburn clearly is of a better class, but readers meet him during an act of violence. The Grangerfords and Shepherdsons are presented through their mindless feud; but they are also in a state of decline, as is the Wilks family. With the exception of Jim, the characters in *Huck Finn* are a fairly sorry lot.

And what of Jim? Much can be made of reducing the adult black male to a figure whose fate rests with an unlettered white teenager. Others might argue that Jim's status is a condescending reminder of that "peculiar institution," forgetting in the process that tales of slavery represent historic fact as well as form a popular literary tradition among those readers who find the work of such writers as Joel Chandler Harris to be a valid portrait of the antebellum period. (In the twentieth century, the popularity of slave romances and Margaret Mitchell's *Gone with the Wind* [1936] suggests that the image of the mythical Old South still lives.) Some readers may decry Jim's superstitious nature and take his reliance on "signs" as an indication of his backwardness. Forgetting that these folkways—like all such customs—explain the inexplicable to primitive people, readers may be inclined to join in poking fun at Jim. Yet he represents a variety of viewpoints and may indeed be most representative of Twain's own ambivalence.

While he demonstrates throughout the novel that he has learned the important lesson of masking his feelings, of living behind the veil, Jim is also a manifestation of an acceptable character type for American readers. At the end of the novel, when he could have saved himself from discovery, he comes out of hiding with the full knowledge that he is jeopardizing his freedom. Perhaps nowhere in American literature has the sacrificial nature of loyalty been more simply presented. Jim, however, is more than a shallow stereotype. When he first appears on Jackson's Island, he has outsmarted his owner, who planned to sell him down the river for eight hundred dollars. His subsequent recitation of his wins and losses in speculative enterprises from banking to livestock—albeit elementary—lends credence to his final assertion that his riches now include himself and he is "wuth eight hund'd dollars." Early, Jim and Huck establish a sense of trust, and the two runaways are mutually protective of each other despite Jim's legal impotence. Between them a force of racial integration takes place. While Huck lies to save Jim (and not without some misgivings), the older man is the instrument of Huck's "education." Whenever Huck is inclined to let the baseness of his human condition assume control, it is Jim who guides him. The bond between the two characters is so strong that if one takes Jim away, Huck—as we know him—ceases to exist.

Clearly, their relationship goes beyond that of free white boy and enslaved black man. Black mammies have become an integral part of American culture. There are still those who nostalgically recall childhood days with them. But little has been done with the black man in fiction. If he is not in the tradition of Uncle Tom or Uncle Remus, then he is often a fugitive from justice or from an enslaving society.

While Jim is all of these, he is also the only "real" father that Huck has. We do not know much about Jim, but we do know that he has great love for his family and longs for the day when he will be free in order to reclaim them. In the meantime, Huck is his family.

For most of the novel one cannot forget that Huck—the free white boy—seems unusually preoccupied with matters of death. On the other hand, Jim—the enslaved black man—is concerned with life and manages to teach Huck something about the meaning of life itself. If Huck comes to demonstrate that conscience is not the captive of man-made laws or that it can transcend the restricting forces of society, Jim displays an affirmation of life that goes beyond the ignoble laws created to enslave. No matter how foolish Jim may appear, and despite the number of times he is called "nigger," in the final analysis he cannot be burlesqued. But the fact that he is not absolutely part of that happy lot of plantation slaves who people American literature is lost on those who reduce the novel to an exercise in name-calling.

Much has been written about Huck's so-called moral dilemma and crisis of conscience. Some readers get misty-eyed over the decision that the youngster must make, without recognizing that Jim has also been forced to make choices. Of course, since it is against the law to help an escaping slave, Huck has to decide whether or not to commit a crime. Constitutional authorities might suggest that unjust laws must and can be changed only through an orderly process, but Huck is not enough in the mainstream to be privy to that process, and consequently he acts on instinct. Thus one can argue that the novel is in reality the story of a boy who learns that the customs of his community really go counter to the best human interests. Needless to say, Huck does not rationalize this on a philosophical level; but if Huck Finn—with his questionable background, limited formal schooling, and restricted world—can learn such a simple lesson, cannot others learn it? Yet what could have been a magnificent tale is so burdened by an excessive use of racial epithets that the story's message is lost to all but the most perceptive.

There is another ambiguity in the novel that not only relates to the nineteenth century but also—in some measure—speaks to the twentieth. If the color of one's skin is important (as some Americans believe), then readers need to look carefully at the description of Huck's father, which features a specific emphasis on his whiteness: "There warn't no color in his face, where his face showed; it was white; not like another man's white, but a white to make a body sick, a white to make a body's flesh crawl—a tree-toad white, a fish-belly white" (chap. 5). If one compares this description of Pap with that of the free black man from Ohio who so angered Huck's father that he refused to vote again or with the presentation of the noble qualities of Jim, "white" does not appear to any particular advantage.

Later in the novel, in a very brief episode, Twain reveals another facet of American ambivalence toward racial issues. There is a tendency to accept blackness when it can be given a foreign air. In the days before public accommodation laws, some blacks pretended to be exotic foreigners in order to stay in hotels and eat in restaurants. It was a joke that delighted blacks and fooled whites. Twain's Duke and King are smart enough to know that a dark-skinned foreigner is acceptable in the world of the Mississippi Valley. Thus they dress Jim as a "Sick Arab." If he does not have to talk, then all of them are safe to travel on the raft during daylight hours.

Questioning the role of organized religion in race relations is as valid today as it was in the nineteenth century, despite the efforts of some churches to become "socially aware." The close relationship between American Christianity and slavery has not been overlooked. Twain, without belaboring the point, shows the love of Bible reading and commitment to the tenets of their church by Miss Watson, the widow Douglas, and the Phelps family. If they find any incongruity between human slavery and what they profess to believe about religion, they keep it to themselves. To make certain that his readers understand that the church supports oppression, Twain—instead of pursuing the slavery/religion issue—introduces in the Grangerford incident a church that permits men to bring guns into the sanctuary. Clearly, then, throughout the novel Twain shows organized religion to be faulty. The fact that Huck learns enough about its heaven and hell to realize that helping Jim will automatically consign him to the latter region is expressed in his famous declaration, "All right, then, I'll *go* to hell," even though his commitment to Jim is not complete enough for him to forget racial distinctions.

Some critics point with pride to Colonel Sherburn's famous speech against the cowardice of the mob. They claim that this is a clear example of Twain's intent. By dropping the voice of Huck, the novelist obviously makes that address stand out boldly. While aesthetically this shift in point of view may weaken the consistency of the work, Sherburn certainly makes a strong statement. But within the context

of the novel, what does the Sherburn incident really mean? Noticeably, it does not alter the action except to save the Colonel from a mob,
although it does allow a brief platform for Twain to express his own
contempt for mobs in an era known for such activities and lawlessness.
However, if this mob is dispersed by the harsh reality of Sherburn's
words, the mob that recaptures Jim at the end of the novel is not
concerned with the niceties of human behavior. If its members were
not aware that they cannot pay for another's property, or if the doctor
did not request that they "be no rougher than you're obleeged to,"
then this mob would surely not be so yielding as the one Sherburn
faced.

An even more telling aspect of Twain's presentation of American
race relations comes in the introduction of Tom's great escape plan
for Jim at the end of the novel. The pragmatic Huck realizes the
stupidity of their actions, as does Jim, but the romantic Tom insists
they must follow him. In these episodic pranks, Jim not only is the
victim but is also coopted to go along in order to humor Tom, who
never considers that he is compromising the dignity of a man. And
Huck's silent assent to the procedure makes him an accessory. In the
end, Tom does not succeed in freeing Jim, who is recaptured and faces
the possibility of even harsher treatment. The central irony should
not escape the reader. While he has been in this final captivity Jim has
in reality been free—a fact that Tom suppresses in order to play his
role and carry out his agenda. In the meantime, Jim's freedom has
come from the old order: "Miss Watson died two months ago, and
she was ashamed she ever was going to sell him down the river, and
said so; and she set him free in her will."

Written during one of the darkest periods of American race relations, *Adventures of Huckleberry Finn* spoke to all segments of
nineteenth-century society. Committed racists would have taken a
perverse delight in the pseudominstrel antics of some of Jim's actions
as well as the legitimizing of the word "nigger" by one of the nation's
most popular writers. Those readers more inclined toward a sense of
fairness would have been able to point with pride to the nobility of
Jim or to his eventual freedom. They could take comfort in Colonel
Sherburn's speech, which, in a day of frequent lynchings, spoke to
that brutality.

Present-day responses to the novel still probably operate on these
two levels. While scholars may speak eloquently of the various themes
to be found in Twain's work, to suggest that the novel is a condemna-

tion of the institution of slavery or that Jim represents the triumph of the human spirit over the most degrading attempts to subdue it might seem to be an optimistic begging of the question when others deplore the apparent elements of racism. That there is much concern with the presence of an objectionable word is perhaps unfortunate, because to focus on an epithet seriously limits one's perception of other aspects of the novel. But such a concern is understandable and cannot be dismissed. It is also symptomatic of those latent attitudes that are so difficult to discard. Ultimately, the status of *Huckleberry Finn* as a "classic" may tell more about the nation than many Americans want to know.

As an expression of the racial ambiguities of the United States, the novel goes beyond a catalog of the ills of the nineteenth century. Although the days of physical slavery have passed, spiritual slavery continues, supported by latter-day versions of Miss Watson, Uncle Silas, and Aunt Sally. Meaning well, they continue to find solace and justifications for their actions within their religion. While the 1880s had a full share of racial romanticists who did not understand the reality of Reconstruction or the depth of feeling that was to mark the antiblack attitudes, modern America has not been free from equally unrealistic visions. Whether or not he intended to do so, Mark Twain satirized those who would romanticize race problems and, in the process, prolong them. The romantic "do-gooders," like Tom, remain among us to conceive elaborate schemes that ultimately fail. Racial epithets are still—unfortunately—too much a part of the spoken and unspoken language of the nation. Notwithstanding desires to the contrary, many Americans' notions of superiority do not vary greatly from Pap's. They seldom stop to think of the illogical conclusions that result. It is "enough to make a body ashamed of the human race." On the other hand, the novel does suggest—and rightly so—that the fates and fortunes of the races are so closely intertwined that one cannot exist without the other. Either consciously or unconsciously, Twain produced a classic statement that weighs the nation in the balance. He described an America that was his and an America that is ours. To ban the novel is to condemn the messenger for the message.

For Further

Reading

Thomas A. Tenney

Bibliographies

The largest single source of information about *Huckleberry Finn* is the annotated checklist of more than six hundred books and articles in M. Thomas Inge, ed., *Huck Finn among the Critics: A Centennial Selection* (Frederick, Md.: University Publications of America, 1985) 317–465. A fuller guide to Twain material is in my *Mark Twain: A Reference Guide* (Boston: G. K. Hall, 1977) and seven annual supplements in the journal *American Literary Realism* that appeared 1977–83; those supplements are continued in the *Mark Twain Circular* (1987—). Most of the annotated entries below are reprinted from those collections, with permission.

Two valuable listings, not annotated, are Carl Dolmetsch, "*Huck Finn*'s First Century: A Bibliographical Survey," *American Studies International* 22.2 (1984): 79–121; and Maurice Beebe and John Feaster, "Criticism of Mark Twain: A Selected Checklist," *Modern Fiction Studies* 14.1 (1968): 93–139. The Dolmetsch list is subdivided into categories such as "Themes," "Techniques," and "International Perspectives," and is preceded by a perceptive seventeen-page introductory essay. The Beebe and Feaster list has the valuable feature of a page-long list of sections on *Huck Finn* in books; this is a welcome step beyond simply listing the books by titles.

Reference librarians can help with the resources at their particular libraries, such as *Current Contents, Literary Criticism Register,* the *Reader's Guide,* and the annual bibliographies of the Modern Language Association and the Modern Humanities Research Association. In addition to these general sources, there are two with a much sharper focus on Twain. The annual *American Literary Scholarship* (Duke UP) for years has included a lengthy section on Twain, with a selective list accompanied by brief but perceptive comments, and organized by topics. Another valuable annual listing is the Twain section of "A Checklist of Scholarship on Southern Literature" in

Mississippi Quarterly; coverage has expanded so that now very little escapes, and there are brief, useful annotations.

Further Reading on Mark Twain and Race

Three works by Twain himself deserve attention: "A True Story, Repeated Word for Word as I Heard It" (1874; reprinted in his *Sketches New and Old*), tells of a slave woman's loss of her family at the auction block and her joy years later when she is reunited with her son; *A Connecticut Yankee in King Arthur's Court* (1889), in which the hero and Arthur experience slavery themselves; although the setting is sixth-century England, the model is the American South, and Twain used slave narratives as sources; and *The Tragedy of Pudd'nhead Wilson* (1894); although this is not Twain's best work, either as fiction or as the picture of an era, it represents one more attempt to deal with the historical fact of slavery in a story where the master's son and the slave's son are switched in their cradles. In addition, there is much of interest in three versions of Twain's autobiography, one edited by Albert Bigelow Paine (1924), one by Charles Neider (1959), and one by Michael Kiskis (1990). There is also a useful anthology, *Mark Twain on the Damned Human Race,* ed. Janet Smith (1962), which includes over forty pages on racial issues.

Three books *about* Mark Twain are of particular interest: Pettit's *Mark Twain & the South* (listed in the next section), Louis J. Budd's *Mark Twain, Social Philosopher* (1962—a solid work), and Philip Foner's *Mark Twain, Social Critic* (1958); although Foner is an avowed Marxist and most available editions of this book are printed in East Germany, he has done his research well and the book is respected and often quoted by Twain scholars. Finally, the books by Walter Blair listed in the next section (and anything else by Blair) are authoritative, important, and valuable.

Annotated Checklist of Criticism

There are a few abbreviations used in this section: MT, Mark Twain; *GA, The Gilded Age* (1873, with Charles Dudley Warner); *HF, Adventures of Huckleberry Finn* (published in England in 1884 and in the United States in 1885; purists do not use the article as *"The" Adventures . . .* , as the first American edition did not); *IA, The Innocents Abroad* (1869); *JA, Personal Recollections of Joan of Arc* (1896); *LOM, Life on the Mississippi* (1883); *P&P, The Prince and the Pauper* (1882); *PW, The Tragedy of Pudd'nhead Wilson . . .* (1894); *TS, The Adventures of Tom Sawyer* (1876).

Allen, Margot. "Huck Finn: Two Generations of Pain." *Interracial Books for Children Bulletin* 15.5 (1984): 9–13.
    At the age of thirteen, and the only black student in a ninth-grade class in Oregon, the writer was extremely uncomfortable with *HF;* three years ago, her son, the only black student in a ninth-grade class in Pennsylvania,

went through the same discomfort when the teacher asked him to read the part of Jim aloud because he had "the perfect voice for it." Mrs. Allen and her husband complained first to the school and then to the Pennsylvania Human Relations Commission and the Pennsylvania NAACP, and she participated in a panel on teaching *HF* (see Chambers 1984). She argues that there is a cost to both black and white students in reading *HF,* and it should not be taught before the upper grades of high school, at the earliest.

Altenbernd, Lynn. "Huck Finn, Emancipator." *Criticism* 1 (Fall 1959): 298–307.

"The purpose of this article is to show that the final episode is the thematic climax of the novel because the rescue of Jim from the cabin is an allegory representing the Civil War": although the South could have freed the slaves voluntarily, romantic nonsense (represented by that of Tom Sawyer) interfered. "What actually frees Jim, and what will actually free the nominally emancipated slave is a voluntary act of human love," first from Huck, then from Miss Watson, who gives him his freedom in her will.

Andrews, William L. "Mark Twain and James W. C. Pennington: Huckleberry Finn's Smallpox Lie." *Studies in American Fiction* 9 (Spring 1981): 103–12.

MT drew on Charles Ball's *Slavery in the United States* as a source for *HF,* and with his interest in the genre it is possible that he also read *The Fugitive Blacksmith: or, Events in the History of James C. Pennington, Pastor of a Presbyterian Church, New York, Formerly a Slave in the State of Maryland, United States* (1849). Like Huck, Pennington deceived some slave catchers with a lie about smallpox, and both *HF* and Pennington's book employ "the lies of a runaway [as] a useful pretext for social criticism and moral reflection." While there is no proof that MT had read Pennington's book, the ex-slave was quite prominent in New York when MT was there in 1853, and MT also would have heard of Pennington through the praise of him in the conclusion of *Uncle Tom's Cabin.* (Gribben, in *Mark Twain's Library* [1980], p. 539, quotes a 1978 letter in which Andrews says he thinks the episode in Pennington was a possible source for *HF.*)

Anonymous. "Huck, Dorothy and the Vigilantes." *America* 146 (24 Apr. 1982): 312–13.

The recent attack on *HF* in Fairfax County, Virginia, reopens the issue of censorship. Books have been banned elsewhere, among them *The Wizard of Oz* ("Dorothy and Toto as countercultural radicals?"), *Mary Poppins,* and *The Grapes of Wrath.* Still, there have been overstatements: *HF* was never actually banned in the Virginia school; some printed material (not *HF*) is unsuitable for young students, and often censorship is merely a way for interest groups "to show muscle in a community." Limiting access to books is a last resort: "Even on the primary and secondary levels, exposure to a variety of ideas—presented with sensitivity to a student's ability to absorb and criticize them—is a basic principle of democracy."

Anonymous. "Huck Finn Tabooed by Denver Library." *Harper's Weekly* 46
(6 Sept. 1902): 1253.

A brief note, concluding: "It all sounds like a practical joke on the
Denver library; but it is an offence against our national common-sense
which ought to be quickly removed."

Anonymous. "'A Little Kind of Low Chuckle.'" *New York Times* 16 Apr.
1982: 26.

An editorial, which says, in part: "Not content with describing 'The
Adventures of Huckleberry Finn' as 'racist trash,' John Wallace, an administrator at the Mark Twain Intermediate School in Fairfax, Va., added that
anyone who taught the book was racist too. Speaking for the school's
Human Relations Committee, he asked that it be removed from the
curriculum. . . . Fortunately, Mr. Wallace and his colleagues have been
overruled by the area school superintendent, Doris Torrice. So the children at the Mark Twain Intermediate School, and their teachers, can all
get back onto the raft with Huck and Jim and travel into one of the
greatest of all American novels."

Anonymous. "Mark Twain's Huck Finn Gets His Mouth Washed out with
Revisions." *Washington Post* 8 Sept. 1983: C5.

An interview with John H. Wallace, a former administrator at the
Mark Twain Intermediate School and the Henry David Thoreau Intermediate School. He has moved to Chicago, founded the John H. Wallace
and Sons Publishing Company, and this week is bringing out the first
edition of ten thousand copies of the *Adventures of Huckleberry Finn
Adapted*. Wallace says he spent two summers working on his version of
HF, improving what has "become a classic because it does ridicule black
people by calling [Jim] a nigger. . . . My book is so much better."

Anonymous. "Selling Huck down the River." *Washington Post* 9 Apr. 1982:
A18.

An editorial on the banning of *HF* in the Mark Twain Intermediate
School (Fairfax County, Virginia): in years gone by, *HF* "offended all
those illiberal and small-minded values that most richly deserved to be
offended," and now it is attacked as racist. "But in fact, the novel *satirizes*
the racist attitudes of the time, and if, as one of its opponents says, it is
asinine to expect seventh-graders to understand satire," then what are
teachers for? Surely they are there to help kids understand things in their
context, to appreciate them.

Anonymous. "Twain's Novels Stay on School's List: Texas Parent Complains
Books Racially Offensive." *Columbia (SC) State* 6 Dec. 1990: 12-A [an
Associated Press dispatch].

The Plano, Texas, school board voted unanimously to keep *TS* and *HF*
on the required list, over the objections of black parent David Perry. Perry
said, however, that he respected the five hundred high school students
who had circulated a petition to keep *HF* and felt the community dialogue
had been useful. Joanne Savage, a high school student, is quoted: "The
book has the ability to provoke much thoughtful discussion about this
problem [racism] instead of ignoring it and pretending that it is solved."

Anonymous. [Banning of *HF* by the Concord Public Library.] *Boston Transcript* 17 Mar. 1885.

> The committee does not call the book immoral, but it "contains but little humor, and that of a very coarse type"; it is "the veriest trash . . . rough, coarse and inelegant, dealing with a series of experiences not elevating, the whole book being more suited to the slums than to intelligent, respectable people."

Anonymous. [Banning of *HF* by Concord Public Library.] *Springfield (Mass.) Republican,* as quoted in *The Critic* 6 (28 Mar. 1885): 155.

> "Mr. Clemens is a genuine and powerful humorist, with a bitter vein of satire on the weaknesses of humanity which is sometimes wholesome, sometimes only grotesque, but in certain of his works degenerates into a grotesque trifling with every fine feeling. The trouble with Mr. Clemens is that he has no reliable sense of propriety. His notorious speech at an *Atlantic* dinner, marshalling Longfellow and Emerson and Whittier in vulgar parodies in a Western miner's cabin, illustrated this, but not in much more relief than the *Adventures of Tom Sawyer* did, or these Huckleberry Finn stories, do."

Auden, W. H. "Huck and Oliver." *Listener* 50 (1 Oct. 1953): 540–41.

> Contrasts attitudes toward nature in *HF* and *Oliver Twist;* observes Huck's stoicism and calls his decision to free Jim "an act of moral improvisation." There is in the book "a kind of sadness, as if freedom and love were incompatible" (from a BBC "Third Programme" broadcast).

Baker, Russell. "The Only Gentleman." *New York Times* 14 Apr. 1982: A23.

> On the banning of *HF* in Mark Twain Intermediate School. In Baker's own school years, "school teachers seemed determined to persuade me that 'classic' was a synonym for 'narcotic,'" and now he waggishly suggests that they all be reserved for adults who can appreciate them—Shakespeare, Dickens, and Melville along with *HF*. Black and white students "might misread Twain as outrageously as Mr. Wallace [John H. Wallace—see below] has in thinking the book is about the dishonesty, dumbness and inhumanity of blacks. This is the kind of risk you invite when you assign books of some subtlety to youngsters mentally unprepared to enjoy them." One must be mature to understand irony such as that of *HF,* which is "full of pessimism about the human race and particularly its white American members." Those Huck and Jim encounter are fools at best, and "the one of honor . . . is black Jim, the runaway slave. 'Nigger Jim,' as Twain called him [actually, Twain didn't] to emphasize the irony of a society in which the only true gentleman was held beneath contempt." But since the racial issue has been raised, "the only sensible thing for the Mark Twain Intermediate School to do is tackle the matter head-on, put aside some other things and conduct a school-wide teach-in to help its students understand what Huck and Jim are really saying about their world."

Banfield, Beryle. "More on the Study . . ." *Interracial Books for Children Bulletin* 15.5 (1984): 10–11.

> A study to determine the effect of reading *HF* on the racial attitudes of

ninth-graders is seriously flawed and should not be used to justify continued teaching of the novel (see Chambers 1984).

Beaver, Harold. "Run, Nigger, Run: *Adventures of Huckleberry Finn* as a Fugitive Slave Narrative." *Journal of American Studies* 8 (Dec. 1974): 339–61.

> Jim is an adult and a slave, and his situation is not Huck's: "If young Huck is taken in by that river-born camaraderie between black and white on a Mississippi raft, it does not follow that his friend (and victim) was equally taken in."

Bennett, Jonathan. "The Conscience of Huckleberry Finn." *Philosophy: The Journal of the Royal Institute of Philosophy* 49 (Apr. 1974): 123–34.

> "I shall use Heinrich Himmler, Jonathan Edwards and Huckleberry Finn to illustrate different aspects of a single theme, namely the relationship between *sympathy* on one hand and *bad morality* on the other." In Huck's case, sympathy wins out over bad morality, as in Himmler's it does not; and the morality of Edwards "was worse than Himmler's," in that he approved of the eternal torment of the damned as good in itself. For further discussion, see Harris (1977).

Berkove, Lawrence I. "The 'Poor Players' of *Huckleberry Finn*." *Papers of the Michigan Academy of Science, Arts, and Letters* 53 (1968) 291–310.

> *HF* is a well-wrought tragedy which denies the possibility of human freedom and reflects the position that "all men are poor players in a drama without significance." The argument is based on the fate-driven device of impersonation, a hoax on readers baited by romanticism, and the revelation that Jim, at the end, is not a free man but an ironic opposite, an f.m.c.—a "free man of color."

———. "The Free Man of Color in *The Grandissimes* and Works by Harris and Mark Twain." *Southern Quarterly* 18.4 (Summer 1980): 60–73.

> Credits George Washington Cable's analogical use of the free man of color in *The Grandissimes* (1880) with having paved the way for Joel Chandler Harris (in "Free Joe and the Rest of the World," 1884) and MT in *HF* similarly to attack the resubjugation of black freedmen in the post-Reconstruction South. (This and the essay by Berkove cited above anticipate Charles Nilon's essay in this volume in significant details, particularly in the parallel between Jim's "liberation," which did not render him truly free, and the plight of black Americans, whose freedom brought by the Civil War was likewise an illusion.)

Bier, Jesse. "'Bless You, Chile': Fiedler and 'Huck Honey' a Generation Later." *Mississippi Quarterly* 34 (Fall 1981): 456–62.

> On Fiedler's essay arguing a homosexual element in *HF* (1948). "Fiedler is an old friend and former colleague of mine, and now that the critical dust has almost settled again, he may not mind a demurral from me as much as from downright hostile quarters." Bier suggests that Jim's relation to Huck is like that of a father, replacing Pap Finn, and he "almost always has his children on his mind." He accuses Fiedler of using evidence very selectively, calling him "always more the critic, even the polemicist, than the scholar."

Black, Ronald J. "The Psychological Necessity of the Evasion Sequence in *Huckleberry Finn.*" *CEA Critic* 52.4 (Summer 1990): 35–44.

Huck carries a burden of guilt, which sometimes he can expiate by his actions; but he feels guilt even when he is blameless, and shoves the guilt into his unconscious. In the final chapters, going along with Tom's charade of freeing Jim, Huck takes his own tumbles for the "crime" of helping a slave escape, and is not disturbed by the discomforts of Jim, "who is the source of that guilt" (41).

Blair, Walter. *Mark Twain & Huck Finn.* Berkeley and Los Angeles: U of California P, 1960.

Blair calls this his "attempt to define the forces which gave *Adventures of Huckleberry Finn* its substance and its form." While considering the importance of MT's boyhood and piloting on the river, he feels that the way they were transmuted into fiction is more important; "therefore I discuss in greater detail the forces shaping such modifications—the man's life, his reading, his thinking, and his writing between 1874 and 1884" (vii). This definitive study concludes with a discussion of *HF*'s popularity abroad in translation, and there is an appendix titled "First New York Edition, First Issue," discussing bibliographical points.

———. *Mark Twain's Hannibal, Huck and Tom.* Berkeley and Los Angeles: U of California P, 1969.

A volume of the CEAA edition of MT's works, consisting of unpublished material on Hannibal and the villagers, and manuscript material dealing with Huck and Tom; includes the texts of "Huck Finn and Tom Sawyer among the Indians," and "Tom Sawyer: A Play."

———. "When Was *Huckleberry Finn* Written?" *American Literature* 30 (Mar. 1958): 1–25.

Contends that Paine is nearer the truth in giving periods of composition as 1876, 1880, and 1883 than is DeVoto in giving only 1876 and 1883. "Furthermore, I believe that both, with most other students of Twain, overestimate the influence of Clemens's Mississippi River trip of 1882 on the novel. If my beliefs prove to be well founded, significant revisions of the story of the genesis of the book will be necessary." The evidence includes letters and recorded conversations, and MT's notes, notebooks, and the surviving manuscript material.

———. "Why Huck and Jim Went Downstream." *College English* 18 (Nov. 1956): 106–7.

William Van O'Connor has called the trip on the raft a flaw, since free territory lay across the river in Illinois; the objection has been made before, by DeVoto and by Dixon Wecter, but takes no account of the activity of slave catchers there, or the fact that Huck's father had got money from Judge Thatcher "to hunt for the nigger all over Illinois with." (MT knew the Fugitive Slave Law was in effect: see Karanovich, below.)

Brack, O. M., Jr. "Mark Twain in Knee Pants: The Expurgation of *Tom Sawyer Abroad.*" *Proof* 2 (1972): 145–51.

In 1893–94 Twain published his sequel to *Huckleberry Finn,* taking Tom, Huck, and Jim to Egypt in a balloon; again, Huck is narrator. The

story first appeared in *St. Nicholas: An Illustrated Magazine for Young Folks,*
edited by Mary Elizabeth Mapes Dodge (author of *Hans Brinker; or, The
Silver Skates*), who made extensive changes to render Huck's dialect more
genteel and to soften or remove references to sweating, alcohol, death,
and organized religion in terms that might offend. Throughout, the word
"nigger" is replaced by other terms (except when Jim himself is speaking);
for example, in the first paragraph of Twain's manuscript Mrs. Dodge
changed "nigger" to "darky." Some improvement!

Brauer, Arlette. "Life Is Still Perilous for Huck Finn." *MD* [a nontechnical
magazine for the medical profession] 28 (June 1984): 117–20, 125, 128,
133.

    This is a substantially researched and workmanlike article directed at a
sophisticated audience whose specialization is not in American literature.
Scholars will not be greatly troubled by a few minor errors concerning
MT's life and works, and in the extensive treatment of the critical reputation of *HF* there is much of interest on the reaction of black parents and
educators of the present time. Brauer reproduces in facsimile most of an
unsigned interview with John H. Wallace in the *Washington Post* for
8 Sept. 1983 (which see), on which is superimposed the front cover of
Wallace's adaptation of *HF* with the language made inoffensive. In her
conclusion Brauer cites a complaint to Pennsylvania's Human Rights
Commission over the teaching of *HF* and the response by "a group from
Pennsylvania State University, which includes the Forum of Black Affairs, . . . studying the effect of the book on 300 white ninth-graders in the
district. The study's report noted that 'Reading *Huckleberry Finn* and
discussing it in class actually enhanced the racial attitudes of whites
toward blacks.' The district has made the reading of the book optional
'pending further study.'"

Briden, Earl F. "Kemble's 'Specialty' and the Pictorial Countertext of *Huckleberry Finn*." *Mark Twain Journal* 26.2 (1988) 2–14.

    Edward Windsor Kemble was twenty-three and relatively inexperi-
enced when he was commissioned to draw the illustrations for *HF*. He
had already published a number of drawings in the old *Life* and *The Daily
Graphic,* some of them comic but not necessarily offensive portrayals of
black subjects. Under pressure of deadlines and sometimes without an
opportunity to see the text he was illustrating, Kemble often resorted to
stereotypes in *HF*. "In retaining Kemble, Twain was in effect authorizing
a pictorial narrative which runs counter to major implications of his verbal
text. For Kemble's drawings re-write the Huck-Jim relationship by reducing Jim, whom Huck gradually recognizes as an individualized human
being, to a simple comic type, a stock figure in an emerging pictorial
tradition." As his career developed Kemble said he became established "as
a delineator of the South, the Negro being my specialty." He created the
Gold Dust Twins once seen on boxes of washing soda, and in 1898
published two books titled *Comical Coons* and *A Coon Alphabet;* the texts
of these books are as offensive as their titles, though many (but not all) of
the drawings are attractive and sympathetic. (Also see Holt, below.)

Brown, Spencer. "Huckleberry Finn for Our Time: A Re-Reading of the Concluding Chapters." *Michigan Quarterly Review* 6 (Winter 1967): 41–46.

The "uneasy amusement" and "irritation" intelligent readers feel over the ending are "the reactions Mark Twain deliberately provoked" in an attack on slavery through showing its effect on ordinary, kind people, and most of all on Huck and Jim: "Thus slavery has corrupted and rendered selfish the best character in the novel" and reduced the manly Jim to a clown.

Brown, Sterling. *The Negro in American Fiction.* Washington, D.C.: The Associates in Negro Folk Education, 1935. Reprint. New York: Argosy-Antiquarian, Ltd., 1969.

On pp. 67–69, depicts MT as sympathetic, tracing his portrayal of Negroes from the "largely traditional" picture in *GA,* and the "bitter memory of cruelty and separation" in "A True Story," to *HF,* where "Jim is the best example in nineteenth century fiction of the average Negro slave (not the tragic mulatto or the noble savage), illiterate, superstitious, yet clinging to his hope for freedom, to his love for his own. And he is completely believable." *PW* is a decline "from the great tenderness and truth of this portrait" and would have been the better for a fuller development of Roxy.

Brownell, Frances V. "The Role of Jim in *Huckleberry Finn.*" *Boston University Studies in English* 1 (Spring–Summer 1955): 74–83.

Jim is passive or absent in most of the episodes involving physical action, and his main role is that of "moral catalyst . . . it is my thesis that Jim's primary function is to further the characterization of Huckleberry Finn: by his presence, his personality, his actions, his words, to call forth from Huckleberry Finn a depth of tenderness and moral strength that could not otherwise have been fully and convincingly revealed to the reader."

Cecil, L. Moffitt. "The Historical Ending of *Adventures of Huckleberry Finn:* How Nigger Jim Was Set Free." *American Literary Realism* 13 (Autumn 1980): 280–83.

Huck's simple plan would have worked, but "Mark Twain chose Tom's plan because it travesties so scathingly the botched way our nation's freeing of the slaves was actually accomplished." Both emancipations were marked by delay, gratuitous cruelty, and a bloody conflict that could have been avoided. (Again, MT never called his character "Nigger Jim.")

Chambers, Bradford. "Scholars and *Huck Finn:* A New Look." *Interracial Books for Children Bulletin* 15.4 (1984): 12–13.

On issues of racism brought up at a conference at Pennsylvania State University, 26–28 April 1984. Participants in some of the sixteen panels (most of them concerned with *HF* on the college or graduate level) seemed unconcerned or insensitive, but the black panel (subtitled "Humor—At Whose Expense?") drew more than half the participants at the conference. "In his opening remarks James Stewart said that the issue was not banning *Huck Finn,* but when and how to teach it." Margot Allen described her pain and her son's pain on reading *HF* in school, a generation apart. Jane Madsden attacked a study purportedly demonstrating that ninth-graders are not negatively affected by reading *HF;* and Terrell Jones, author of the study, responded that his findings were only tentative, but he had urged that *HF* not be taught below grade 11 or 12, and that area schools undertake a racism-awareness program. "Twain's effective use of irony to satirize social evils was acknowledged by everyone, but the dialogue raised a second question: What is the age level at which children can understand the irony? By the end of the discussion, there was considerable agreement that the humor in *Huck Finn* was too sophisticated for use in elementary school, but several participants wondered if high school students are any better equipped." Chambers "met the following day with representatives of the Penn State College of Education and the Black Studies Program. We agreed to jointly develop a set of lesson plans that teachers might use with *Huck Finn.*"

Cummings, Sherwood. "What's in Huckleberry Finn?" *English Journal* 50 (Jan. 1961): 1–8.

> An analysis geared to teaching in high school. Students are accustomed to television dramas in which the moral values are clear and nothing is left to inference; but MT tells the story through Huck, who himself is unaware of what MT is implying. The two major themes are Huck's rejection of society and his struggle with his conscience.

DeMenil, Alexander Nicholas. "Samuel L. Clemens." In *The Literature of the Louisiana Territory.* St. Louis: *St. Louis News,* 1904. 197–202.

> MT's literary career was "a puzzle to me. It had always seemed to me impossible that a writer who violated nearly all the canons of literary art and whose themes were so thoroughly commonplace, should become so extensively known and so widely popular as Mr. Clemens has become. Of course, his fame is only of to-day, but it is wonderful that it is so widespread and hearty, even if it is merely ephemeral." MT "deals of the everyday and commonplace—he is often coarse" (as in *HF*); he is "irreverent, if not blasphemous" (as in *IA*), and he is "unnatural and straining after effect" (as in *TS*). "As a humorist, he paints no typical characters," and "as a novelist, what could possibly be more wretchedly untrue to history and to human nature than his *Personal Recollections of Joan of Arc*— a twentieth-century Joan labelled fifteenth century? Mark Twain lacks the education absolutely necessary to a great writer; he lacks the refinement which would render it impossible for him to create such coarse characters as Huckleberry Finn." He is popular because he makes people laugh.

Dickinson, Asa Don. "Huckleberry Finn Is Fifty Years Old—Yes; But Is He Respectable?" *Wilson Bulletin for Librarians* 10 (Nov. 1935): 180–85.

> A librarian, Dickinson wrote to MT in distress when he heard at a meeting of the Public Library that *HF* was to be moved from the children's rooms to the adult sections in the various branches. MT replied (21 Nov. 1905):

>> I am greatly troubled by what you say. I wrote Tom Sawyer & Huck Finn for adults exclusively, & it always distresses me when I find that boys and

girls have been allowed access to them. The mind that becomes soiled in youth can never again be washed clean; I know this by my own experience, & to this day I cherish an unappeasable bitterness against the unfaithful guardians of my young life, who not only permitted but compelled me to read an expurgated Bible through before I was 15 years old. None can do that and ever draw a clean sweet breath again this side of the grave. Ask that young lady—she will tell you so.

Most honestly do I wish I could say a softening word or two in defense of Huck's character, since you wish it, but really in my opinion it is no better than God's (in the Ahab & 97 others), & those of Solomon, & Satan & the rest of the sacred brotherhood.

If there is an Unexpurgated in the Children's Department, won't you please help that young woman remove Tom & Huck from that questionable companionship?

This letter and other correspondence between MT and Dickinson may also be found in the *New York Times* (2 Nov. 1935) and in *Mark Twain's Autobiography.* Ed. Albert Bigelow Paine. 2 vols. New York: Harper & Brothers, 1934. 2: 333–39.

The first two sentences have been widely quoted without the rest of the letter, to give the false impression that *TS* and *HF* were never intended to be children's books in the first place.

Doughty, Nanelia S. "Realistic Negro Characterization in Postbellum Fiction." *Negro American Literature Forum* 3 (Summer 1969): 57–62, 68.

Defends MT against the accusation that his Negroes are ridiculed as stereotypes. In *HF,* "like all Clemens' blacks, Jim is a *pre-war* slave. His submissiveness is the necessary bearing of the wholly-owned chattel—*not* a synthetic attitude decreed by the author." In *GA,* Uncle Dan'l may resemble the comic stereotype, but he is in fact a kindly, devout Negro from before the war. In *PW,* Roxy's courage and gaiety are emphasized, but her color is not: "So Clemens ignored mere color as a causative factor. He also discards heredity. The crucial element in the development of Tom's character is environment."

Du Bois, W. E. B. "The Humor of Negroes." *Mark Twain Quarterly* [later *Mark Twain Journal*] 5.3 (Fall–Winter 1942–43): 12.

Contrary to American opinion (in the 1940s), Negroes are not humorous by nature. Africans Du Bois had seen were dignified and solemn, but in America and the West Indies, "the Negroes are humorous; they are filled with laughter and delicious chuckling. They enjoy themselves; they enjoy jokes; they perpetrate them on each other and on white folk." Their humor is partly defense, partly a source of pleasure otherwise limited for an oppressed people, but also "there is an undercurrent of resentment, of anger and vengeance which lies not far beneath the surface and which sometimes exhibits itself at the most unexpected times and under unawaited circumstances." Although Du Bois has not made an analytical study, he notes "the dry mockery of the pretensions of white folk" and a gift for "the apparently innocent but really sophisticated joke" that disarms the hostile white man.

"Then among themselves Negroes have developed a variety of their own humor. The use of the word 'nigger,' which no white man must use, is coupled with innuendo and suggestion which brings irresistible gales of laughter. They imitate the striver, the nouveau riche, the partially educated man of large words and the entirely untrained. . . . One can only say, that to the oppressed and unfortunate, to those who suffer, God mercifully grants the divine gift of laughter. These folk are not all black nor all white but with inborn humor, men of all colors and races face the tragedy of life and make it endurable."

Edwards, June. "Morality and *Huckleberry Finn*." *Humanist* 44 (Mar.–Apr. 1984): 35–36.

"It's a terrible book to give to a child—if one believes in absolute values and admits no hierarchy of moral reasoning." Censors of the right oppose a supposed undermining of traditional values and fail to see that Huck respects sincerity and has "much natural wisdom." Others object to the portrayal of blacks and the use of the word "nigger," missing MT's ironic point.

Egan, Michael. *Mark Twain's "Huckleberry Finn": Race, Class and Society.* London: Published for Sussex UP by Chatto & Windus, 1977.

"Twain's novel is one of the very best histories of its period because it details and concretises . . . the full experience of an entire way of life" (134). Grim in its concerns, "its intellectual somberness is supported by images of gloom and midnight so persistent they must be accounted deliberate and thematic" (10). Egan's topics include (in chapter titles) "Dialectic of Form and Structure," "Twain's Fiction and the Reading Public," "Racism, Slavery and Freedom," and "The Religion of Violence."

Ellison, Ralph. "Change the Joke and Slip the Yoke." *Partisan Review* 25 (Spring 1958): 212–22. Reprinted in *Shadow and Act* (1964), 45–59, and in the second Norton Critical Edition of *HF* (1977).

An answer to an essay by Stanley Edgar Hyman on Negro American literature and folklore (immediately preceding). On *HF,* Ellison argues that "Twain fitted Jim into the outlines of the minstrel tradition, and it is from behind this stereotype mask that we see Jim's dignity and human capacity—and Twain's complexity—emerge." MT was still too close to the Reconstruction to escape "the white dictum that Negro males must be treated either as boys or 'uncles'—never as men. Jim's friendship for Huck comes across as that of a boy for another boy rather than as the friendship of an adult for a junior; thus there is implicit in it not only a violation of the manners sanctioned by society for relations between Negroes and whites, there is a violation of our concept of adult maleness." Ellison suggests that it was concern over this question that led Leslie Fiedler to argue a homosexual relationship in "Come Back to the Raft Ag'in, Huck Honey!" Fiedler was "so profoundly disturbed by the manner in which the deep dichotomies symbolized by blackness and whiteness are resolved that, forgetting to look at the specific form of the novel, he leaped squarely into the middle of that tangle of symbolism which he is dedicated to unsnarling and yelled out his most terrifying name for chaos."

―――. *Shadow and Act.* New York: Random House, 1964.

Includes "The Seer and the Seen" (1946; published in *Confluence* [Dec. 1953]: 24–44); "Change the Joke and Slip the Yoke" (*Partisan Review* [Spring 1958]: 45–59); "The Art of Fiction: An Interview" (*Paris Review* [Spring 1955]: 167–83); "Some Questions and Some Answers" (*Prevues* [May 1958]: 261–72). On Huck, who, "like Prometheus . . . embraces the evil implicit in his act in order to affirm his belief in humanity," and the recognition of Jim's humanity (and on "Hemingway's blindness to the moral values of *Huckleberry Finn* despite his sensitivity to its technical aspects"; 29–36). On MT's failure to represent Jim as an adult (50–51); again on the central moral question in *HF* (182–83). On language, Ellison speaks of "having inherited the language of Shakespeare and Melville, Mark Twain and Lincoln and no other," although American Negro speech has been important to our language (266–67).

Ensor, Allison. "Twain's *The Adventures of Huckleberry Finn,* Chapter 37." *Explicator* 26 (Nov. 1967): item 20.

MT had already quoted in *IA* from Acts 17, and would have known Paul's statement that God "hath made of one blood all nations of men for to dwell on all the face of the earth"; thus, the fact that Uncle Silas Phelps was preparing next week's sermon from the same chapter may be an ironic thrust at his dual role as minister and slave owner.

Ferguson, DeLancey. "Clemens' . . . *Huckleberry Finn.*" *Explicator* 4 (Apr. 1946): item 42.

A reply to a query by P. B. A. in *Explicator* 4 (Nov. 1945): Q. 7 [In *Mark Twain at Work,* p. 54, DeVoto says MT disregards the fact that Jim could have reached free soil by crossing the river to Illinois; can any reader comment?]. Ferguson explains: Jim could not escape directly across the never into Illinois, because he would be quickly captured for a reward; his chances would be better if he entered free territory some distance from where he had escaped. (See Karanovich, below: MT knew fugitive slaves were not safe even in Elmira, N.Y.)

Fiedler, Leslie A. "Come Back to the Raft Ag'in, Huck Honey!" *Partisan Review* 15 (June 1948): 664–71.

As in *HF,* other American novels (*Moby Dick,* the Leatherstocking tales) are marked by an affection between a white and a nonwhite male that Fiedler terms "homoerotic"; the title of this essay is not a quotation from *HF.*

―――. "*Huckleberry Finn:* The Book We Love to Hate." *Proteus* 1.2 (1984): 1–8.

HF is currently under fire for supposed racism, but over the years has been condemned as immature, unstructured, coarse, and immoral, a poor model for children. "It was therefore predictable from the start that scarcely a year would pass during the century since its publication that has not seen Twain's book forbidden somewhere in the United States. . . .

What is surprising . . . is that even as *Huckleberry Finn* has remained a banned book, it has also become a *required* one. . . . Its "persistent popularity . . . has in fact, always troubled members of any elite, esthetic, moral, or political, whose members feel they know better than the unredeemed masses what is good for them."

Fields, Howard. "The First Amendment. Principal in Fairfax County, Va. Recommends Restriction of 'Huckleberry Finn.'" *Publishers Weekly* 221 (17 Apr. 1982): 18.

A short news story on the controversy over *HF* at Mark Twain Intermediate School; for additional details see the entries above for two anonymous newspaper editorials, and articles by Russell Baker, Dorothy Gilliam, and John Wallace.

Fischer, Victor. "Huck Finn Reviewed: The Reception of *Huckleberry Finn* in the United States, 1885–97." *American Literary Realism* 16 (Spring 1983): 1–57.

Despite a failure of major journals to review it (in part because of MT's own interference with sending out review copies), *Adventures of Huckleberry Finn* was not ignored by American critics . . . to the extent supposed (See Vogelback 1939), nor were the reviews as uniformly unfavorable or as ignorant of what Mark Twain achieved as has been thought." Fischer lists 14 reviews of the chapters of *HF* as they appeared in the *Century*, 33 reviews of the book between 1884 and 1885, 30 later reviews (1886–1910), 58 articles and editorial comments on the banning of *HF* by the Concord Public Library (many supported MT), 4 news items on the illustration that had been mutilated to make it obscene (by adding a penis), 4 comments on the bust by Karl Gerhardt used as a frontispiece, and 23 news stories on the suit against Estes and Lauriat (the Boston booksellers that had advertised *HF* for sale at a price below that charged by subscription agents).

Fishkin, Shelley Fisher. "Race and Culture at the Century's End: A Social Context for *Pudd'nhead Wilson*." *Essays in Arts and Sciences* (U of New Haven) 19 (May 1990): 1–27.

The stories of *HF* and *PW* were each "hijacked" by another story, of race and slavery: "Two of the most powerful and most powerfully flawed books in American literary history were the result. The subliminal subject of American race relations (discussed here at length) at the time when the books were written helps account for the unresolved contradictions and ironies in both books.

———. "Twain, in '85." *New York Times* 18 Feb. 1985: A17.

An "Op-Ed" page defense of *HF* against charges of racism: the book itself is an attack on racism through an irony some readers fail to recognize. When MT attacked mistreatment of the Chinese in a story for a San Francisco paper in the 1860s, his editor bowed to the prejudices of readers and refused to publish it. In 1870 he treated the theme ironically in "Disgraceful Persecution of a Boy," about a boy arrested for stoning Chinese, even though everything he had learned from his elders taught him that it was "a high and holy thing" to abuse them.

Gibb, Carson. "The Best Authorities." *College English* 22 (Dec. 1960): 178–83.

> Tom and Huck "believe niggers and people are two different things," but MT is not ending *HF* "with a burst of spleen" aimed at "two likable youngsters"; his target is the culture that has shaped their attitudes.

Gibson, Donald B. "Mark Twain's Jim in the Classroom." *English Journal* 57 (Feb. 1968): 196–99, 202.

> On the twentieth-century problems arising from the stereotyped portrayal of Jim in *HF* and from MT's ambivalent attitude toward him.

Gilliam, Dorothy. "Banning Huck." *Washington Post* 12 Apr. 1982: B1.

> Argues that *HF* is not actually banned at the Mark Twain Intermediate School (Fairfax County, Virginia), just removed from the required reading list. Still, the subject is sensitive, and "if 'Huck Finn' is going to be discussed, it should be taken up under the guidance of a teacher or a librarian who is trained to discuss the historical context of the book and the author. This is the way we develop the sensibilities that will eliminate the banning of books once and for all. 'Huckleberry Finn' is a classic. But the messages it carries for both black and white children are at best mixed, and it cries out for careful interpretation. That is what the school wants to give it."

Gillman, Susan, and Forrest G. Robinson, eds. *Mark Twain's Pudd'nhead Wilson: Race, Conflict, and Culture*. Durham: Duke UP, 1990.

> A collection of essays from a conference on *PW,* a structurally flawed but important book dealing with issues of race and slavery ten years after *HF*. Among the essays are Eric J. Sundquist, "Mark Twain and Homer Plessy" (of the landmark *Plessy vs. Ferguson,* "separate but equal" Supreme Court decision); Susan Gillman, "'Sure Identifiers': Race, Science, and the Law in *Pudd'nhead Wilson*"; Myra Jehlen, "The Ties That Bind: Race and Sex in *Pudd'nhead Wilson*"; John Carlos Rowe, "'By Right of White Election': Political Theology and Theological Politics in *Pudd'nhead Wilson*."

Gloster, Hugh. *Negro Voices in American Fiction*. Chapel Hill: U of North Carolina P, 1948. 106–7. [Not seen; quoted in Haslam (1969).]

> Gloster contends "that 'the foundations' of the present tendency to depict Negroes as human beings in literature 'were laid in the last quarter of the nineteenth century in the works of such writers as Albion Tourgée, G. W. Cable, and Mark Twain.'"

Gollin, Richard, and Rita Gollin. "*Huckleberry Finn* and the Time of the Evasion." *Modern Language Studies* 9 (Spring 1979): 5–15.

> The authors suggest reading the final chapters "as an Aesopian satire on enlightened white attitudes toward the freed black men, not in the 1840's, when the story is set, but in the 1880's, when the chapters were written."

Griska, Joseph M., Jr. "Two New Joel Chandler Harris Reviews of Mark Twain." *American Literature* 48 (Jan. 1977): 584–89.

> After a one-page introduction on the acquaintance of MT and Harris, their extant correspondence, and the Harris review of *P&P,* reprints

"Two New Books" and " 'Huckleberry Finn' and His Critics" from the
Atlanta Constitution of 11 June 1882 and 26 May 1885. The first of these,
on *The Stolen White Elephant,* is interesting for comment on MT's artistry
and "habit of looking keenly after his interests" in his dealings with
publishers. The *HF* review lambastes the critics who have taken their cue
from the action of the Concord Public Library (which banned the book)
and unjustly called *HF* coarse and inartistic; Harris praises *HF* for the
artistry and the example of "manliness and self-sacrifice."

Gullason, Thomas Arthur. "The 'Fatal' Ending of *Huckleberry Finn.*" *American Literature* 29 (Mar. 1957): 86–91.

The concluding episode, "based on Tom's lie, cannot be considered
fatal because Huck settles conflicts presented earlier in the novel. Important themes, which are repeated and varied, furnish the key." In the last
chapters Huck rejects "Tom's romantic irresponsibility . . . and society's
cruel nature [and] . . . understands Jim's true worth." Huck's honest
and humble facing and resolving of the conflicts shows his developing
strength of character (91).

Hansen, Chadwick. "The Character of Jim and the Ending of *Huckleberry
Finn.*" *Massachusetts Review* 5 (Autumn 1963): 45–66.

Jim was Huck's "moral burden" in that "by his constant presence, and
his constant decency, and his constant humanity he forces Huck to do
something more than drift with the river. He forces Huck to come to
grips with that part of himself which belongs to society." In the ending
Huck and Jim both allow themselves to be drawn into Tom's romantic
schemes, but not without reservations. The closing sentences represent
"for Huck an emotional, if not an intellectual rejection of civilization,"
and an escape both for Huck and for Jim.

Harris, Joel Chandler. [Letter to the editor.] *Critic* 7 (28 Nov. 1885): 253.

Praises MT and singles out *HF:* "There is not in our fictive literature a
more wholesome book."

Harris, John. "Principles, Sympathy and Doing What's Right." *Philosophy:
The Journal of the Royal Institute of Philosophy* 52 (Jan. 1977): 96–99.

Bennett errs in "The Conscience of Huckleberry Finn" (Bennett
1974), because Huck has no organized moral principles of his own. "To
represent Huck as facing a dilemma is misleading, for Huck does not
decide to give way to the pressure of his conscience, he just collapses under
it."

· Haslam, Gerald W. "*Huckleberry Finn*—Why Read the Phelps Farm Episode?" *Research Studies* (Washington State University) 35 (Sept. 1969):
189–97.

Although the ending of *HF* is weakened by stylistic excesses, and
defenses based on form are unsatisfactory, it can be justified "as a logical
extension of the often-emphasized moral texture of the novel. . . . [T]he
dissonance one senses in the final episodes of the novel is largely a product
of Twain's fictional projection of the seminal moral dilemma of a slaveholding society: human beings viewed as commodity."

Haupt, Garry. "The Tragi-Comedy of the Unreal in Ralph Ellison's *Invisible*

Man and Mark Twain's *Adventures of Huckleberry Finn.*" *Interpretations* (Memphis State University) 4 (1972): 1–12.

Emphasis is on Ellison and his novel, and on *HF* only to explore parallels and influence. "Ellison found his American literary roots in the nineteenth-century novel because he felt it presented a rounded picture of the Negro, saw the Negro as symbolic of general American problems, and communicated a strong sense of social responsibility. All of these factors bind Ellison to Twain, as he himself has pointed out." In *Invisible Man* an overdependence on the outside world causes loss of self, while Huck's moral development puts his instinctive self in conflict with a false self. "The moral conflict is a pseudo-conflict, because the norms of society as they exist in Huck's mind are unreal."

Head, John. "It's Absurd to Accuse Twain of Being Racist." *Atlanta Journal and Constitution* 26 Nov. 1990: A-13.

On attempts by David Perry, a black city councilman in Plano, Texas, to remove *HF* and *TS* from required reading lists in local schools. Although Perry denies an attempt to censor, "That's not true. I suspect that the people who seek to control what other people read, hear or see believe that they are acting with the best of intentions. But having good intentions doesn't guarantee you'll be right. In this case Mr. Perry is surely wrong, for he has found Mark Twain and his books guilty of offenses they didn't commit." In fact, MT, "measured by the standards of his day, was progressive, even radical, on race. His books don't promote racism, they lampoon the stupidity of it. The first problem is that Mr. Perry doesn't get it. The second, and larger, problem is that he firmly believes students won't get it either." With proper teaching about background and context, "they'll learn something valuable from a great writer's portrait of racism's silly and downright ugly face." (John Head is black, a *Constitution* editorial writer.)

Hearn, Michael Patrick. "Expelling *Huck Finn.*" *The Nation* 235 (7–14 Aug. 1982): 117.

HF has been under fire as a racist book at schools around the country, most conspicuously at Mark Twain Intermediate School, in Fairfax County, Virginia. Hearn defends *HF* and concludes: "Because of the recent public outcry, Fairfax County has ruled that *Huckleberry Finn* may be taught, but only with 'appropriate planning.' One wonders how it must have been presented before this ruling. The problem is the teaching, not the novel. How could anyone assign the book and not place it within its proper historical context? Should any class fail to discuss the humanity of Mark Twain's novel, then the school board should keep *Huckleberry Finn* and chuck the teacher."

Hentoff, Nat. *The Day They Came to Arrest the Book.* New York: Delacorte P, 1982.

A novel about censorship in a high school, with particular focus on the furor over an attempt to remove *HF* from a reading list and the library as racist, sexist, and immoral. The presentation is balanced; except for the school principal there are no fools or villains, but only honest and well-

meaning persons whose convictions collide. The issue for Hentoff is not
racism, sexism, or immorality; it is the free and open exchange of ideas.

———. "Huck Finn and the Shortchanging of Black Kids." *Village Voice*
18 May 1982: 8.

In Warrington, Pennsylvania, a black eighth-grader allegedly was "harassed verbally and physically" after his class read *HF*. Details are uncertain, but the school removed *HF* from the junior high reading list.
Hentoff argues that *HF* is not difficult to understand; it is a major novel,
and any conflicts over the themes treated provide a teaching opportunity.

———. "Huck Finn Better Get out of Town by Sundown." *Village Voice*
4 May 1982: 8.

Begins a four-part series on current efforts by black parents and John
Wallace to remove *HF* from the schools. *HF* has met opposition from the
beginning, though until recently on the grounds of irreverence and emphasis on the lower classes.

———. "Is Any Book Worth the Humiliation of Our Kids?" *Village Voice*
11 May 1982: 8.

A sensitive exploration of the various motives of censors and book
banners, some sincere and some politicized. Hentoff has talked with black
parents who object to *HF* and Jewish parents who object to *The Merchant
of Venice*. "I think they're wrong in wanting to throw out or hide these
works, but they do raise questions about how to teach certain books.
Questions that go even more deeply into the nature of teaching itself."

———. "Romeo, Romeo, I Can Hardly Hear You." *Washington Post* 23 Nov.
1984: A27.

On censorship of books in the schools. Three young-adult novels by
Judy Blume have been removed from school libraries in Peoria despite
their high recommendation by the American Library Association, and a
school edition of *Romeo and Juliet* published by Scott, Foresman is bowdlerized, despite false statements to the contrary in the accompanying
teacher's guide. And Huck Finn is in trouble again, not only in America
(in Waukegan, Illinois, this time) but also in England: "The Inner London Education Authority is currently ordering all of its employees, including non-teachers, to take 'race consciousness' courses. In one of those
courses, certain books are condemned for their infectious racism. One of
them is 'Huckleberry Finn.' Well, Huck never did think he and 'sivilization' had much in common."

———. "These Are Little Battles Fought in Remote Places." *Village Voice*
25 May 1982: 4.

On his conversation with an official in an unnamed school district who
is fighting to keep *HF* as required reading for ninth-graders for the
following reasons: it is told by an adolescent, it is simple in its form, and it
ties in well with nineteenth-century American history; moreover, it is
about Huck's own maturing. The official recognizes the sensitivity of
black parents: "I can assure them we teach it sensitively, and they'll say, 'It
still hurts my child.' And I'll say the child can choose another book. But
what book can replace *Huckleberry Finn?*"

Hoffman, Daniel G. "Jim's Magic: Black or White?" *American Literature* 32 (Mar. 1960): 45–54.

    Jim's "superstitions are used structurally to indicate his slavery while a slave and his spiritual freedom with Huck"; freed from credulity with his escape from bondage, "he becomes a magician able to read the mysterious signs of nature."

———. "Mark Twain." *Form and Fable in American Fiction*. London and New York: Oxford UP, 1961.

    "Black Magic—and White—in *Huckleberry Finn*" (317–42) shows three attitudes toward life, indicated in supernatural terms: both "the conventional piety of the villagers" and "the irrelevant escape of the romantic imagination" are "morally inadequate." "The third—which pays homage to the river god—gives dignity to human life" through the world of supernatural omens understood by Jim, who undergoes growth in the story. This article is a complete revision of "Jim's Magic: Black or White?" (1960).

Hoffman, Michael J. "Huck's Ironic Circle." *Georgia Review* 23 (Fall 1969): 307–22.

    HF "is not a novel about a boy's moral awakening, nor a polemic against slavery, nor a book about how good instincts are stronger than an evil society. We have always overestimated Huck Finn and have likewise underestimated his creator. . . . The dynamic theme that runs throughout *Huckleberry Finn* is an unresolved dialectic between the moral responsibility of the individual and the morality of the society in which he moves and against which he must function." Huck does not share the perceptiveness of MT and the reader; he never truly learns to regard Jim as an equal; he believes in property rights and the institution of slavery, and he follows the leadership of Tom Sawyer. The ending is consistent with this unimaginative Huck: "The irony of the book has now come full circle in that Huck has not rejected society's standards at all. He just feels personally inconvenienced by things like school, and clothes. But he still believes just as strongly that society is right."

Holland, Laurence B. "A 'Raft of Trouble': Word and Deed in *Huckleberry Finn*." *Glyph* (Johns Hopkins Textual Studies) 5 (1979): 69–87. Reprinted in Eric J. Sundquist, ed. *American Realism: New Essays*. Baltimore: Johns Hopkins UP, 1982. 66–81.

    "What *Huckleberry Finn* is about is the process, with its attendant absurdities, of setting a free man free." Jim is rescued repeatedly, but futilely, "and Twain it was, though with more complex motives than Tom's, who thought up the crude sport that is condemned in Tom, the 'adventure' as Tom calls it to which Twain devoted so much of *The Adventures of Huckleberry Finn*. Twain's conscience is therefore stirred not only as a Tom Sawyerish, fish-belly white citizen who never freed a slave in his life, but by the lie he perpetrated in the very act of forming his fiction" on what MT called elsewhere a "lie of silent assertion."

Holt, Elvin. "*A Coon Alphabet* and the Comic Mask of Racial Prejudice." *Studies in American Humor* 5.4 (Winter 1986–87): 307–18.

On the 1898 book by Edward Windsor Kemble, illustrator of *HF,* reproducing a number of the racial caricatures appearing there. (Also see Briden, above.)

Howe, Irving. "Anarchy and Authority in American Literature." *Denver Quarterly* 2 (Autumn 1967): 5–30.

On the raft, "itself so wonderful a symbol of the isolation, purity and helplessness on which the anarchist vision rests," Huck and Jim "create a community of equals," but the idyllic existence is constantly threatened by the world and cannot last (22–25).

Howell, Elmo. "Uncle Silas Phelps: A Note on Mark Twain's Characterization." *Mark Twain Journal* 14 (Summer 1968): 8–12.

"Mark Twain was a friend of the Negro . . . and he never failed to speak out against the injustice he suffered, particularly in the South," but he "also loved those Valley people who enslaved Jim. . . . Thus *Huckleberry Finn* is built around paradox": the Phelps family "are among Mark Twain's favorite people, and Uncle Silas Phelps is his finest portrait of a good man," kindly and decent rather than clever.

Jehlen, Myra. "Gender." *Critical Terms for Literary Study.* Ed. Frank Lentricchia and Thomas McLaughlin. Chicago: U of Chicago P, 1990. 263–73.

Arguing that "culture, society, history define gender, not nature" (263n), uses *HF* as an example (265–73): "This man's book about a boy" takes Huck "into a limbo of gender." (Jehlen's arguments apply equally well to race as an artificial notion.) When he hurries back to the raft, telling Jim "They're after us," "they" are literally after Jim, not Huck, who is by race one of "them," but identifies with Jim in his situation as fugitive.

Karanovich, Nick. "Sixty Books from Mark Twain's Library." *Mark Twain Journal* 25.2 (1987, 1990): 9–20.

The sixty books in the Estelle Doheney Collection at St. John's Seminary in Camarillo, California, were sold at auction by Christie's, between October 1987 and May 1989. Of particular interest is William Still's *The Underground Railroad* (Philadelphia: William Still, 1883). MT's ownership of the latter book reveals his interest, while he was finishing *HF,* in the actual means by which a slave could reach freedom and safety. Furthermore, a flyleaf inscription in his handwriting indicates that he was well aware that a slave did not become free by entering a free state, and of course Jim could not win freedom simply by crossing the river to Illinois:

> Mrs. Luckett was a slave in Richmond, with a daughter 3 years old. Her brother, Jones, an escaped slave, lived in Elmira (1844). He cut two hearts out of pink paper, & wrote on one, "When you see this again, you will know." No other word accompanied it. After a while a white man went [to] Richmond with the other heart, called on the woman's mistress on some pretext which brought in the slaves: Mrs. L. saw & recognized the duplicate heart; she escaped, with her child in the night, joined the man at a place appointed, (Annapolis,) & thence got through safely to Elmira. She lives in Canada, now (whither she had to flee when the fugitive slave law was passed 1850), & the child is also married & lives in Binghamton, N. Y. (1884). This account given by Mother, who knew the several parties.

[Elmira, New York, was the home of MT's Langdon in-laws, who had left their church over the issue of slavery and helped found a new congregation; their home was a station on the Underground Railway.] This inscription is also printed in Gribben, *Mark Twain's Library,* 666.

Note: This article, which discusses events of 1987–89, was actually published in 1990, although the journal issue is dated 1987.

Kelly, James J. "They're Trying to Kill *Huckleberry Finn.*" *Mark Twain Journal* 13 (Winter 1965–66): 13–14.

Kelly misinterprets the objections to *HF* as required reading. Moreover, Kelly's own racist opinions make him a part of the problem: "Whole organizations, such as the N.A.A.C.P. and the Urban League, have registered ceaseless objections to *Huck Finn* for the liberal use of the term *nigger* throughout the book. Another frequent complaint is against the diction used by the book's Negro characters in their dialogue. To ostracize either book or author for such cause is unreasonable and unrealistic. For any individual or organization to deny the fact that the American Negro, generally, and with the exception of a small minority, speaks a limited and lower-vulgate English is ridiculous. . . . It is hardly the fault of Samuel Clemens if the average American Negro remains inarticulate in English after being in this country for three-hundred years. The blame for such verbal limitation surely can not lie with Samuel Clemens, *Huckleberry Finn,* its publishers, or the readers who enjoy it."

King, Bruce. "*Huckleberry Finn.*" *Ariel: A Review of International English Literature* (University of Calgary) 2 (Oct. 1971): 69–77.

"*Huckleberry Finn* is a spiritual autobiography. Its main themes are the development of Huck's acceptance of Jim as an equal . . . and his willingness to be rejected by society and risk damnation so that Jim may escape." The trip down the river has as its archetype "the traditional allegory of the soul's pilgrimage through this world." It is a radical book, though not in the sense that it would substitute populism: consider Pap Finn. "Huck, isolated, uncorrupted, true to himself, could never be assimilated into any society."

Kolb, Harold H., Jr. "Mark Twain, Huck Finn, and Jacob Blivens: Gilt-Edged, Tree-Calf Morality in *The Adventures of Huckleberry Finn.*" *Virginia Quarterly Review* 55 (Autumn 1979): 653–69.

HF shows patterns in which Huck gradually learns of Jim's humanity, but also reveals that he has not fully learned his lesson; furthermore, other passages suggest that Huck "has an instinctive compassion for Jim from the beginning. . . . These three patterns—moral development, moral backsliding, moral stasis—complicate but do not contradict the lesson of honesty, justice, and mercy first recognized by Joel Chandler Harris." He shares qualities with pious fools in MT's works such as Jacob Blivens, "The Good Little Boy Who Did Not Prosper." *HF* ends in Tom Sawyerish burlesque because "Tom is the rightful hero of Mississippi Valley society; Jim's debasement and Huck's suppression are precisely what the whole novel is about . . . even though Mark Twain created a spotless moral hero he was reluctant to let his hero triumph." He never wrote another *HF* because "it became impossible for him to believe in his hero."

Krause, Sidney. "Huck's First Moral Crisis." *Mississippi Quarterly* 18 (Spring 1965): 69–73.

Huck's moral awareness of Jim does not come in the fog episode in chapter 15 (as Lionel Trilling suggests), since his response there is psychological rather than moral; apologizing to Jim and recognizing him as a person prepare Huck for the following chapters, in which he "saves Jim by dint of courage and wit" from slave hunters.

Krauth, Leland. "Mark Twain, Alice Walker, and the Aesthetics of Joy." *Proteus* 1.2 (1984): 9–14.

In *HF* and *The Color Purple* "a dark universe of human inhumanity becomes the precondition of the joy that eventually dominates each work." For Jim, for example, the famous "trash" episode which leads Huck to apologize is "a claiming of self," as Celie's is when Mr. —— tells her she is poor, black, ugly, a woman, "Goddam . . . you nothing at all," and then she asserts herself. "In each case, the agency of joy—a surprising release of the self from the world of pain—involves nothing less than the novel's controlling moral vision." Walker's characters change dramatically for the better, and in *HF* bad characters are replaced by better ones as the novel progresses: "As Pap is replaced by Jim, Emmeline Grangerford by Mary Jane Wilks, Judge Thatcher by Lawyer Levi Bell, the Grangerfords and Shepherdsons by Silas and Sally Phelps (and perhaps even the Duke and the King by Tom and Huck), we witness the reality of human goodness."

Levy, Leo B. "Society and Conscience in Huckleberry Finn." *Nineteenth-Century Fiction* 18 (Mar. 1964): 383–91.

The critical view that equates what Huck calls "conscience" with the views of the society in which he lives are basically correct, but "criticism of the novel has suffered from too much insistence upon its schematic or doctrinal aspects." Natural man is not necessarily innocent—cf. the degraded Pap—and the growing closeness of Huck and Jim is "the recognition and fulfillment of mutual needs so strong that they can transcend racial barriers"; hence Huck's decision to help Jim escape may be not rebellious and isolating" but "a socializing decision through which he begins to discover a deeper bond with society than any he has known."

Lewis, Stuart. "Twain's Huckleberry Finn, Chapter XIV." *Explicator* 30 (Mar. 1972): item 61.

While Huck takes the traditional view of Solomon's wisdom in proposing to divide a baby, "Jim realizes the terror of one man's holding absolute power over another. . . . The test is too close for comfort."

Lofrith, Erik. "Huck, for Short; or One Hundred Years of Solicitude." *Studia Neophilologica* 62 (1990): 61–77.

An extensive survey of Swedish translations of *HF,* none of them true to MT's book. They are generally shortened, with significant omissions, and bowdlerized to reduce or remove references to nakedness, chafing at authority, and moral ambiguity. Some of the translation is merely bad, but too often Huck is made to sound more educated than he really is, and Jim is sometimes made to speak in a kind of bad Swedish that makes him sound like a buffoon.

Logan, Rayford W. *The Negro in American Life and Thought: The Nadir, 1877–1901*. New York: Dial, 1954.

Describes MT as "both a traditionalist and a non-conformist" in his attitude toward Negroes, and quotes Sterling Brown's praise for the depiction of Jim in *HF*.

Long, William J. *American Literature: A Study of the Men and the Books That in the Earlier and Later Times Reflect the American Spirit*. Boston and New York: Ginn, 1913.

Criticizes MT's crudity in *IA* and *CY*, but also in *TS*, with its "dime-novel sensationalism," its emphasis on "the lawless, barbarous side of boy-life . . . its self-assertion without its instinctive respect for authority" (466–67). *HF* "ends not with a moral climax" but in Jim's rescue "by the most approved dime-novel methods. The portrayal of all these astonishing scenes is vivid and intensely dramatic; one needs hardly to add that it is a portrayal, not of the great onward current of American life, but only of its flotsam and jetsam." Still, MT portrayed character and scene vividly, and "was at heart a reformer" (467–68). Some critics believe his "more dignified works," such as *P&P* and *JA*, will last longer (466).

Lynn, Kenneth S. "Huck and Jim." *Yale Review* 47 (Mar. 1958): 421–31.

In *HF* there is a succession of biblical themes, especially that of Moses—and a parallel in that when Moses led the Israelites toward freedom he moved toward death, and the movement carrying Jim to freedom will separate the two friends. Huck undergoes rebirths in a cycle of initiations culminating in deaths, and Jim passes through successive bondages.

McDowell, Edwin. "From Twain, a Letter on Debt to the Blacks." *New York Times* 14 Mar. 1985: 1, 16.

A letter of 24 December 1885 to Francis Wayland, dean of the Yale Law School, blunts recent accusations that *HF* reflects racism on the part of the author. MT inquires about helping with the expenses of a black student. He would be less willing to do so for a white, "but I do not feel so about the other color. We have ground the manhood out of them, & the shame is ours, not theirs, & we should pay for it." The student, Warner T. McGuinn, was commencement orator at his graduation in 1887 and became a lawyer in Baltimore, where he was twice elected to the city council; Supreme Court Justice Thurgood Marshall called him "one of the greatest lawyers who ever lived." The letter was authenticated by Shelley Fisher Fishkin; collectors Richard and Nancy Stiner made it available after reading her article (see Fishkin 1985) contending that *HF* ironically attacked racist attitudes. Fishkin adds that MT planned to aid another black Yale law student, and did pay the tuition of A. W. Jones at Lincoln University; he also supported the European apprenticeship of Charles Ethan Porter, a black painter, and interceded with President Garfield to prevent the dismissal of Frederick A. Douglass as marshal of the District of Columbia. History professor Sterling Stuckey of North-western University called MT's letter "a clear condemnation of the larger society for what it had done and was doing to black people. It couldn't be a clearer, more categorical condemnation of racism in American life and I'm not at all surprised to find that it came from Twain." As for complaints that *HF* is racist, Stuckey says: "My sense of the criticism is that it comes mainly from the nonacademic side of the black community, not from black intellectuals. In my judgment, 'Huck Finn' is one of the most devastating attacks on racism ever written."

McIntyre, James P. "Three Practical Jokes: A Key to Huck's Changing Atti-tude toward Jim." *Modern Fiction Studies* 14 (Spring 1968): 33–37.

Beginning with Chadwick Hansen's 1963 study, the article traces Huck's growing awareness of Jim's humanity: first Tom hung Jim's hat on a tree, then Huck nearly killed him in a joke involving a rattlesnake skin, but it was only through offending Jim's human dignity in the "trash" episode that Huck fully recognized his companion as an individual rather than a type. McIntyre's interpretation contrasts with Hansen's picture of Jim as developing from a minor figure to a symbol of man.

MacKethan, Lucinda H. "Huck Finn and the Slave Narratives: Lighting out as Design." *Southern Review* 20 (Apr. 1984): 247–64.

The slave narratives were a popular genre in the 1840s and 1850s, and MT knew, borrowed from, or showed parallels to books by Charles Ball, William Wells Brown, Frederick Douglass, James Pennington, and others. There are similarities between Brown's narrative both in tone and in the point of view of a young boy written down by an older man. MacKethan argues convincingly that excising the "raftmen's passage" from chapter 16 brings *HF* closer to the conventions of slave narratives. Jim's failure in his first escape attempt means little: Douglass and Brown also failed the first time.

Mailloux, Steven. "Interpretation." *Critical Terms for Literary Study*. Ed. Frank Lentricchia and Thomas McLaughlin. Chicago: U of Chicago P, 1990. 121–34.

On the question of to whom an interpretation must be acceptable, uses the "trash" episode in chap. 15 of *HF* as one example of how "interpretation takes place in a political context, and each interpretive act relates directly to the power relations (whether of nation, family, gender, class, or race) involved in that context."

Matthews, Greg. *The Further Adventures of Huckleberry Finn*. New York: Crown, 1983.

A sequel to *HF*. Huck's father is alive after all, and murders Judge Thatcher, but Huck is accused. He flees toward California with Jim (whose wife and children were bought out of slavery by Huck but then died in a fire at the widow Douglas's), pursued by the man hunter Chauncey Thermopylae Bartlett. They journey with emigrants, Indians, and even for a time with a traveling brothel known as "The McSween Heavenly Angels Choir." The word "nigger" is pervasive once more, though Huck reproves one white man who calls Jim a "nigger" (302).

Huck tells black slaves in California they are free, and when necessary Jim strikes white men. There are the "boundless suspense, thrills, and cliff-hangers" promised on the dust jacket, but not quite the "unerring reproduction of Twain's distinctive style."

Mills, Nicolaus. "Prison and Society in Nineteenth-Century American Fiction." *Western Humanities Review* 24 (Autumn 1970): 325–31.

Cooper, Hawthorne, Melville, and MT all found the structure of society imprisoning. "Throughout *Huckleberry Finn* slavery is seen imprisoning whites as well as blacks." *CT* shows that MT "saw exploitation characteristic of society as a whole, not merely the antebellum South."

Nagel, James. "*Huck Finn* and *The Bear;* the Wilderness and Moral Freedom." *English Studies in Africa* 13 (Mar. 1969): 59–63.

Both MT and Faulkner saw the South as cursed by its history of slavery, with the Negro a continuing reminder; the old order, founded on injustice and maintained by brutality, could not endure. In *HF* and *The Bear* a white boy too young to share the cultural guilt is paired with a Negro male, a victim of the old order, with a good heart and a simple but practical mind. Most probably the pairing is not homoerotic, as Fiedler suggests (1948), but rather an attempt to reduce race relations to basic human relations. In both stories physical isolation produces "a social vacuum in which basic human essence floats freely." Both stories "appeal to a latent wish for moral freedom" and "parallel on several levels the experience of each man as he grows up."

N[ock], S. A. "Editorial Comment." *College and University* 33 (Winter 1958): 202–3.

A lengthy discussion of MT's portrayal of Negroes, and white attitudes toward them, in *HF,* which has just been removed from New York City schools: "Anyway, a whole big cityful of youngsters may no longer, it seems, discover for themselves the magnanimity of Jim, and may no longer see for themselves how magnanimity encourages gentleness and thoughtfulness in others. What is probably the most powerful defense of the Negro ever written is now banned."

Ornstein, Robert. "The Ending of Huckleberry Finn." *Modern Language Notes* 74 (Dec. 1959): 698–702.

Miss Watson's freeing of Jim in her will is not a sacrifice but "perhaps the crowning act of selfishness and pious greed: the desire to make the best of all possible worlds." Tom's childish intervention can be explained in personal terms: he could free a slave, as MT could attack slavery, when it had become safe to do so.

Perry, Thomas Sergeant. "Mark Twain." *Century* 30 (May 1885): 171–72.

A review of *HF.* The use of Huck as narrator lends unity and truthfulness; the ending seems contrived. Perry applies terms of humor to questions now taken differently, as in Huck's "mixed feelings about rescuing Jim, the negro, from slavery. His perverted views about the unholiness of his actions are most instructive and amusing."

Pettit, Arthur G. *Mark Twain & the South*. Lexington: UP of Kentucky, 1974.

Provides an extensive account of MT's views on race, and their changing and maturing from his boyhood in the slave state of Missouri. Pettit
shows that MT came to a humane and decent view eventually, and wrote
helpful things about blacks, but argues that MT never fully outgrew his
racism.

Piacentino, Edward J. "The Significance of Pap's Drunken Diatribe against
the Government in *Huckleberry Finn*." *Mark Twain Journal* 19 (Summer
1976): 19–21.

No mere digression, the passage introduces the ironic method MT
used throughout *HF*, "establishes as a recurring motif the pattern of
hypocritical behavior exhibited in the action of many of the characters
Huck encounters," and "initiates Huck's as well as the reader's education
into the inhuman, pretentious ways of antebellum southern white society."

Rodnon, Stewart. "*The Adventures of Huckleberry Finn* and *Invisible Man*:
Thematic and Structural Comparisons." *Negro American Literature Forum*
4 (July 1970): 45–51.

There are similarities in "the journey concept, the education motif,
and the essential theme," as well as something deeper than "a satiric
examination of . . . American society" and a "basic-goodness-of-the-heart
theme." "The novels are stylistically alike in at least four areas: language,
folklore, humor, and narrator point-of-view." In *Shadow and Act* (1964),
Ellison has commented on Jim's role as a symbol of humanity for Huck,
whose decision to help him escape represents MT's acceptance of a personal responsibility.

Rubin, Louis D., Jr. "Southern Local Color and the Black Man." *Southern
Review* 6 (Oct. 1970): 1011–30 [on *HF*, 1026–30].

Huck provides a voice, and Jim a basis, for evaluating "the moral
worth of the town and the countryside along the river." MT may not
have recognized the importance of his theme of Jim's yearning for freedom; Ralph Ellison has argued that Jim's character could be more fully
rounded, though he is a triumph of characterization and understanding, a
symbol of humanity.

Sage, Howard. "An Interview with Ralph Ellison: Visible Man." *Pulp* 2
(Summer 1976): 10–11, 12.

In a general discussion of American authors, the American experience,
and the search for a national literature, Sage notes the central position of
the race problem as a moral concern, the literary importance of oral lore as
seen in MT, and the significance in *HF* of "Afro-American speech, superstition, humanity." Like other American writers of the nineteenth century,
MT was not academic, and he knew both the black and the white oral
traditions and folklore of the Mississippi River and elsewhere, and used
what he could of the available traditions and conventions. There is a
concern for a national voice in the novel, and "how to get a particular
ethnic accent on the page. Even Mark Twain manages to caricature the
speech of Jim in the book, not because he meant to do so, but because the
tradition, the convention out of which he worked, was that of the minstrel

show and Afro-American speech was considered implicitly funny in those days."

Seelye, John. "The Craft of Laughter: Abominable Showmanship and *Huckleberry Finn*." *Thalia: Studies in Literary Humor* 4 (Spring–Summer 1981): 19–25.

The conclusion "recommends itself to us precisely because it *is* bad . . . like the greatest of literary problems, Hamlet's hesitation, it is essential to an understanding of art as entertainment." Resenting his position as popular entertainer, MT played a practical joke on the reader. Deceptions and trickery pervade *HF:* in the end we learn that Jim has been free for weeks, Pap dead, and the flight down the river unnecessary; Huck, of course, would have known all this as he began his narration.

———. "'De Ole True Huck'": An Introduction." *Tri-Quarterly* 16 (Autumn 1969): 5–19.

Consists of the introduction and the final chapters of Seelye's *The True Adventures of Huckleberry Finn*. In the introduction Seelye summarizes objections to MT's *HF* by librarians, pressure groups, and critics; Seelye's version will retell the story as the "crickits" would have it.

———. *The True Adventures of Huckleberry Finn*. Evanston, Ill.: Northwestern UP, 1970.

A rewriting of *HF* to give the critics a version that answers their objections, this is a comic tour de force.

Sidnell, M. J. "Huck Finn and Jim: Their Abortive Freedom Ride." *Cambridge Quarterly* 2 (Summer 1976): 203–11.

MT was more perceptive than critics who view the ending of *HF* as flawed: "Life on the raft has offered a beautiful vision of what might be the relationship of negro and white, but the vision is not, and cannot be, a representation of America as it really is." Huck "must return to the trivially vicious world of Tom Sawyer's America," at the end "utterly changed not in itself but in our perception of it."

Sloane, David E. E. *"Adventures of Huckleberry Finn": American Comic Vision*. Boston: Twayne, 1988.

Furnishes context (including useful mention of others, among them Henry Ward Beecher, who objected to the conventional "good boy" novel on grounds of both realism and ethics) and summary of critical reception, followed by a sequential reading through "the major moments of the book" that sees the conclusion as "a symphonic elaboration of the first three chapters." Sloane carefully examines the painful issues of race and bothersome use of the word "nigger" throughout (see his index), arguing that MT unflinchingly portrayed the vicious racism of the time, "to make the reader uncomfortable" with it. "He intended to be aggressive in putting forth the most blatant symbol of that American and universal shortcoming [racism]; here, it is 'nigger'" (29).

Sollors, Werner. "Ethnicity." *Critical Terms for Literary Study*. Ed. Frank Lentricchia and Thomas McLaughlin. Chicago: U of Chicago P, 1990. 288–305.

Grouping "ethnic, racial, or national identifications" as based on contrast, cites *CY* (on 290–304) as a useful example "because of its apparent distance from any immediate ethnic sensibilities" while treating such topics as politics, social justice, and slavery. (MT's hero, sent back to the sixth century, encounters injustices that existed in other ages, including human slavery—inflicted on whites in *CY*—which is drawn from books on black slavery in the nineteenth century.)

Starke, Catherine Juanita. *Black Portraiture in American Fiction: Stock Characters, Archetypes, and Individuals*. New York: Basic Books, 1971.

On *HF* (175–80): "Mark Twain is an early, major novelist to give qualities of an individual to a Negro in our literature; because he gives him characteristics of a submissive slave and end-man comedian also, Jim's is a transitional image of a Negro as an individual." A trend had been established by 1884, when *HF* appeared in England, and "since then, other, more fully realized images of slaves who are also individuals have appeared in literature."

Stein, Jean. "The Art of Fiction XIII: William Faulkner." *Paris Review* 12 (Spring 1956): 28–52.

"This conversation [with Faulkner] took place in New York City, midwinter, early 1956." On Sherwood Anderson: "He was the father of my generation of American writers and the tradition of American writing which our successors will carry on. . . . Dreiser is his older brother and Mark Twain the father of them both" (46). On favorite characters in literature: "Huck Finn, of course, and Jim. Tom Sawyer I never liked much—an awful prig" (47).

Stein, Ruth. "The ABC's of Counterfeit Classics: Adapted, Bowdlerized, and Condensed." *English Journal* 55 (Dec. 1966): 1160–63. Condensed as "Counterfeit Classics." *Education Digest* 32 (Apr. 1967): 39–41.

Uses school editions of *HF* as an example of the disservice done the reader when vocabulary is altered to fit word lists, passages are trimmed or toned down, and episodes are removed. "Transmission of our cultural heritage is accomplished partially through the teaching of the classics. Those that survive have an intrinsic merit of their own. It should not be snuffed out of existence by precautionary or hygienic measures. . . . It is a foolish waste of money, time, and effort to settle for any of the inferior revisions."

Stevenson, E. Burleson. "Mark Twain's Attitude toward the Negro." *Quarterly Review of Higher Education among Negroes* 13 (Oct. 1945): 326–64.

Argues that MT's attitude toward the Negro was "affectionate and friendly," as exemplified in *TS, HF, GA, PW,* and *LOM.* His attitude was sometimes mistaken, and MT failed to take "what might seem to us the manly stand on issues pertaining to the Negro. It is, however, an attitude that can be followed in building up strong racial ties." Documentation is from familiar sources, and this article will be most useful on the introductory level.

[Television debate.] "Freeman Reports." Cable News Network 14 Mar. 1985.

Shelley Fisher Fishkin has recently authenticated an 1885 MT letter to the dean of Yale Law School on paying the expenses of a black student (for text see McDowell 1985). Here she talks with John H. Wallace, who has been trying since 1972 to ban *HF* from high school classrooms; Sandi Freeman moderates. Wallace dismisses blacks with opposing views as subservient to white money (as in the case of an NAACP official) or "brainwashed" (as in the case of a black high school student who telephoned the program from Richmond, California, to say that she had recently read *HF* in an advanced English class, felt she had learned an important moral lesson, and did not feel inferior or injured). Wallace repeats essentially what he has said elsewhere, dismissing *HF* as "racist trash," although he would be willing to see it kept in the schools for optional outside reading, and "I really have no problem with this book being used at the college level." He contends that too many teachers are inept or racist. Professor Fishkin argues that both MT and *HF* are antiracist, that good teaching and informed debate are essential, and that children must learn the lessons of history; for her own children the painful history is that of the Holocaust, in which two of their great-aunts died. She makes a strong case for encouraging a diversity of opinion and more sophisticated discussion.

[Television debate.] "Nightline." ABC-TV 4 Feb. 1985. (Transcript $2.00 from Journal Graphics, Box 234, Ansonia Station, New York, NY 10023.)

Jeff Greenfield in Chicago and Ted Koppel in New York interviewed Meshach Taylor, who was currently playing Jim in a stage production of *HF* at Chicago's Goldman Theater; Nat Hentoff, who had written a number of times in defense of *HF* against those who would ban it; and John H. Wallace, "researcher for the Chicago School Board who has been fighting to ban *Huckleberry Finn* from schools since 1972." Wallace condemns *HF* as "racist trash" harmful to black children, but Taylor says he has played the part of Jim in performances abroad and all over the United States, many times before school groups, and has found students capable of learning to understand what he says he himself found to be "one of the best indictments against racism that I had ever read." Hentoff has visited classes over the years and has observed *HF* being taught: it is difficult at first, "and the kids will say, 'yeah, when I started that . . . it was pretty awful,' but then they begin to read the book, and see what's happening, and what happens to them then is what is called education."

Vedder, Henry C. "Charles Dudley Warner." In *American Writers of To-Day*. New York, Boston, Chicago: Silver, Burdett, 1894. 87–103.

"Mr. Samuel L. Clemens has published certain books in serious literature, without in the least persuading the public to take him seriously. Many read *The Prince and the Pauper* through with misgiving, lest a huge jest might after all be concealed beneath the apparently sober tale. They failed to enjoy the story, because they were continually and nervously looking for some hidden snare. It is only when, as 'Mark Twain,' he writes some such trash as *The Adventures of Huckleberry* that this really capable writer can make sure of an appreciative hearing" (94).

Vogelback, Arthur Lawrence. "The Publication and Reception of *Huckleberry Finn* in America." *American Literature* 11 (Nov. 1939): 260–72.

Chiefly on the chorus of complaint that the book was "vulgar," "coarse," and "inelegant." (See Fischer entry above.)

Wallace, John H. *The Adventures of Huckleberry Finn Adapted.* Falls Church, Va.: John H. Wallace & Sons Company, 1983 ($3.95 plus fifty cents postage; write to John H. Wallace & Sons, P.O. Box 216506, Chicago, IL 60621.)

Consists of MT's text virtually unchanged, except for replacing the word "nigger" throughout with less offensive terms, generally "black."

———. "Huckleberry Finn Is Offensive." *Washington Post* 11 Apr. 1982: B8.

An administrator at the Mark Twain Intermediate School, Fairfax County, Virginia, defends banning the book: "'Huckleberry Finn' uses the pejorative term 'nigger' profusely. It speaks of black Americans with implications that they are not honest, they are not as intelligent as whites and they are not human. All this, of course, is meant to be satirical. It is. But at the same time it ridicules blacks. This kind of ridicule is extremely difficult for black youngsters to handle. I maintain that it constitutes mental cruelty, harassment and downright racial intimidation to force black students to sit in a classroom to read this kind of literature about themselves. I read 'Huck Finn' when I was in high school—and I can remember feeling betrayed by the teacher. I felt humiliated and embarrassed. Ten years ago, my oldest son went through the same experience in high school, until I went to talk to the teachers about it; and he lost all interest in English classes." However, Wallace has no objections to having *HF* in a school library, and "it's perfectly all right for college class use, especially at the graduate level."

Weaver, Thomas, and Merline A. Williams. "Mark Twain's Jim: Identity as an Index to Cultural Attitudes." *American Literary Realism* 13 (Spring 1980): 19–29.

A sociological study tracing Jim's successive portrayal by the critics as "a kind, simple, child-like being," a noble savage, the product of social circumstances, a family man, a Christ figure, and so on. Here, Jim is depicted as "far from the innocent victim." He has "an active impulse to chicanery which parallels the artful subterfuge of Huck Finn, Tom Sawyer, or any of the other notorious tricksters and confidence men appearing throughout Twain's fiction."

Will, George F. "Huck at a Hundred." *Newsweek* 105 (18 Feb. 1985): 92.

"Huck's story resonates in America's heart because it is about freedom understood in a distinctively American way, as the absence of social restraints, and obedience to the promptings of a pure heart." Will praises MT's language and dismisses those who find *HF* racially offensive as "ninnies."

Williams, James D. "The Use of History in Mark Twain's *A Connecticut Yankee.*" *Publications of the Modern Language Association* 80 (Mar. 1965): 102–10. Reprinted in Allison R. Ensor, ed. *A Connecticut Yankee in King Arthur's Court.* New York: Norton, 1982. 368–83.

In a broad and thorough examination of MT's sources over a number of historical periods, Williams shows that he borrowed several incidents in the *Yankee* book from Charles Ball's *Slavery in the United States,* and for a time considered printing excerpts in an appendix to show that those scenes were authentic. He shares with Ball the belief that slavery made the slaveholders brutal, and that for slaves death was an escape, even for children; the church, with its condemnation of suicide, was no friend to the slave. (Also see Andrews entry, above.)

Wiseby, Herbert A., Jr. "The True Story of Auntie Cord." *Mark Twain Society Bulletin* 3.2 (1981): 1, 3–5.

On Mary Ann Cord, the cook for Theodore and Susan Crane, in Elmira, New York. She told MT her story at Quarry Farm, where the Clemenses spent their summers. Like "Aunt Rachel" of "A True Story," she was reunited with her son Henry after the Civil War; he had escaped from slavery in 1858, at the age of thirteen, and made his way to Elmira; it was there that he had enlisted, then made his way south as a Union soldier.

Woodard, Fredrick, and Donnarae MacCann. "*Huckleberry Finn* and the Traditions of Blackface Minstrelsy." *Interracial Books for Children Bulletin* 15.1–2 (1984): 4–13. Reprinted in Donnarae MacCann and Gloria Woodard, eds. *The Black American in Books for Children: Readings in Racism.* Metuchen, N.J.: Scarecrow Press, 1985. 75–103.

"The tradition of white men blackening up to entertain other white people at the expense of black people's humanity is at the center of *Huck Finn*'s portrayal. . . . This dimension is important to a full interpretation of the novel and should be considered essential to any classroom use of the book." As early as 1843, the Virginia Minstrels put on a program, and their successors enjoyed great popularity. Mark Twain enjoyed the outlandish costumes and stage quarrels, and seems to have drawn on the tradition for scenes he included both in *Huck Finn* and in stage readings on his lecture tours.

Standard Edition

Adventures of Huckleberry Finn. Ed. Walter Blair and Victor Fischer, with the assistance of Dahlia Armon and Harriet Elinor Smith. Published in cooperation with the U of Iowa. Berkeley: U of California P, 1988. Also available in the Mark Twain Library Edition (U of California P, 1985) without the extensive textual notes, but with the same meticulously established text, the "Raftsmen's Passage" which was cut from the first edition of *HF* for nonliterary reasons, and the original illustrations (from the first edition of *HF*).

Contributors

Richard K. Barksdale is Emeritus Professor of English at the University of Illinois at Urbana-Champaign. He is editor (with Keneth Kinnamon) of *Black Writers in America: A Comprehensive Anthology* (1972) and author of *Langston Hughes: The Poet and His Critics* (1977). Currently he is editing an anthology of British antislavery literature and revising his 1977 study on Hughes. He has published several articles on Afro-American literature in scholarly journals.

Bernard W. Bell is Professor of English at the University of Massachusetts, Amherst; he received his Ph.D. there, and his B.A. and M.A. degrees from Howard University. A former chairman of the Five College Afro-American Studies Committee, he is also a founder and former acting head of the W. E. B. Du Bois Department of Afro-American Studies at the University of Massachusetts. He is the editor of *Modern and Contemporary Afro-American Poetry* (1972) and the author of *The Folk Roots of Contemporary Afro-American Poetry* (1974), the prize-winning *The Afro-American Novel and Its Tradition* (1987), and many articles and reviews on black literature and culture.

Mary Kemp Davis is Assistant Professor of English at the University of North Carolina at Chapel Hill, where she received her Ph.D. in American literature. She earned her B.A. at Florida A. & M. University and her M.A. at Atlanta University. She has published articles on Arna Bontemps, Sherley Anne Williams, and Frederick Douglass. Her special interests are the slave narrative and American fiction treating slavery, slave resistance, and slave insurrections. She is currently at work on a book entitled *Nat Turner Before the Bar of Judgment: Fictional Treatments of the Southampton Slave Insurrection of 1831*.

Thadious M. Davis is Professor of English at Brown University; she has also taught at the University of North Carolina at Chapel Hill. She holds a Ph.D. from Boston University. She is the author of *Faulkner's "Negro": Art and the Southern Context* (1983) and coeditor of six volumes on Afro-American writers in the *Dictionary of Literary Biography*.

Peaches M. Henry is currently a graduate student at Columbia University, working on a doctoral dissertation tentatively titled "The Role of Truth in Autobiography." Before entering the graduate program at Columbia, she taught English for four years at Stephen F. Austin High School in Austin, Texas.

Betty Harris Jones, now deceased, was a member of the English Department at Rutgers University, where she received her A.B. degree; she received her M.A. and Ph.D. degrees at Bryn Mawr College. In addition to publishing a number of articles on British and American literature, she was active in the National Humanities Faculty as an NHF scholar, visitor, and faculty coordinator, working with high schools in the Excellence in Teaching English program (funded by the National Endowment for the Humanities and the Rockefeller Foundation). She conducted a number of seminars on American literature, some specifically on *Huckleberry Finn*.

Rhett S. Jones is Professor of History and Afro-American Studies at Brown University, where he earned his Ph.D. in history and served for twelve years as chairperson of the Afro-American Studies Program. An honors graduate in sociology from the University of Illinois, he also holds an M.A. in sociology from the University of Connecticut and an M.A. in history from Brown. His book *Truncated Societies: The Normative Origins of Black Life in the New World* is forthcoming from Temple University Press. He has published numerous articles in anthropological, historical, literary, and sociological journals.

James S. Leonard is Associate Professor of English at The Citadel and editor of the *Mark Twain Circular*. He has published numerous articles on nineteenth- and twentieth-century American literature and is coauthor of *The Fluent Mundo: Wallace Stevens and the Structure of Reality* (1988). He holds a Ph.D. in English from Brown University.

Julius Lester, a graduate of Fisk University, is a Professor in the Department of Afro-American Studies and the Judaic Studies Program at the University of Massachusetts, Amherst. He is the author of *To Be a Slave* (1968) and twelve other books of nonfiction, fiction, and poetry.

Donnarae MacCann is a doctoral candidate in American studies at the University of Iowa. She holds a B.S. degree from the University of California at Berkeley, and an M.L.S. degree from UCLA. She is coauthor of *The Black American in Books for Children* (1972; 2nd ed. 1985), *Cultural Conformity in Books for Children* (1977), and *The Child's First Books: A Critical Study of Pictures and Texts* (1973). She is a member of the Editorial Advisory Board of the Council on Interracial Books for Children.

Charles H. Nichols is Professor of English at Brown University. He holds an A.B. degree from Brooklyn College and a Ph.D. from Brown University. He is author of *Many Thousand Gone: The Ex-Slaves' Account of Their Bondage and Freedom,* and editor of *African Nights: Black Erotic Folk Tales* and *Arna Bontemps, Langston Hughes: Letters 1925–1967.* He has published numerous articles and reviews on American and Afro-American literature.

Charles H. Nilon, now retired, was Professor of English and director of the Black Studies Program at the University of Colorado, Boulder. He holds a B.S. degree from Tennessee State College, an M.A. from the University of Kansas, and a Ph.D. from the University of Wisconsin. He has taught a variety of courses and has delivered papers and participated in seminars in American literature and black literature and culture. His publications include *Faulkner and the Negro* (1965), major work in bibliography, and a number of journal articles.

Arnold Rampersad is Professor of English at Princeton University. He previously taught at the University of Virginia, Stanford University, Rutgers University, and Columbia University. He holds B.A. and M.A. degrees from Bowling Green State University, and A.M. and Ph.D. degrees from Harvard. His wide-ranging publications include *The Art and Imagination of W. E. B. Du Bois* (1976) and a two-volume biography of Langston Hughes, *The Life of Langston*

Hughes, vol. 1: *1902–1941: I, Too, Sing America* (1986) and *The Life of Langston Hughes,* vol. 2: *1941–1967: I Dream a World* (1988).

David L. Smith is Associate Professor of English at Williams College. He received his B.A. at New College in Sarasota, Florida, and his M.A. and Ph.D. from the University of Chicago. He has taught and presented numerous papers in various areas of American and Afro-American literature; the article that appears here was the basis for the keynote address he delivered at the *Huckleberry Finn* Centenary Conference at the University of Missouri on 18 April 1985. He has been active as a member of various college committees and has chaired the Afro-American Studies Program and the Faculty Steering Committee. He has been a panelist for the National Endowment for the Humanities and the Smithsonian, and he is currently at work on a book to be titled *Racial Writing, Black and White.*

Carmen Subryan coordinates the English skills component of a developmental program at Howard University. Born in Guyana, South America, she attended Guyana Teachers' College; she received B.A., M.A., and Ph.D. degrees at Howard University. Her doctoral dissertation is titled "Mark Twain's Portrayal of Blacks in Selected Works."

Thomas A. Tenney is editor of the *Mark Twain Journal.* He holds a Ph.D. from the University of Pennsylvania and has taught at Rutgers University and the College of Charleston; he currently teaches at The Citadel. He is author of *Mark Twain: A Reference Guide* (1977) and is currently working on a second volume of that *Guide* and on a documented day-by-day record of Mark Twain's life.

John H. Wallace has long been involved in controversy over the place of *Huckleberry Finn* in the schools. He was the official at Mark Twain Intermediate School (Fairfax County, Virginia) most involved in opposition to the novel, which he has repeatedly and strenuously denounced; nonetheless, he has also repeatedly said he sees no reason why the book should not be used at the college level. Wallace comes from a strongly religious background; his mother was an evangelist in the Pentecostal church. He opposes *Huckleberry Finn* largely on the ground of improper language, and has produced his own edition with the words "nigger" and "hell" removed. He holds a B.A. from Central State University in Ohio, and an M.A. in psychology from Chicago State University; he has done work at Northwestern University toward the doctoral degree. He is now a consultant for the Chicago public schools.

Kenny Jackson Williams is Professor of English at Duke University. She holds a B.A. from Benedict College, an M.A. from De Paul University, and an M.A. and Ph.D. from the University of Pennsylvania. Her publications in American and Afro-American literature include *They Also Spoke: An Essay on Negro Literature in America, 1789–1930* (1970) and *A Storyteller and a City: Sherwood Anderson's Chicago* (1988); she is coeditor of *Chicago's Public Wits: A Chapter in the American Comic Spirit* (1982).

Fredrick Woodard is Professor of English, Associate Vice President for Academic Affairs, and Associate Dean of the Faculties at the University of Iowa. He holds a B.A. degree from Iowa Wesleyan College, and M.A. and Ph.D. degrees in American studies from the University of Iowa. He has written extensively on W. E. B. Du Bois, and collaborated with Donnarae MacCann on the article "*Huckleberry Finn* and the Tradition of Blackface Minstrelsy."

Index

Library of Congress Cataloging-in-Publication Data

Satire or evasion? : Black perspectives on Huckleberry Finn / James S.
  Leonard, Thomas A. Tenney, Thadious M. Davis, editors.
     p.   cm.
  Includes bibliographical references and index.
  ISBN 0-8223-1163-1 — ISBN 0-8223-1174-7 (pbk.)
  1. Twain, Mark, 1835–1910. Adventures of Huckleberry Finn.
2. Twain, Mark, 1835–1910—Characters—Afro-Americans. 3. Twain,
Mark, 1835–1910—Political and social views. 4. Slavery and slaves
in literature. 5. Afro-Americans in literature. 6. Race relations
in literature. 7. Racism in literature. I. Leonard, J. S. (James S.)
II. Tenney, Thomas Asa. III. Davis, Thadious M., 1944–   .
PS1305.S27   1991
813'.4—dc20   91-14315
                                                CIP